Ethnic Entrepreneurs, Crony Capitalism, and the Making of the Franco-Mexican Elite

Ethnic Entrepreneurs, Crony Capitalism, and the Making of the Franco-Mexican Elite

José Galindo

The University of Alabama Press | Tuscaloosa

The University of Alabama Press
Tuscaloosa, Alabama 35487-0380
uapress.ua.edu

Typeface: Minion Pro

Cover design: David Nees

Cataloging-in-Publication data is available from the Library of Congress.
ISBN: 978-0-8173-2080-5
E-ISBN: 978-0-8173-9336-6

Contents

Illustrations

FIGURES

TABLES

Preface

One morning in December 2000, while walking through the streets of Florence, Italy, I observed a group of Mexican compatriots of both genders sitting by the fountain of Neptune. In their loud conversation, I observed in them the great need to attract attention, to show that they came from the Mexican elite and that they were wealthy. They laughed and showed superficial attitudes toward the historical area that surrounded them at that moment and attitudes of contempt toward passersby. As a master's student at the University of Oxford in those years, I felt a great need to theorize, analyze, and explain, from an academic point of view, the origin of these types of people who shared the same background as me.

After those days in Florence, I chose the origin and persistence of the economic elite in Mexico as the subject of my next research project. Conducting a field study in Mexico City in the summer of 2001, I had an opportunity to undertake an interesting case study of a family of French origin who had immigrated to Mexico toward the end of the nineteenth century. Further research into several of these French families and other immigrant groups gave me the first clues that the wealth of the elite families of independent Mexico had not necessarily been inherited from the highest spheres of colonial society. There were also groups of immigrants, like these French, who had arrived in Mexico during the second third of the nineteenth century in conditions of poverty and had accumulated wealth over the years. The Mexican environment had favored them because they were white, Catholic, and of Latin origin. In a relatively short time, by the beginning of the twentieth century, they had been capable of ascending to the highest spheres of Mexican society.

When, in 2011, I decided to dedicate myself full-time to academia after finishing my PhD (2009) and working at the Comisión Nacional de los Derechos Humanos (2005–10). I was invited by the Department of History at the University of California, Berkeley as a visiting scholar for a two-year period (2012–14). There, I decided to take up the case analyzed in my 2001 research, transforming it into a study on crony capitalism in Mexico. That is, my new research focused on determining the way in which modern capitalism had emerged in Mexico toward the end of the nineteenth century. I sought mainly to answer questions about how the links between politicians and businessmen, who shared the economic profits of business, had been fundamental to the emergence of modern capitalism in Mexico, and how these links and profits had evolved over time. I also became interested in studying whether this type of capitalism came from institutional weakness and whether its implementation had any effect on the development and operation of formal institutions in Mexico.

These questions, together with my need to understand the economic elite and the role of ethnic entrepreneurs in Mexico, are what motivated the writing of this book. At the same time, my research into contemporary corruption in Mexico has provided evidence of the evolution of crony capitalism since the Porfiriato, leading to what today can be classified as collusive corruption. These links of the past and the present are analyzed in detail in the last chapter and conclusion of this book.

This is an exhaustive study not only about the links between politicians and entrepreneurs but also about the strategies, some common and some individual, that French entrepreneurs used in Mexico, as well as the social networks that each of them created to enrich themselves. To this end, this work includes analyses of specialist studies in cronyism, as well as primary sources, such as historical and notary archives, and interviews with members of the French community in Mexico and of the Jean family in particular.

Most of the primary data concerning the Jean family and other families of the Barcelonnette group was processed using UCINET. With this free software for social network analysis, I measured the centrality of members and associates of the Jean family within its network. This measurement considers the number of connections of a given member of the network and the connections of those to whom that member is connected. More specifically, in graph theory and network analysis, "centrality" refers to a possible measure of a vertex (node) in that graph, which determines its relative importance within the network. By recognizing the centrality of a node, we can determine the impact of a person involved in a social network. In this theory, the centrality nEigenvec is a measure of the influence of the node in the network. This methodology assigns scores to all nodes in the network, based on the concept that connections with high-score nodes contribute more to the score of the node in question than equal connections to the low-score nodes.

Throughout the work, I also analyzed cliques and ties between family members and the other members of the network. This data analysis enabled me to verify the importance of the general French social network present in Mexico in that period to the specific economic development of the Jean family and to establish whether the Jean network was independent or interwoven with the general French network, as was the case for other entrepreneurial French families. Moreover, the analysis shows how this successful French family used certain common strategies to expand its wealth, including connections with politicians and other strategies beyond those of co-nationals. These connections with politicians provide the main topic of this research; as the study will show, it is through these links that crony capitalism developed in Mexico and has been strengthened to the present day.

Acknowledgments

I want to thank all those who, over the years, had an influence on the evolution and development of this book. I am especially grateful to Alan Knight at the University of Oxford and to Margaret Chowning at the University of California, Berkeley. I also want to thank the Consejo Nacional de Ciencia y Tecnología (Conacyt), who supported me with funding, and the Programa para el Desarrollo Profesional Docente (PRODEP), which also financed part of this research. I am also grateful to the Chevening awards program; the Fondo para el Desarrollo de Recursos Humanos (FIDERH), managed by Banco de México; and the Fundación Mexicana para la Educación, la Tecnología y la Ciencia (FUNED). All of them funded different stages related to this research. I also want to thank the University of Alabama Press, particularly Wendi Schnaufer, who supported the publication of this research, and all the assistants and other professionals who collaborated with me in this project and publication process, especially Diana Méndez, Susie Jackson, Susan Harris, Alejandra Lozano, Jeff Cole, Miriam Guadarrama, and Andrés Martínez. Last but not least, I appreciate all the facilities that the Universidad Veracruzana has made available to me to be able to conclude this work. This university opened its doors to me in February 2014, and I found in it a serious space of international scope to carry out research and teaching in the field of history.

Abbreviations

AFMSB	Asociación Franco Mexicana, Suiza y Belga de Beneficencia
Banamex	Banco Nacional de México
BLM	Banco de Londres y México
BMM	Banco Mercantil Mexicano
BNM	Banco Nacional Mexicano
CANACINTRA	Cámara Nacional de la Industria de la Transformación
CBPM	Compañía Bancaria de París y México
CGT	Confederación General del Trabajo
CIASA	Compañía Industrial de Atlixco
CIDOSA	Compañía Industrial de Orizaba S.A.
CISAASA	Compañía Industrial de San Antonio Abad
CIVSA	Compañía Industrial Veracruzana S.A.
CROM	Confederación Regional Obrera Mexicana
CTM	Confederación de Trabajadores de México
MDC	Meyran Donnadieu y Compañía
Nafinsa	Nacional Financiera
NG	New Group

PRI	Partido Revolucionario Institucional
SFIM	Sociedad Financiera para la Industria en México
VJC	Veyan Jean y Compañía

Ethnic Entrepreneurs, Crony Capitalism, and the Making of the Franco-Mexican Elite

Introduction

This book explores historical, political, and economic perspectives of crony capitalism in Mexico, a practice in which success in business depends primarily on the relationships between business leaders and government officials. It shows how this practice can have both positive and negative effects on an economy, depending on the formal institutional development of a country.[1] When capitalism emerged, crony capitalism was necessary for the development of capitalist economies around the world.

When capitalism took off with greater force in Mexico during the Porfiriato, a period of Mexican history dominated by Pres. Porfirio Díaz (1876–80 and 1884–1911), there was little formal institutional development; for this reason, cooperation between entrepreneurs and politicians, implying monetary benefits for both groups, was of enormous importance in making the productive apparatus work. This informal practice in Mexican business favored connections between political and economic elites, bypassing the formal institutional frameworks while ignoring negative effects on the emergence of new entrepreneurs. However, over the years, this arrangement has been difficult to control and has played against the strengthening of institutions that it originally compensated.

In contrast, some developed economies have been able to construct stronger institutions and a culture of respect for the law, despite maintaining a certain level of crony capitalism in the productive processes of their economies. The different perceptions that societies have of the importance of the common good has undoubtedly played a role in this, as have other variables, to be mentioned throughout this work.

To scrutinize crony capitalism and its effects, I use the case study of a family of French migrants from the region of Barcelonnette: the Jean family. I study the Jeans from their arrival in Mexico at the end of the nineteenth century to the consolidation and subsequent weakening of the economic power of some of their members by the mid-twentieth century. The wider immigrant community of so-called Barcelonnettes represents a clear example of networking and ethnic entrepreneurship, meaning that their business network shared a common national background and migration experiences, and this facilitated their success with regard to weak formal institutions.

By the time the first member of the Jean family arrived in Mexico, the Barcelonnette business network was strongly interwoven and dense, with 86 percent of its members of French origin. In addition, the dynamics of big business in Mexico were, to a large extent, based on friendships within the highest and most important sociopolitical spheres of the country. Ethnic entrepreneurs are thus a useful subject of inquiry for this study and the Díaz government is a key period from which to begin the search for abundant evidence of crony capitalism in Mexico.

The importance of studying the Jean family is primarily that its experience in Mexico differs from that of the rest of the French community. They arrived in the country during a later period than the already studied (traditional) Barcelonnette migration to Mexico. The first waves of Barcelonnettes in Mexico arrived mostly around the mid-nineteenth century. However, most of the Jean brothers arrived in the country at the beginning of the twentieth century, close to the end of Díaz's presidency. This had a direct effect on the type of business strategies they implemented: more individual, without relying so much on the general support network built by other Barcelonnettes, but linked to key sectors of the economy such as banking.

In addition, they faced different historical realities at different stages of their development, compared with the rest of the Barcelonnettes established in Mexico. Most significant were the Mexican Revolution (1910–20) and the agrarian reform processes, which intensified between the 1920s and 1930s in the center of the country. This led them to build business relationships with the new revolutionary governments and entrepreneurs, which has permitted some members of the family to persist within the economic elite until today. This part of the history of the Jean family differs from other Barcelonnettes established in Mexico, who could not survive the triple effect of the Mexican Revolution, the First World War (WWI), and the Great Depression. The study of this family and its historical context will allow the reader to understand a singularly unique story of a family from Barcelonnette in Mexico, highlighting particularities worth stressing beyond the traditional historiography of this migratory group.

In that sense, this book represents the beginning of the construction of a new historiography about the final stages of the Barcelonnette migration in

Mexico. In addition, this microstudy gives readers a clear vision of the origin of crony capitalism in Mexico and other elements that assured the success of this French community in the country. The book also delves into the factors that helped or hindered some members of the Barcelonnette community in remaining within the Mexican economic elite. Finally, it analyzes corrupt practices that remain in the present and how they have been perpetuated.

The term *crony capitalism* is of recent origin. In the late 1990s, academics and analysts from around the world developed a particular interest in crony capitalism in East Asia, as it was considered one of the primary causes of economic collapse in the region after 1997. As the term gained currency, it was used to contrast the virtues of American-style capitalism with the economic model of other countries that allowed close links between government and large businesses.

However, numerous scandals have come to light in recent years to show that the United States has always had a considerable amount of crony capitalism. The approach to analyzing this subject has, therefore, changed over the years, giving the concept a more global application.[2] Thus, in many countries, crony capitalism has served to strengthen specific political and economic interests over time, transforming both business environments and political systems through the evolution of formal and informal institutions, both public and private, even in nations considered democratic and liberal.

Microstudies of crony capitalism, such as the one presented here, offer insights into specific relationships between political and business classes in diverse contexts and conditions. This allows the identification of similarities and differences in the development and adaptation of this phenomenon within societies. Accordingly, this work analyzes the specific networks forged by the Jean family to adapt to and exploit business practices in Mexico in a context of partially weak formal institutions. My study presents considerable in-depth empirical evidence to demonstrate the multifaceted and persistent problem of crony capitalism—which today can be classified within the more ample concept of collusive corruption—combining qualitative and quantitative methods, and supported by detailed insights into nineteenth- and twentieth-century Mexican history.

Since corruption is largely an economic phenomenon with micro- and macroeconomic consequences, much of the focus of this work is associated with those aspects. This book falls under the field of study of the economics of corruption. In fact, most of the benefits that come from corruption, directly and indirectly, are related to a change (usually an increase) in personal wealth, where individuals, acting through networks, appropriate what is public for their personal benefit.[3]

Stephen Haber defines crony capitalism in Latin America as a system "in which those close to the political authorities who make and enforce policies receive favors that have great economic value."[4] From that starting point, he studies the relationship between economic and political agents through concessions and privileges in the competitive market. Most books on Mexico written by neo-institutionalists, however, fail to recognize the complexity of the institutional framework during the Porfiriato and the stronger legal and political constraints to the president's power. The Porfirian judicial system, for example, set important limits on the government. *Institutions and Investment*, by Edward Beatty, proves that there were many more formal institutions operating in business during the Porfiriato than neo-institutionalists recognize. Businesses benefited from but were simultaneously restricted by specific policies, patents, and economic programs promoted by the Díaz government.

A different view of crony capitalism in Mexico, from both historical and economic perspectives, can be built from an in-depth analysis of the circumstances, factors, and significant agents that surround this phenomenon. This is one of the main objectives of this book. In fact, research affirms that crony capitalism in Porfirian Mexico lies somewhere between neo-institutionalist explanations and the analysis of Porfirian capitalism made by authors such as Edward Beatty. Neo-institutionalists employ a theory-heavy and empirically light approach to understanding corruption, whereas Beatty exaggerates the role of formal institutions in the Mexican economy in that period.

Recent studies that have a cultural focus on corruption—such as those by Rosenmüller and Ruderer,[5] who argue that corruption is culturally determined—fail to explain the institutional factors and interests that lie at the center of the causes and consequences of corruption. From that point of view, the economic aspect is a key consideration in the study of corruption, that is, how corruption affects economic incentives and what the economic effects of corrupt practices are, including the consolidation, or lack thereof, of formal institutions. Cultural studies on corruption that address the economic aspect are, therefore, more applicable to problem solving, if the objective is to make a contribution that can influence public policy and even promote cultural change.[6]

I do, however, agree with historical and anthropological relativists, who are more associated with cultural studies of corruption, that premodern political systems needed what is known today as collusive corruption as a lubricant to function and provide a degree of stability to their economies. This lubricant was maintained in the Latin American region after its independence.[7] In addition, at the end of the nineteenth century, political, social, and economic instability in Latin America gave way to rulers, such as Díaz, whose economic reforms were supported by global liberalism and cliques of powerful friends.

With such support, they were able to replace weak formal institutions with informal practices that gave a degree of certainty to key elements of the economy, including property rights and an increase in credit, which had previously been very scarce.

Beyond the cultural and economic approaches, corruption in Mexico has also been analyzed from other points of view, such as the political and religious. Each perspective contributes to the understanding and interpretation of the phenomenon in a given context, providing a definition of it, a form of analysis, and a proposal to combat it. Also, the profiles of people who have written about corruption in Mexico vary considerably. Most of the substantive literature on corruption has been written by political scientists and/or sociologists, such as Stephen D. Morris, María Amparo Casar, and Mauricio Merino Huerta; anthropologists, such as Claudio Lomnitz-Adler; journalists, such as Roberto Blanco Moheno and Juan Miguel de Mora (both from a previous period); consultants and members of civil associations, such as Juan E. Pardiñas, Max Kaiser, and José Octavio López Presa; and cultural and economic historians, such as Horst Pietschmann, Christoph Rosenmüller, and Stephen Haber.

It was only in the last decades of the twentieth century that corruption began to be studied. In Mexico, from the mid-1950s, governmental authorities were aware of the negative consequences of corrupt practices, as can be observed in the moralizing policies implemented during the administration of Pres. Adolfo Ruiz Cortines (1952–58). However, when Stephen Morris, a key author of the first academic studies of corruption in Mexico from a political science perspective, began investigating corruption in the 1980s, there was almost no systematic analysis of the subject.

There was no sign of any civil society organization dedicated to fighting corruption, although it was clearly a growing problem.[8] In 1979, journalists wrote two of the first works that addressed corruption: *La corrupción en México* by Roberto Blanco Moheno and *Ladrones en el gobierno* by Juan Miguel de Mora. The former surveyed prominent men, their families, friends, and sometimes their partners or accomplices who had shaped Mexican history while being involved in cases of corruption. The latter reveals increasing corruption in Mexico since the revolution.

Both of these early works, however, are journalistic and descriptive. Yet, they represent a first effort that captured the attention of academics regarding the possibility of systematizing and analyzing the information with a different methodology. To that end, the classic work of Stephen D. Morris in *Corruption and Politics in Contemporary Mexico* addresses the causes, effects, and dynamics of corruption in Mexican politics by employing sophisticated methods and analyses.

Morris continued to study corruption. In *Corruption and Democracy in Latin America*,[9] a comparative book edited in conjunction with Charles Blake, the authors note that certain countries in this region appeared to use corruption as a way to maintain the privileges and welfare of specific sectors of the population but also to decrease struggles and political threats. Furthermore, according to that study, "substantial evidence suggests that in much of Latin America corruption permeates daily life. . . . Corruption is often the rule rather than the exception."[10] Morris and Blake then mention that the dynamics of corruption have historical backgrounds that adapt into social mechanisms, meaning new generations inherit corrupt practices, and the public institutions created to combat it have proved less powerful than those practices. These authors suggest that a better understanding of corruption might contribute to the creation of ways to combat it. Certainly, the study of corruption, not only in Mexico but also in the whole world, has increased considerably in recent years.

In general, Morris's work on corruption outlines the state of affairs that led to the political change that occurred in Mexico in 2018.[11] Morris saw that the issue of political corruption directly affected election results. The best proof of this was that the official party, the Partido Revolucionario Institucional (PRI), lost the presidency in 2000 and, although it recovered it between 2012 and 2018, it lost again overwhelmingly in 2018 due to causes directly related to corruption. Morris's ideas certainly influenced the writing of this book; for example, looking for the roots of corruption in the past and the role of corruption in the maintenance of privileges for certain members of society, or groups, who are clearly associated with crony capitalism.

However, an issue that Morris does not address explicitly, which presents an opportunity for this book, is that crony capitalism has been immune to political changes. It has been a persistent element in every single administration. Even the new president, Andrés Manuel López Obrador, has a new group of allied business leaders who are favored in a similar way to other business people allied with the previous administrations. This is an area where public resources clearly disappear, and it is difficult to trace them.

Following Morris's legacy in the field of political science, studies on corruption in Mexico have advanced in the direction of defining corruption, explaining how the fight against it has been undertaken, and giving new tools to analyze and confront it. In *México*, María Amparo Casar notes that "although it has always been part of the landscape of national politics, the fight against corruption in Mexico was not incorporated into the public agenda and debate until the 1980s. It was then that it began to be perceived and defined openly as a harmful practice for public life, and formal institutional mechanisms to limit and punish it were developed."[12] She notes that, for this reason, the Secretariat of the Comptroller General of the Federation (SECOGEF) was founded in 1982—a starting point for the creation of formal institutions and laws to combat corruption within the Mexican government.

In addition, in the more stable climate after the Cold War, the World Bank, and later the International Monetary Fund (IMF), began to consider corruption as a systemic obstacle to the development of capitalism, creating new ways of measuring the level and forms of corruption.[13] Accordingly, corruption in Mexico has been an increasing focus of research from a multidisciplinary perspective. In 1998, José Octavio López Presa—an actuary who has been more involved with the implementation of public policies than in the academic field—coordinated a book titled *Corrupción y cambio*, which studied the phenomenon of corruption systematically and in depth. It analyzed the factors that propitiate it, exposed some cases of corruption, and discussed how it has been combated, prevented, and corrected.[14]

Many of the most recent studies on corruption in Mexico follow this trend. They focus on contemporary corruption and possible solutions to the problem. People involved in civil associations, nongovernmental organizations (NGOs), and public administration have carried out most of this work. For example, the Instituto Mexicano para la Competitividad (IMCO), directed by Juan E. Pardiñas, published *La corrupción en México: Transamos y no avanzamos* (Corruption in Mexico: We cheat and we do not advance) in 2015. The title is based on a popular saying, suggesting that although there may be individual benefits of corruption in the short term, the republic foots the bill in the end.[15]

In addition, in María Amparo Casar's aforementioned book, she presents indexes, indicators, and measurements of corruption in Mexico and describes efforts to combat it, including some results. Similarly, Irma Eréndira Sandoval, the current federal secretary of public function and a former academic at the Universidad Nacional Autónoma de México (UNAM), has proposed strategies for reform in the fight against corruption in the absence of a culture of legality in Mexico.[16]

All these recent books focusing on contemporary corruption have influenced my work—particularly in my last chapter, where I approach this topic more closely. However, the studies by Mauricio Merino Huerta and those of the academic program that he coordinates, the Programa Interdisiplinario de Rendición de Cuentas (PIRC-CIDE), have been particularly important for my understanding of contemporary corruption. For example, my own definition of collusive corruption, which I use in this work as an alternative to and more ample term than crony capitalism, takes elements from Transparency International, which defines corruption as the abuse of public power for private benefit, and Merino Huerta, who defines it as the illegitimate capture or appropriation of the public.[17]

For this work, collusive corruption is defined as the phenomenon by which a public official (supported by a network of bureaucrats under his orders and sometimes by other officials of the same hierarchy) abuses public power in the exercise of his functions and appropriates in collusion with elements of the private sector what belongs to the inhabitants of a nation (the public) in an illegitimate manner, either following the laws or not (or, in some cases, even supporting modification of specific laws in the short or long terms) to favor the individual's interests.

It is important to make clear that my definition refers particularly to acts committed by members of the public sector or people who manage public resources and who are linked in some way to the private sector. In addition, it includes an aspect that is difficult to measure but fundamental to consider: when the corrupt person or network carries out acts of corruption without violating the law. This situation is presented continuously, for example, in the processes of tenders for goods, services, and public works. That is to say, a "theater" is set up in almost every procurement process, where all the laws are fully complied with but the public authorities' favored bidders for goods, services, and public work get the benefit. The profits from these contracts are then distributed among the elements of the private and public sectors that participate in these processes.

Despite the economic focus of my work, and despite the neo-institutionalist influence in some of my definitions (institutions, for example), such diversity in study perspectives and forms of corruption coincides more closely with a heterodox approach. My multidisciplinary academic background and professional experience have given me particular authority to investigate the subject. When I first became interested in collusive corruption, my perspective was more focused on contemporary corruption and my vision was restricted to that of an economist. However, I decided to undertake historical research to delve deeper into the subject. From the evidence I discovered, I deduced that some contemporary corrupt behaviors were a legacy of past practices. That is why I include a brief discussion of contemporary corruption in the final chapter in this book. This contemporary analysis is linked to the main issues addressed in the other four chapters. The last chapter also recaps the major themes of the study and reflects on how the decline of the Porfiriato did not reduce crony capitalism. In addition, the chapter expands on the critique of neoliberalism for failing to change the underlying characteristics of the business community and its practices. In other words, it tells the reader what the past can reveal about Mexico's future.

As mentioned, this book is also about the role of ethnic entrepreneurs in the implementation of capitalism in Mexico. Migration has been a pillar of the capitalist system worldwide. It contributes to the promotion of industrialization, scientific and technological development, labor, increased domestic and foreign investment, the exchange of goods, and the transformation of political, economic, and social apparatuses. For this reason, ethnic groups of various nationalities and regions, such as different European, Jewish, Chinese, and Middle Eastern groups, were able to migrate to Mexico in search of better opportunities, welfare, and security.

It is important to mention that, among all of these ethnic entrepreneurs that migrated to Mexico, the Barcelonnettes (the subject of this book) were not the only ones who employed crony capitalistic strategies to amass fortunes and prevail in the Mexican elite up to the present day. And this is precisely one of the key reasons for the title of this book. I wanted to keep the relationship between crony capitalism and ethnic entrepreneurs clear without excluding other participants of this system of practices that created the particularities of capitalism in Mexico. Lebanese migrants in a later period, for example, employed these strategies as well, with Carlos Slim being a prominent example. His parents were both Maronite Catholics of Lebanese origin. His father, Julián Slim Haddad, arrived directly from Lebanon in the early twentieth century at the age of fourteen and his mother, Linda Helú, was born in Parral, Chihuahua, in Mexico. Carlos Slim, currently the richest man in Mexico and one of the richest men in the world, is well-known for his enterprises in telecommunications (TELMEX and TELCEL) and department stores (Sanborns and Sears), among many other companies.

When discussing ethnic entrepreneurship specifically, we should understand it as "a set of connections and regular patterns of interaction among people sharing common national background or migration experiences."[18] Much has been written and theorized about ethnic entrepreneurs, in Mexico and other countries. For example, in the book *Immigrant Businesses*, several authors theorize about the spatial and institutional context, social capital, globalization, and migratory networks of ethnic entrepreneurs.[19] They observe that immigrants contributed to the increase of small-scale entrepreneurs who developed local economies: "Numerous immigrants—making use of their own capital and favourable economic conditions—successfully made the transition to self-sufficiency via entrepreneurship."[20]

This pattern adequately encompasses the case of the Barcelonnettes in Mexico. The first wave of these immigrants arrived after 1821 with no capital. However, they began working in the retail trade, especially in textiles. The second and third waves of migration of this group toward the middle and end of the nineteenth century had support from the business network generated by the first wave. The latter had diversified their production from textiles to all kinds of manufacturing and had also become the main partners of the most important department stores and banks in Mexico. From their arrival, second- and third-wave immigrants were assured jobs in shops and later in banking and factories.

Another influential work about ethnic entrepreneurs is by Robert Kloosterman and Jan Rath: *Immigrant Entrepreneurs*. They make a theoretical exploration of the institutional context around immigrant entrepreneurs who made an impact on urban life and played an important role in the communities where they settled.[21] Although this study focuses on immigrant entrepreneurship in the last decade of the twentieth century in "advanced economies," it provides a useful theoretical framework for understanding key aspects shared by most ethnic entrepreneurs, such as social cohesion and specific practices that are exclusive to each individual group and nationality.

For their part, Flap, Kumcu, and Bulder make a sociological review of the human and social capital of ethnic entrepreneurs and the importance of these to their success: in particular, a tight community based on their own principles and a desire to elevate their social status. This was shared by the group studied in this book and particularly the Jean family.[22]

More specifically for Latin America, Monica C. DeHart offers an ethnographic approach to specific cases of ethnic entrepreneurs in different parts of the region. Although her book, *Ethnic Entrepreneurs*, focuses on indigenous communities not necessarily composed of immigrants, it is worth mentioning because she finds that groups with similar ethnic characteristics who participate in productive processes that were previously alien to them share certain attributes. For her, the figure of the "ethnic entrepreneur takes multiple forms, all of which embody values, relationships, and forms of knowledge deemed particularly useful for the community-based, participatory development paradigm."[23] All these aspects shared by these communities contribute to national economies, which in turn provide keys to their development—something that also emerged from the knowledge and values that the Barcelonnettes offered to the Mexican economy, eventually making them a powerful economic group in Mexico.

The particular case of French migrants—the Barcelonnettes, coming from the Ubaye valley in the French Alps—provides evidence on the process of settlement, integration, and incorporation into Mexico's social, political, and economic life. Barcelonnette migration to nations across the Atlantic was principally motivated by socioeconomic and political circumstances at home, which included the effects of the European industrial revolution.

Mexico offered these French migrants opportunities unavailable to most non-Europeans in that period. This is because racial and cultural arguments (imaginary constructs based on notions of "Western," "European," and "modern") were significant in the development and transformation of the Latin American nations, especially in the nineteenth century. It was thought that European immigrants could help build nations similar to those of their places of origin. French immigrants were, therefore, not an obstacle for governments and their policies. On the contrary, the same governments saw these individuals as potential economic and political allies in the "Europeanization" of Mexican society and modernization of the economy, as happened during the Porfiriato.

For that reason, immigrants during that period enjoyed many privileges and concessions, some of which were established through specific laws that favored them. For example, the Naturalization and Aliens Act, enacted in 1886, permitted foreigners who acquired real estate in Mexican territory to be naturalized as Mexican citizens provided they renounced their foreign nationality.[24] For its part, much of Mexican society preferred foreign migration composed of Catholics and farmers of Latin origin, especially Spanish, French, Belgian, and Italian, as they were "more easily assimilated," although in practice foreign migration was not limited to these nationalities.[25]

Delving further into the characteristics of the Porfiriato, which saw the greatest flourishing and expansion of the Barcelonnettes in Mexico, we find it to roughly coincide with what is known as the first "modern" globalization of the international economy. Díaz's presidency was characterized by the centralization of political power and economic achievements through policies aimed at the liberalization of trade, industrialization, and the welcoming of foreign migration and capital. Despite what traditional views of the Porfiriato claim, the privileges and concessions obtained did not subjugate the Mexican economy.

Díaz and his allies also strengthened the banking system. However, its operations focused on short-term rather than long-term needs. French bankers—though without ties to the Barcelonnette group at first—were crucial in establishing the main banks during the Porfiriato, such as the Banco Nacional Mexicano (BNM) in 1881 and 1882. This bank had the authorization to issue bills and was a pioneer in conducting credit operations between a bank and the government, financing the latter. Progressively, in the following three decades, the Barcelonnettes obtained more importance in the banking sector in Mexico, becoming the banks' main investors.

These characteristics of the Porfirian economy coexisted within a very fragmented internal market that only allowed significant processes of specialization and development in specific regions of the country. Although the

Porfirian state contributed to the development of internal markets through the construction of a railway network and the fight against the internal customs tariffs (*alcabalas*) in states and municipalities until their abolition in 1896, "it failed . . . in criteria such as the rectification of spatial inequality and economic and distributive efficiency."[26]

In the northeast, for example, there appeared a virtuous circle, fed by a mining-metallurgical-railway integration that stimulated the development of a durable business culture and network. Cotton cultivation in La Laguna and the development of its urban center, Torreón, is another example of the economic expansion of the north in this period. However, many southern regions, such as Tabasco, Chiapas, Guerrero, Oaxaca, and parts of the states of Michoacán and México, remained stagnant. In addition, the economic policies prioritized the development of specific sectors, such as manufacturing and the export economy.

However, economic growth in general was insufficient and affected by multiple distortions, as has been shown in various studies of the goods and factor markets. In Riguzzi's words, "there were industries but no industrialization; a banking system but little long-term credit; and salaried labour that coexisted with coercive mechanisms. And in the primary sector, there were no substantial improvements in efficiency of allocation of resources, meaning that as far as the internal market was concerned, Mexican agriculture remained far below international yields."[27] Also, the structure of the economy mainly benefited specific privileged groups of society, the Barcelonnettes and other members of Díaz's network being clear examples of this. This condition particularly affected the distributive efficiency of the Mexican economy.[28]

When Díaz took power in 1876, he faced several obstacles. Formal institutions were not strong and the governments that preceded him had experienced financial constraints as a result of the precariousness of public finances and tax collection, as well as foreign interventions and power struggles between different factions in different regions. The result had been economic stagnation and political disorder. Díaz confronted these challenges with a series of mechanisms to consolidate his authority. For example, he partnered with state elites in building alliances and sought other alliances with foreign interests that could benefit his government. The Porfirian era ushered in the first period of durable political stability in Mexico after independence.

At the same time, French culture, education, architecture, and lifestyle had an important influence on Mexican society, especially on the elites and on Díaz himself, who was to spend his last days in exile in Paris in the company of some of his closest collaborators. During his first presidency, Díaz reestablished diplomatic relations with the French—relations that had been complicated by Napoleon III's intervention in Mexico—allowing French capital and bankers to play an important role in the economy and industry of this country. With these measures, Díaz wanted, in part, to minimize the economic weight of the United States in Mexico, attracting mainly investment from European countries. As a result, waves of French migrants accelerated their entry to Mexico in that period with almost no restrictions through the Gulf of Mexico, the location of ports of entry from Europe; some settled nearby, while others progressively expanded to other regions. These dynamics and social mobilizations allowed many French families to ascend to the highest spheres of Mexican society.

In addition, the doctrine of positivism, founded by the French philosopher Auguste Comte (1798–1857), had an enormous influence on the ideology of the Porfirian regime and the political system. In 1891, some intellectuals and members of the elite who supported Díaz formed a political group based on Comte's positivist principles, calling themselves *científicos* (scientists). They believed that scientific methods should be applied to the study of society and solving its problems and that science and technology were the key to the progress of the nation.

José Yves Limantour, one of the heads of the científicos, became finance minister of the Porfirian government in 1893. He had French origins, as his parents had been born in France in the regions of Brittany and Bordeaux. This is one of many examples of the special treatment that the French received from the Porfirian regime, some of whom penetrated not only the business sector but also politics, which eventually facilitated the development of crony capitalism.

The Porfiriato needs to be revisited to understand what it brought to Mexico in terms of institutional development, which is one of the main goals of this book. As defined earlier, institutions are related to formal aspects (laws, constitutions, property rights) and informal aspects (customs, traditions, taboos, sanctions, codes of conduct) of a society, which affect its economy. At the same time, since certain behavioral patterns of the Mexican political and economic elite have repeated themselves over the years, it is also essential to identify parallels between the Porfiriato and the present day. With that in mind, the story addressed in this book affords a critical analysis of the relationship between politicians and business leaders in Mexico throughout the twentieth century.

OVERVIEW OF THE BOOK

This book is organized into five chapters, the last of which includes a discussion of contemporary corruption in Mexico. The chapters form a chronological narrative that analyzes many aspects of crony capitalism, its effect on institutions, and its relationship with specific ethnic entrepreneurs in the country.

Chapter 1 introduces the different currents of French migration in Mexico between 1815 and 1910 and their regions of expansion throughout the country. It then explains the characteristics of one of the four main currents of migration that came from France in that period: the Barcelonnettes. These were a group of ethnic entrepreneurs who, through dedication and effort, as well as the strategic creation of networks, were able to consolidate a number of successful businesses. Some of these businesses, such as the department stores Liverpool and El Palacio de Hierro, still have great national importance. This chapter presents the contextual foundation on which its main arguments are based.

Chapter 2 presents an analysis of crony capitalism as a mechanism or dynamic exploited by business and political elites, to their mutual benefit, to thrive and remain in power. While the phenomenon of crony capitalism has already been studied and debated, I suggest this has become a persistent form of corruption that has plagued Mexico and specifically allows business and political elites to collude and prosper. In this chapter, I offer, from a theoretical and practical perspective, a new way of understanding how crony capitalism in the early twentieth century fundamentally changed the future of Mexico.

One important discovery of my research is that crony capitalism was fundamental and necessary for the development of capitalist economies around the world, including Mexico's economy during the Porfiriato. However, as time passed, some developed economies built more robust institutions and a culture of respect for the law, which has not occurred to the same degree in Mexico and other developing countries.[29] My hypothesis is that crony capitalism is the main reason that institutions remain underdeveloped or weak.

In this chapter, I also create a theoretical framework that includes not only the concept of crony capitalism but also different concepts of elite and power elite, as well as key aspects to explain the persistence of the economic elite in Mexico. For this, I analyze specific cases of industrialists and landowners in the country. The mechanisms of crony capitalism and the strategies for accessing and persisting within the economic elite are two key aspects that will allow better understanding of the general experience of the Barcelonnettes in Mexico and the specific case of the Jean family.

In chapter 3, using large databases elaborated mainly from information obtained from notarial archives, I employ a sophisticated social network analysis software to construct and analyze the social network of the Jean family and the companies in which their members were involved. I explain the strategies the Jean family used to build wealth and to remain one of the most successful business families in the country during the twentieth century, surviving events such as the Mexican Revolution (1910–20) and the effects of the agrarian reform programs of the 1920s and 1930s on their economic expansion and properties.

Moreover, the Jean family built their wealth in one of the most important industrial sectors in Mexico in the first half of the twentieth century: cotton textiles. I explain how they also diversified into many other businesses, mainly in central Mexico, in the following years. I trace what, in some ways, is a classic trajectory—the rise and fall of a great family—but with attention to the particular circumstances and strategies the family used to preserve and improve its position.

Although not all members of the Jean family were equally successful, some employed effective strategies to maintain their positions as part of the economic elite over the years, which I study in chapter 4. In fact, Emilio Azcárraga Jean, the great-grandson of the first Jean (Adrián Jean) to immigrate to Mexico in the late nineteenth century, is currently the head of an important mass-media company for Spanish-language content, Televisa, whose television programs have reached China, Russia, and India. This company has been linked to Mexican politicians and to most federal and local governments since its foundation in 1955. In this chapter, I also study the fate of members of other families of the Barcelonnette community that established themselves in Mexico. This will permit the reader to understand some aspects that allowed members of different families of French origin to endure within the Mexican economic elite.

In the final chapter of the book, "Reflections on Corruption in Mexico," I examine how and to what extent crony capitalism has permeated Mexican business culture. I explain the evolution of Mexican public institutions in the twentieth century, briefly addressing topics such as anticorruption legislation and controls, crony capitalism, the rule of law, and the advance of corruption. I also discuss the strategies and processes that recent Mexican governments have employed to favor friends in economic sectors. In particular, I show how the privatization of public companies, implemented mainly by Pres. Carlos Salinas de Gortari (1988–94; hereafter Salinas), created a new group of wealthy Mexican businessmen, different from the traditional entrepreneurs that had maintained control of the economy in Mexico since before the Mexican Revolution.

This final chapter demonstrates how and why old business practices persist in modern Mexico and continue to hinder the creation of a strong institutional environment supported by the rule of law.

CHAPTER ONE

The Development of the French Business Community in Mexico during the Nineteenth Century

After 1821, and throughout most of the nineteenth century and the first decade of the twentieth, a poor French community managed to migrate en masse to Mexico. This wave of migration came from Barcelonnette in the Ubaye valley, located in the region of Provence, France, a popular vacation spot today. The specific characteristics of the group's internal organization in their workplace, the values they shared, and the business networks they created, which included Mexican politicians, allowed a proportion of them to become wealthy.

By the beginning of the twentieth century, the Barcelonnettes could count among their assets almost all the department stores established in Mexico and approximately 55 percent of the manufacturing industry. They had also become the majority shareholders of the Mexican banks and some of them even penetrated the Mexican economic elite. For example, members of the Jean family reached the highest sphere of Mexican society, a position they were able to maintain over the years, in part, by marrying into the Azcárragas—the owners of Televisa, one of the current leading media companies in Latin America.

Although Mexican policies to attract foreign migrants were not as successful as in other Latin American countries, there were waves of migration from other countries, which in some periods coincided with the Barcelonnette migration. These included, for instance, people from Lebanon and Syria who began to arrive at the end of the nineteenth century. These men likewise came to Mexico to seek wealth and also constructed networks with members of the Mexican elite, including public servants. By employing business strategies similar to those of the Barcelonnettes, some members of these communities in Mexico are currently among the richest people in the world, notably Carlos Slim, who is of Lebanese descent.

In this chapter, I explain the events and characteristics that enabled the great economic flourishing of the Barcelonnette group in Mexico in terms of wealth creation and the level of investment in key economic sectors. Some immigrants from Barcelonnette experienced diminished wealth and position by the trifecta of the Mexican Revolution, WWI, and the Great Depression; others, including a branch of the family studied in this book, still remain powerful members of Mexico's economic elite in the present day.

I also describe other waves of French migration within Mexican territory and the places where migrants became established, as well as the varied economic activities they carried out throughout the nineteenth century. This will allow a clear location of the Barcelonnette migration in time and space, in relation to the rest of the French migration currents that existed in Mexico during the nineteenth century. Additionally, I address the persistent myth regarding the success of all the members of the Barcelonnette community in Mexico. This is a myth that transcends this migrant group, so it is important to clarify in this chapter that not all the Barcelonnettes became rich nor did most of the foreigners who came to Mexico seeking a better future; only a minority achieved this goal.

THE OVERALL PICTURE OF FRENCH MIGRATION TO MEXICO

Before analyzing specific waves of French migration, how the French became distributed around Mexican territory, and their occupations in nineteenth-century Mexico, this introductory section explains the evolution of the size of the French population established in Mexico from the late colonial period to the first third of the twentieth century.

French migration to Mexico, while not as widespread as US or Spanish migration, has been considered particularly important due to the impact French immigrants had on the Mexican economy by the end of the nineteenth century through participation in key sectors such as industry, banking, and commerce. However, French migration to Mexico is more complex and extensive than that of the entrepreneurs from Barcelonnette who exploited those sectors. The various waves of French migration to Mexico between 1815 and 1910 can be helpfully categorized as (1) military migration, (2) expeditionary migration, (3) Barcelonnette migration, and (4) other dispersed waves.

The military and expeditionary waves are related to French interventions in Mexico and to specific policies to attract immigrants and were diverse regarding their regions of origin in France. On the contrary, and as its name implies, Barcelonnette migration focused on a specific regional migrant pole of exit: the Ubaye valley within Provence in southeastern France. Mexican policies to attract foreign migration bolstered this wave, but it eventually became closely linked to specific sectors of the Mexican economy, whose origins were in the retail textile trade. Geographically, the Barcelonnettes also became established in cities within commercial and industrial states, while other waves of migration spread to different regions of the country, including rural areas.

The literature on French migration in Mexico is limited.[1] Economic historians have focused primarily on the study of US and Spanish capitalists in Mexico during the Porfiriato because of the larger comparative size of their colonies. However, migration from France is of interest, in part, because it was different from the migration from other nations of the world. French migration to Mexico took place on a smaller scale compared to immigration from other countries, but it was fundamental for the Mexican economy. As a result of the actions of the Barcelonnettes, most of the economic sectors in which they participated had been radically transformed by the turn of the twentieth century.

French migration in Mexico became especially important in the second half of the eighteenth century as a consequence of the change of the royal house of Spain from the Habsburgs to the Bourbons. Although the number of French migrants in Mexico remained small at the end of the eighteenth century, those that came to Mexico participated in such economic sectors as culture, education, food, and fashion or else they became low- or medium-ranking bureaucrats. However, it is difficult to estimate the actual size of the French community in Mexico at this time, as no formal censuses were undertaken. In fact, according to Jean Meyer, during most of the colonial period and the first years of the nineteenth century, one could only hear French names in New Spain when individuals of French origin became targets of inquisitorial processes.[2] Indeed, in those years, some of the French faced serious problems, primarily related to their so-called revolutionary stances and ideas that opposed orthodoxy.[3]

The size of the French colony in Mexico began to increase after independence in 1821. This was in part the result of specific government policies implemented to attract foreign migration to Mexico. Additionally, Mexico's new status as an independent country attracted foreigners who were looking for new economic opportunities to subsist—or to become rich. As shown in table 1.1, by 1832, the French had become the largest group of immigrants in Mexico, with around six thousand French-born people living in Mexican territory.

One of the reasons French migration surpassed Spanish migration during this period was that the Spanish had been expelled from the country beginning in 1827; by 1832, fewer than four thousand Spaniards remained in Mexico.[4]

TABLE 1.1. French population living in Mexico, 1800–1950

Year	French-born population in Mexico	As % of the total foreign population in Mexico	Rank of French population in Mexico compared with those from other countries
1800	700	—	—
1832	6,000	—	1
1849	1,775	—	—
1855	2,048	—	—
1895	3,897	6.9	4
1900	3,970	6.8	4
1902	3,500	—	—
1910	4,729	4.0	6
1912	4,300	—	—
1921	3,947	3.9	7
1930	4,949	3.0	8
1940	1,801	2.6	9
1950	1,997	1.8	6

Source: Data from Pérez Siller, "Los franceses," 340.

The first law for the expulsion of Spaniards from Mexico was enacted in 1827, and a second, in 1829, complemented it.

The expulsion of the Spaniards came as a result of the measures taken against them by the nation-states that emerged from the Spanish-American Wars of Independence. It was a process that extended across the continent and that had its origin in political acts, including Spanish threats of territorial reconquest. This initiative was at first directed against individuals who had occupied positions in the Spanish administration; however, when Spanish troops invaded Mexican lands in a failed attempt in 1829, the initiative expanded to target the entire Spanish population.

As a result of these two laws, more than seven thousand people were expelled from Mexico due to their Spanish origin between 1827 and 1829. Some studies affirm that there were fewer than two thousand Spaniards in the country by 1830.[5] However, although small, migration from Spain never fully stopped in this period. Spain officially recognized Mexican independence in 1836, and this recognition would again cause increasing waves of migration from Spain to Mexico, mainly in the second half of the nineteenth century.

It is interesting to note the decline in the French population in Mexico after

1832 (see table 1.1). This can be explained in part by the Mexican-American War (1846–48), which resulted in Mexico's loss of California in a period when significant amounts of gold were discovered there. The decline may also be due to the Pastry War, a war between Mexico and the French from 1838 to 1839 that led to anti-French sentiment and ultimately to the expulsion of some of the French from Mexican territory.[6] The Pastry War is also known as the first French intervention in Mexico.[7]

The figure for the French population of Mexico in 1849 was taken from the report entitled *Registre de la Population Francaise au Mexique*. However, the author of this report, J. Levasseur, only included heads of family (1,775). As a result, Pérez Siller estimates the number of French inhabitants in Mexico in 1849 to be around 4,000.[8] This underestimation appears in other figures presented in table 1.1,[9] so the population figures after 1850 were also at least twice the size. As can be observed in the table, the French population in Mexico rose again slightly in the second half of the nineteenth century. This resulted from the increase in chain migration from Barcelonnette to Mexico, which had begun in 1821. Various regional studies have acknowledged the concentration of Barcelonnette migration in that period, although it is unclear just what percentage of the total French population in Mexico came from this specific region.[10]

By 1895, the year of the first official population census in Mexico, the French population had escalated to 3,897 (see table 1.1). This figure increased to 4,729 in 1910, at which point the French population in Mexico reached its peak, subsequently decreasing as a result of the Mexican Revolution and WWI. In the year 1910, the Barcelonnettes, as a group, reached their highest level in terms of their contributions (investment and production levels) to the Mexican economy in the main sectors where they participated: industry, commerce, and banking. However, the revolution and WWI would also negatively affect these contributions, with some exceptions. As an example of these exceptions, the main Jean family companies continued to grow between 1910 and 1920 as they reinvested their increasing profits.

Considering the underestimation of data on the French community in Mexico, we see that its size ranged, on average, between six thousand and eight thousand individuals over the course of the nineteenth century. These numbers are small compared to those of other foreign immigrant groups. For example, throughout most of the nineteenth century (except for a period during the 1830s), the Spanish population was more numerous than the French population in Mexico. Moreover, by the turn of the century, the US, Chinese, and Guatemalan populations were also much larger than the French community in Mexico, as can be observed in figure 1.1.

As these numbers show, French migration in Mexico cannot be considered

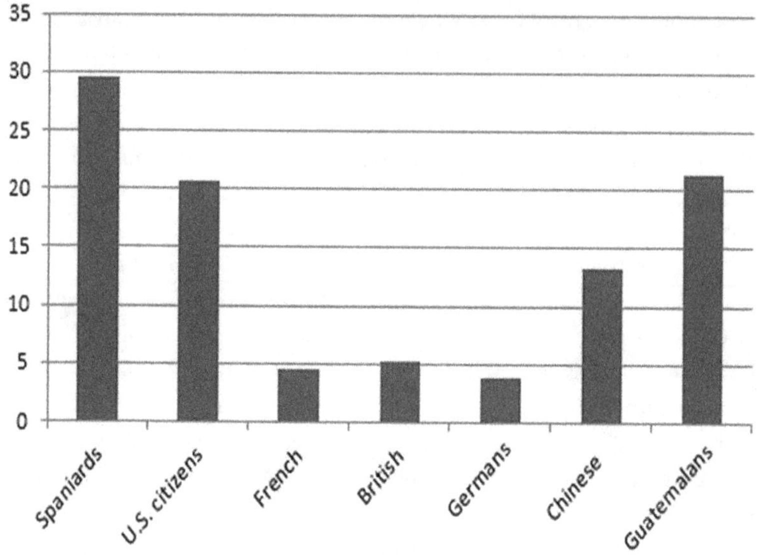

Figure 1.1. Selected foreign nationals in Mexico, 1910 (in thousands). Based on Instituto Nacional de Estadística y Geografía, "Censo de Población y Vivienda 1910," accessed November 5, 2014, https://www.inegi.org.mx. (José Galindo)

a demographic expansion, as was the case for European migrations to other Latin American countries during this period. For example, in Argentina, the Italian, French, and Spanish populations were much more important than any colony of foreigners in Mexico. However, the significance of the small French community established in Mexico lies in its contributions to the Mexican economy. This was particularly the case of the Barcelonnette group, which capitalized at a specific moment in Mexican history—during the Porfiriato (1876–1911)—and transformed commerce, manufacturing, electricity generation, housing, and finance in Mexico.

Next, we delve into the waves of French immigrants in Mexico in the nineteenth century other than the Barcelonnette group.

Waves of French Migration and Their Impact

Following independence, there were three main waves of French immigration into Mexico in the nineteenth century, independent of that of the Barcelonnettes: as part of the French army (military); in expeditions intended to colonize land (expeditionary); and in other dispersed waves (others). Each of them will be briefly analyzed here to contextualize the Barcelonnette migration that will be explained later in this chapter.

Military Migration

Between 1815 and 1820, at the end of the Napoleonic Wars, while Mexico was still struggling for its independence from Spain it received around one thousand retired French soldiers. Many of these soldiers entered through northern Mexico and settled in different regions of the country. A number of these soldiers became established in the state of Veracruz, in Acayucan, and San Andrés Tuxtla, among other places. The population of French soldiers at Veracruz attracted other migrants to this region. In fact, Veracruz was ultimately the port of entry for 60 percent of French migrants between 1820 and 1830.[11] However, little is known about this first migration process and its aftereffects.

Another clearly defined period of nineteenth-century French military migration took place during the second French intervention in Mexico in the 1860s. This was an intervention that initially resulted from the precarious state of public finances in Mexico. The Public Treasury disaster obliged Pres. Benito Juárez to issue the law of July 17, 1861, which decreed a two-year suspension of the debts that Mexico owed to three foreign countries: Great Britain, France, and Spain. This measure produced a European response: the London Convention of October 31, 1861. By means of this diplomatic agreement, the signatory powers agreed to send naval and military forces to Mexico, demanding that it recognize and honor its debts. However, the emperor of France, Napoleon III, had other intentions regarding Mexico that aligned with the desire of some conservative Mexicans to resolve the country's internal problems through the arrival of a foreign ruler and the establishment of a monarchy. Napoleon III wanted to expand and install his power on the new continent, collect the enormous debt Mexico owed to France, and subjugate Mexico "to form a Latin empire that would contain the encroaching and expansionist march of the United States."[12] Paradoxically, he was following the Anglo-Saxon country's example in light of successful attempts to appropriate territory and wealth that had belonged to Mexico and that had been seized some years earlier during the war between Mexico and the United States (1846–48). Napoleon III also took advantage of the situation in which Mexico found itself, with a constant power struggle, several internal wars, and poor economic conditions, as well as the United States's internal conflict at that time. The latter would last until 1865 and prevent the United States from focusing attention on Mexico and protecting the country from this European threat.

This eventually led to the establishment of a French empire in Mexico in 1864, led by Maximilian of Hapsburg (Maximilian I)—the second in line of the Hapsburg brothers, with little chance of governing in Europe—accompanied by his wife, Charlotte of Belgium. The idea of a French empire was initially supported by Maximilian's older brother, Franz Joseph, emperor of Austria, who approved Napoleon III's plan despite considering the latter a political rival due to his power. In addition, Franz Joseph was not unhappy to have his brother far away from Austria, given his alternative political ideals. However, he would later doubt his brother's success, due to Mexico's political and economic instability.

The emperor couple arrived in Mexico to face a more complex reality than the French emperor had warned them about. They tried to implement liberal policies that would bring serious negative consequences for the emperor, as they affected the economic interests of the Catholic Church and wealthy landholders who were part of the conservative groups who had originally supported Maximilian in establishing an empire in Mexico. As his control began to weaken, Charlotte traveled to France in mid-1866 to seek help from Napoleon III and the pope. She asked Napoleon III to continue the support that he had rescinded upon realizing that there was no chance of sustaining the empire in Mexico with benefit to him. However, the response from both was negative. Between January and March 1867, most of the French armed forces would leave Mexican territory.

Maximilian could have left Mexico too, but he hoped to reconstitute a Mexican imperial army with figures like Miguel Miramón and Tomás Mejía—two Mexicans who had supported him as emperor. Maximilian fought the Mexican republicans, led by Benito Juárez, until he was taken prisoner in Querétaro. The empire ended with Maximilian's execution alongside Miramón and Mejía on June 19, 1867, in the Cerro de las Campanas, Querétaro.[13]

This intervention brought with it new French migrants, due in part to army desertions and special permission requests made by militiamen to remain in Mexican territory.[14] However, it has proven difficult to determine the exact number of soldiers that remained in Mexico after the end of the French empire in 1867. An approximate figure is nine hundred individuals, some of whom married Mexican women and established themselves permanently in the states of Durango, Jalisco, Michoacán, Aguascalientes, Oaxaca, Veracruz, and México, among others.[15]

Expeditionary Migration

During the 1830s, the Mexican government implemented migration policies to encourage foreign migration to the country. These policies fell within the social, political, and economic goals of the new nation. The idea was to populate different regions of Mexico, to solve agricultural scarcity in virgin lands using international migration, and to "improve the Mexican race." The government supported foreign expeditions to contribute to this process. European migration was particularly favored by this policy, and France undertook various expeditions organized in what have been referred to as colonization companies.

There is a tragic episode of one of these migration attempts. Between 1829 and 1834, around six hundred French migrants, primarily from the southeast regions of Vaucluse and Drome, arrived in Coatzacoalcos, Veracruz. Most of these immigrants ultimately died as a result of a combination of tropical weather and diseases, shipwrecks, and river floods. Those who survived dispersed through various parts of the states of Veracruz and Oaxaca. Some of them also migrated to the southeastern state of Tabasco a few years later.[16]

A more successful expedition was led by Stéphane Guenot, a former treasurer of the French army. In 1833, he established himself in Jicaltepec, Veracruz, along with eighty Burgundians primarily from the region of Champlitte. The Jicaltepec settlement prospered, and throughout the nineteenth century, it became the main point of entry for many arriving immigrants, primarily from Bourgogne and Franche-Comté.[17]

This wave of migration was predominantly rural, and some of these migrants became wealthy Mexican farmers, producing mainly vanilla and corn, among other crops. Between 1840 and 1880, they also colonized the town that came to be known as San Rafael, across the Nautla River from Jicaltepec (fig. 1.2).

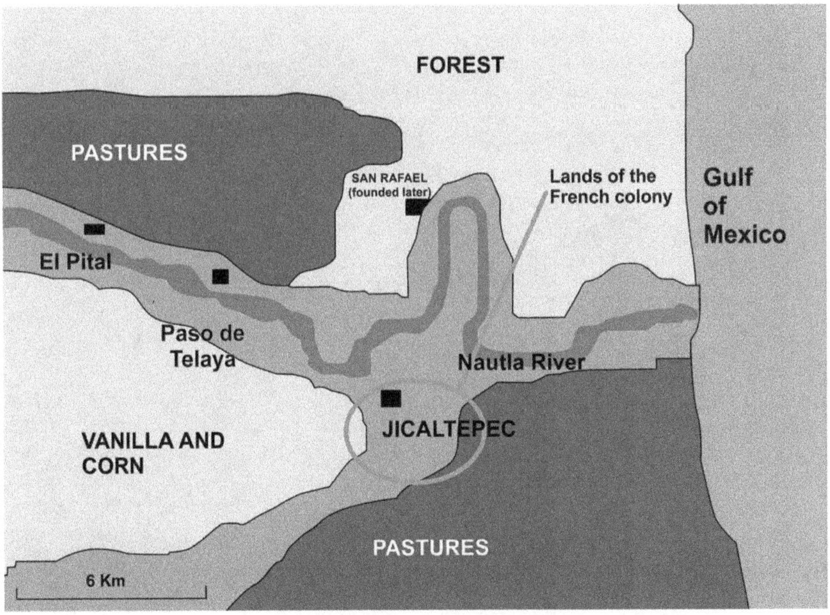

Figure 1.2. Land use in Jicaltepec, 1833. Based on the Archivo Museo de San Rafael collection and David Skerritt Gardener, *Colonos franceses*, 100. (José Galindo)

Figure 1.3. Traditional way to cross the Nautla River from Jicaltepec to San Rafael, 2014. (José Galindo)

Figure 1.4. Typical French building in Jicaltepec, 2014. (José Galindo)

They crossed the river in rowboats, as can be observed in figure 1.3. In addition, they built beautiful houses in both towns using French architecture and style (fig. 1.4). At the turn of the twentieth century, the inhabitants of Jicaltepec and San Rafael were still promoting French migration to Mexico.

In addition, by the second decade of that century, they began to relax the customs that had kept them isolated from the non-French inhabitants of this region. This was reflected in greater economic spillovers and benefits for the region, as well as an increase in marriages and miscegenation in the area. A series of letters from different years, sent between inhabitants of this French colony and authorities in France, describe the living conditions in Mexico and in these colonies in particular.[18]

There were other colonizing projects led by French colonization companies, such as the Franco-Mexican Colonization Company. It was founded in 1833 and established two new colonies in Veracruz, Mexico: one along the Xaltepec River and another in Tepijolote. Other French colonization projects failed in Texas, Chihuahua, and Sonora in the 1850s. The original idea behind these projects was to establish agricultural colonies in those regions, attracted by the success of the agricultural colonies in Veracruz. These efforts were part of the leading role that the Mexican government also undertook in foreign migration in the 1850s. Indeed, in 1854, Pres. Antonio López de Santa Anna issued a general law regarding this subject.[19]

Other French Migrations to Mexico

Other waves of French migration to Mexico have not been studied in detail. These were mainly the result of isolated individuals who, like their countrymen, decided to migrate in the hope of a better future. Many were driven by the difficult political or economic situations in France during the nineteenth century or simply by the desire to construct something new. These isolated individuals actually constituted the bulk of the French community in Mexico. Immigration from southwest France stands out in particular; however, little is known about the Basque-Bernese migration from the Atlantic Pyrenees. These very diverse immigrants did not generate a group identity that distinguished them, unlike the Barcelonnettes and the French established in Jicaltepec and San Rafael.[20]

There are numerous ways by which the French reached Mexico indirectly. For example, around twenty thousand French immigrants arrived in California in 1853, attracted by the Gold Rush. They were comprised largely of former Republicans, soldiers, and artisans. However, they were victims of xenophobia in the United States so some of them ultimately settled in Mexico, in the northern state of Sonora.[21] This was a sizable population, one that adopted Mexican traditions and culture very quickly, and they did "not keep anything of their origin but their names."[22] In Meyer's words, the French who were fully incorporated into Mexico "are numerous but are lost to the historian, unable to evaluate the phenomenon."[23]

Expansion of the French Colony within Mexican Territory

This section will show, with the support of the available data, where all the population of French origin was distributed within Mexican territory by the mid-nineteenth century and how this changed over the next seventy years when the Barcelonnette colony clearly expanded.

By the mid-nineteenth century, the French had become distributed in cities located in three primary geographic areas: Mexico City; the main ports of Tampico, Veracruz, and Tabasco in the Gulf of Mexico and Guaymas in the Pacific; and in the capital cities of mining and commercial states from Oaxaca to Chihuahua, including the states of Hidalgo, Guanajuato, San Luis Potosí, Zacatecas, Durango, and Guadalajara (fig. 1.5).

These places of residence have much to do with mandatory points for the transit of goods, particularly silver. Two-thirds of the immigrants were

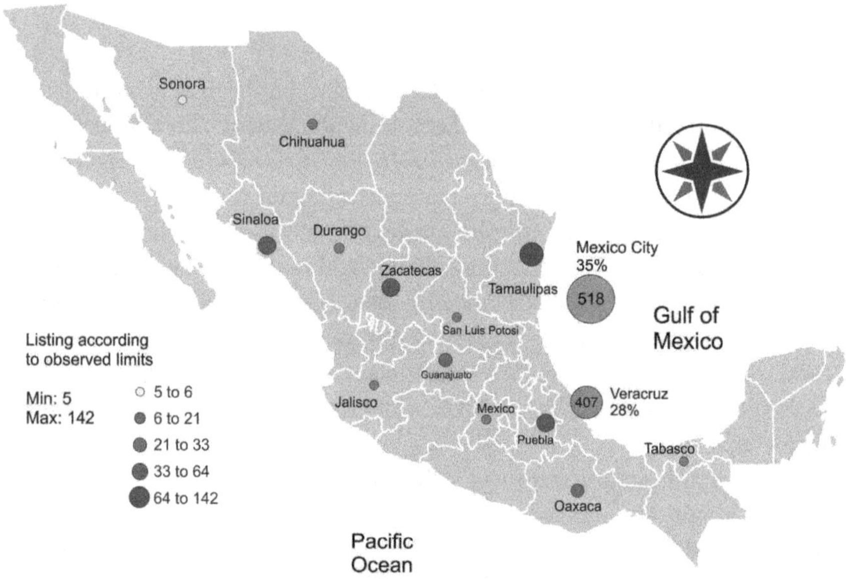

Figure 1.5. French immigrants in Mexico by state, 1849 (1,470 people in total). Based on data from Pérez Siller, *Los franceses*, 358. (José Galindo)

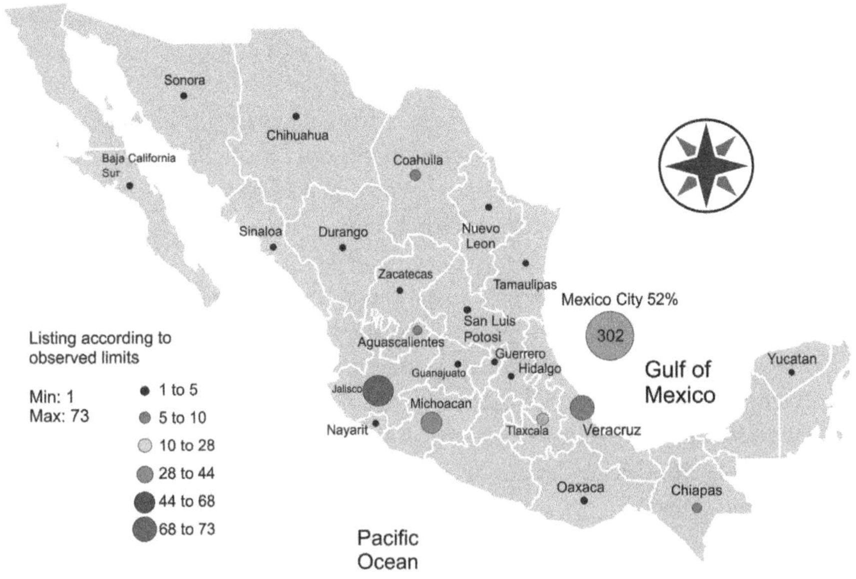

Figure 1.6. French immigrants in Mexico by state, 1914–1918 (580 people in total). Based on data from Pérez Siller, *Los franceses*, 359. (José Galindo)

concentrated in the Puebla-Veracruz-Mexico corridor. The profile of immigration was dependent upon the local economy, and it changed over time to become completely different by 1914 (fig. 1.6).[24]

As seen in figure 1.6, the concentration of the French population in Mexico City had deepened, with more than half of the French immigrants established there. More generally, the French were primarily established in the central part of the country, between Veracruz and Guadalajara. Some were also established in the south, in the states of Oaxaca, Chiapas, and Yucatán, and in the north, they were primarily established in the state of Coahuila.

The Veracruz population constituted 12 percent of all French immigrants during this period. Within Veracruz, the French settled mainly in the textile regions near Orizaba and in cities such as Cordoba and Xalapa. They also settled in agricultural regions where companies such as the Paraíso Novillero Sugar Mill produced crops like sugar in the central zone of the state or in agro-urban settlements such as those previously mentioned in Jicaltepec and San Rafael. Additionally, there were numerous traders and brokers who moved to the port of Veracruz. Immigration to the state of Veracruz was thus multifaceted and oriented to very different economic sectors: rural, industrial, and commercial.

In the west and the rest of the country in general, we find that immigrants most frequently established themselves in the capitals and major cities of the states. In fact, four-fifths of the total identified sample of the French population in 1914 lived in five cities: Mexico City, Guadalajara, Morelia, Puebla, and Orizaba. Others became established in cities such as Saltillo, Tulancingo, Aguascalientes, Chihuahua, Monterrey, León, and Oaxaca; this confirms the predominantly urban character of French immigration in the second period analyzed.[25]

When we compare 1849 (see fig. 1.5) and 1914 to 1918 (see fig. 1.6), the transformation of French immigration is readily apparent: the French left the ports and mining areas to concentrate on the major cities in the center and west of the country with their migration becoming urban in character. The migration of the Barcelonnette group, mainly urban and accentuated in the second half of the nineteenth century, contributed to this change in the nature of French migration in Mexico.

The Occupations of the French Community in Nineteenth-Century Mexico

As the French population became concentrated in cities during the second half of the nineteenth century, the economic activities of French immigrants also narrowed in focus. By 1915, the proportion of French immigrants engaged in trade had increased considerably and a large number of commercial houses founded by that time belonged to the French community.

It is important to note that French immigration to Mexico in the late nineteenth century largely coincided with the "Frenchification" of Mexico, due to a taste among Mexican elites for French fashion, wine, and other luxury goods, and a concurrent interest by Mexican presidents in French liberalism and modernization. Both of these elements helped the Barcelonnette community in Mexico grow, since they were able to capitalize on the Porfiriato era's interest in economic progress.

What was the socioprofessional profile of French immigrants? During the mid-nineteenth century, the French continued to carry out economic activities already predominant in the eighteenth century. In 1845, the range of jobs and professions was extensive, but they can be grouped into categories that allow for clearer comparisons with later data. Traders were the largest category, representing around 26 percent. Following close behind were artisans, at 25.8 percent (carpenters, joiners, locksmiths, jewelers, goldsmiths, engravers, painters, vintners, and shoemakers, among others). There was a large group dedicated to working in the food industry (around 11.1 percent);

these included bakers, pastry chefs, and restauranteurs. Farmers and workers (mainly in textiles) represented around 10.5 percent, while fashion designers and hairdressers represented 6 percent. The other 20.6 percent was comprised of other professionals and employees, including public servants, other servants, and the unemployed.

This composition changed over time. Beginning in 1891, but more pronounced in 1914 to 1918, the number of immigrants engaged in trade (dealers, employees, brokers, or sellers) increased substantially. In 1891, this group represented more than 50 percent of the immigrant population, but by the second period analyzed (1914–18), it represented two-thirds.[26] By the second period, new categories had also appeared, such as owners of commercial houses or founding partners, officers, directors, and managers. This indicates the proliferation of commercial establishments. Additionally, it points to the transformation of small textile shops called *cajones de ropa*, founded in the years 1840 to 1850, into import and novelty shops during the 1860s and 1870s.

There was another stage in this evolution: the construction of department stores from the late 1890s to 1910. The Barcelonnettes contributed significantly to all these changes. By 1910, the number of French commercial houses spread across the country reached more than 300, of which 240 belonged to the Barcelonnettes. Within their productive network, the Barcelonnettes also participated in the manufacturing industry, which provided products to their commercial houses. They also participated in national and regional banks, in which by that same year they controlled more than 60 percent of the banks' shares.

The Frenchification of Mexico

Before analyzing the growth of the Barcelonnette community in Mexico, it is important to explain how the Mexican elites developed a taste for French goods and culture, which coincided with the period in which the Barcelonnettes expanded in Mexico. The Maximilian Empire (1863–67) saw a burgeoning taste for luxury, especially among the Mexican elites. At the time, many countries around the world associated this luxury with all things French, including Mexico. One Barcelonnette highlights this growing taste: "The avidity of the Mexican elites to participate in the French civilization is amazing, ridiculous, and pathetic. The members of the elite speak a Spanish full of Gallicisms, and walk in the afternoon, especially on Sundays, wearing crinoline dresses, tuxedos, and top hats. . . . Clothing and military uniforms are tailored to what Parisian fashion dictates. Mexican elites also bring French hairdressers, dressmakers, tailors, shoemakers, and chefs to cook for them. The cafes, such as La Concordia and El Progreso, car rides, dances in halls, so similar to ours, . . . are all products of Frenchification, . . . as when the bourgeois or the elegant woman wearing a fur coat dreams of the Bois de Boulogne."[27]

Arnaud, a notary public of French origin, affirmed that "from 1863 to 1864, French silk exports to Mexico grew abruptly from 2,959,329 to 9,653,999; French cotton fabrics increased from 1,823,047 to 4,782,177; wool fabrics increased from 2,855,318 to 15,309,351; and linen fabrics grew from 155,083 to 310,946."[28]

The French army also became an important inspiration for Mexican generals, and French science permeated Mexican scientific and educational institutions in the country beginning in the 1860s. In addition, French architecture in general and Haussmann's Paris in particular inspired many architects and urban planners throughout the world—Mexico was no exception.

Haussmann was chosen by Emperor Napoleon III to undertake a massive urban renewal program of new public works, boulevards, and parks in Paris. This is commonly referred to as Haussmann's renovation of Paris. His vision of the city still dominates central Paris, and its influence can be seen, for example, in Mexico City's avenue currently named Paseo de la Reforma, which was built during the French empire in Mexico.

Haussmann's influence is also evident in the attempts to zone and decentralize cities in Mexico. Service networks were created in Porfirian Mexico, usually located in the periphery so as not to obstruct bureaucratic activities. For example, the stations of the Central and Mexican Railroad, the Mexican National Railroad, the Interoceanic Railroad, and the trams in the capital were constructed in this period. Mexico and Paris also shared a decentralization of certain urban facilities, such as cemeteries, slaughterhouses, hospitals, insane asylums, and prisons, all of which were not deemed sanitary enough to be located in the center of the city.[29]

The French in Mexico also enjoyed more autonomy and freedom under liberal presidents Benito Juárez (1867–71), Sebastián Lerdo de Tejada (1871–76), and Porfirio Díaz (1876–1911), as they were not associated with the imperialist invasion of Napoleon III. In fact, the French Revolution, which overthrew the monarchy in France, had served as an inspiration and model for freedom in the Latin American independence movements and its ideas were still very present in the Mexican liberal presidents of the last third of the nineteenth century.

Although liberalism of Juárez's era was different from Porfirian liberalism, British and French liberalism significantly influenced these Mexican presidents. Jeremy Bentham's ideas, for example, penetrated Mexican liberalism throughout the nineteenth century. Bentham was the founder of modern utilitarianism (a philosophical thought in which pleasure and pain ultimately motivate human actions). Bentham's utilitarianism, in some ways, underlined

Enlightenment ideas of the rights of man. Although he "rejected the French Declaration of Rights of 1789 as 'mere bawling on paper,' [he] ended up justifying on the basis of utility the very rights which the French were claiming on grounds of nature."[30]

Utilitarian doctrine dominated the social and economic aspects of Mexican liberal thought, including agrarian aspects. In addition, utilitarianism clearly influenced the thought of José María Luis Mora, one of the main supporters of Mexican liberalism and secular thought. "We find [Mora] speaking in 1827 of 'the wise Bentham' and agreeing that not only is utility the origin of all law, but also the principle of all human actions."[31]

The differences that appeared between the Juárez and Díaz regimes' concept of liberalism—and between the policies that each applied to achieve liberty and equality as the main values of their philosophy—relate to the Porfirian regime's growing interest in economic development and the promulgation of positivist philosophy, ideas that emerged from the works of the French philosopher Auguste Comte during that period. Positivism proposed that the only valid knowledge is scientific, and that authentic knowledge is susceptible to verification through the scientific method.

This principle included knowledge in social disciplines. In addition, this philosophy emphasized the importance of order and progress in society. One consequence of the adoption of these new ideas was that Díaz clearly favored economic progress over democracy, which he considered to be unfeasible at the time he took office.[32]

Scientific racism also became more influential in Mexico in the Porfirian era. Herbert Spencer's Social Darwinism influenced the avant-garde liberal ideas of the time, and particularly those of John Stuart Mill, another proponent of utilitarianism and a former student of Bentham. If liberalism had been conceived as a philosophy of individuals in the beginning, with Mill it now expanded to recognize its relationship with social institutions and their development. Mill's liberalism also adopted the idea of survival of the most capable individuals. This corresponded to the popular concept of "survival of the fittest" in Darwin's biological scheme and was now applied racially, as adherents claimed the white race was the most capable of achieving economic progress. These ideas also had an impact on Díaz's policies. For example, although he proclaimed that all foreigners should be treated with absolute respect, there was a preference for white immigrants as part of a plan to "whiten" the Mexican population.[33]

Under the historical and ideological context and the background on French migration discussed above, the next section specifically delves into a case study of the Barcelonnettes.

THE BARCELONNETTE CASE STUDY

The Growth of the Barcelonnette Community in Mexico

Following independence, Mexico struggled to find an effective ruler until Juárez formally took power again in 1867, after the French intervention. The presidents that governed Mexico before him faced constant foreign interventions and invasions, internal divisions between liberals and conservatives, widespread regionalism with caudillos and caciques governing different areas, and frequent bankruptcy. Juárez died unexpectedly in 1871, and Sebastián Lerdo governed following his death—with the persistent threat of Díaz seizing power. After Díaz took office in 1876, he continued the process of centralizing power and implementing conditions conducive to stimulating the Mexican economy.

The Barcelonnettes capitalized on this situation. The story of the group's immigration came as a result of the many challenges they experienced in their native France. During the first half of the nineteenth century, itinerant sales, the basis of life in the lower Alps, began to decline. The appearance of regular salaried jobs created competition and traveling merchants began searching for other jobs, from modest administrative positions in the cities to unskilled labor.

Moreover, the textile industry began to compete with handmade items, which families in the mountains had historically manufactured during the winter. The initial industrialization efforts in the lower Alps failed because of winter frosts, partly because they interrupted communications, generating a serious obstacle to production and trade. Nonetheless, by 1850, the decline of handmade textiles sold door to door was accelerating, and the manufacture of silk articles had already collapsed. By the mid-nineteenth century, the process of emigration from the lower Alps to other regions had increased, especially during the winters (fig. 1.7).

This process of migration benefited not only itinerant merchants but also shepherds, priests, and teachers. In fact, Barcelonnette stopped supplying priests and teachers to the surrounding regions of France when urban Mexico began to offer better alternatives.[34] The first family of Barcelonnettes that arrived in Mexico in 1821, the Arnaud brothers, departed for America in the early 1820s after closing down their silk workshop in Jaussiers, a town close to Barcelonnette. The Arnaud brothers opened the first novelty shop in Mexico City in 1829: Las Siete Puertas. This business was not very prosperous, but it served as a seed for other businesses. For example, other Barcelonnettes (Eugène Caire, Gabriel Derbez, and Alphonse Jauffred, who was a former employee of the

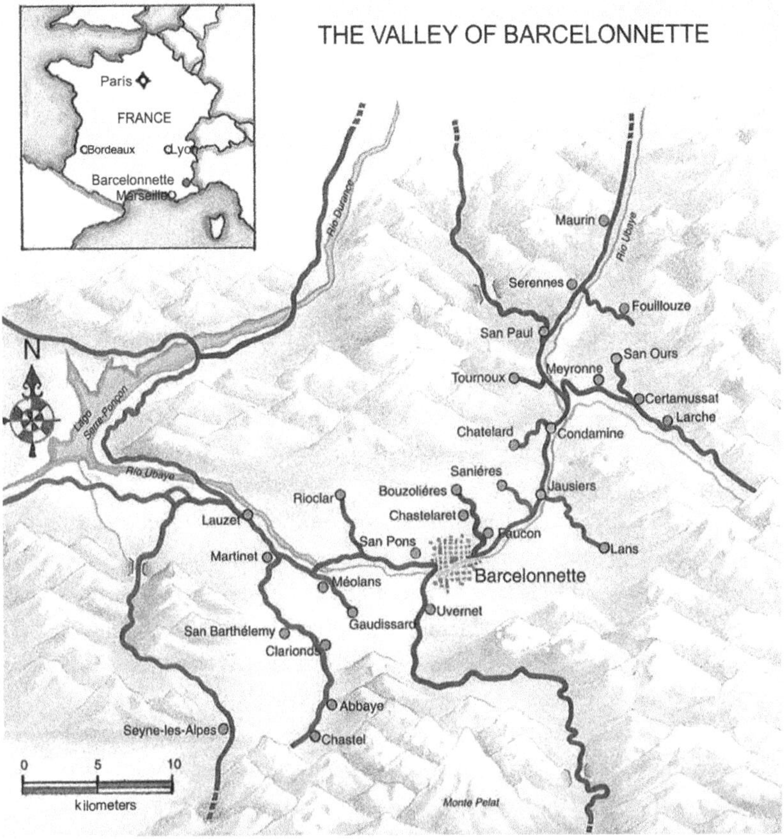

Figure 1.7. Valley of Barcelonnette. (Base map courtesy of Editorial Clío, Libros y Videos, S.A. de C.V.; modified by José Galindo)

Arnauds) opened a similar store in 1838 that was more successful. In fact, the positive results from their store allowed them to return rich to France in 1845. Some authors mention that, when they returned to France, each of the partners of the store brought back 50,000 Mexican pesos, which were equivalent to 200,000 gold francs. This represented a fortune in the location in which they had originally lived in France.

From that moment on, a significant percentage of the youth population of Barcelonnette and its surrounding areas began to dream about becoming rich in Mexico and emigrated to that country, finding support and employment offered by fellow countrymen who had already established themselves there.[35] Thus, initial economic success created a chain of migration from that region. The characteristic specific practices and values of this group came to include the construction of a closed business network, mainly composed of members of the same community but also including other key entrepreneurs from Mexico and other countries, as well as Mexican public servants. It was this complex network that eventually defined the group's distinctive identity.

By the mid-nineteenth century, the Barcelonnettes had already established nine retail houses in Mexico. Five were located in the capital, and the rest were in the capital cities of the states of México, Zacatecas, Puebla, and Jalisco.[36] These trading houses exclusively sold common fabrics, mainly to produce linens and underwear. Overall, products on offer were poorly diversified and of poor quality and sold in small establishments. At that time, Spaniards and Mexicans controlled retail and intermediate trade. The Barcelonnettes obtained their first products from wholesale houses in Mexico City, where they received acceptable credit conditions: they had a payment term of eight months with an interest rate of 1 percent per month thereafter.[37]

The organization of the Barcelonnettes' first shops was disciplined and overly strict. The hierarchy was divided among the bosses (the founding partners who managed the shops), the salaried employees (who enjoyed a portion of profits), and the apprentices in training. Employees' lives were characterized by austerity and hard work, and they shared an environment that kept them isolated from the Mexican reality and entirely dependent on their employer. Once recruited, immigrants worked at least a year in simple jobs for extremely low wages. When they had enough understanding of Spanish and business operations, and had earned the respect of their bosses, they could serve behind the counter. After a time, they might be eligible for promotion to fill posts as traveling representatives or accountants. Some could later establish businesses on their own or enter into partnerships. It is noteworthy that, after arrival, it took the Barcelonnette immigrant an average of four to six years to start their own (typically small) businesses.[38] For the successful, the prospect of saving profits over a few decades might allow them to return to France and marry there.[39] In that case, the management of the businesses would be transferred to compatriots or relatives, while the main owners retained ownership back in France.

The Barcelonnettes had several advantages upon their arrival in Mexico. They integrated with ease due to their status as Europeans and because they shared the most practiced religion in Mexico: Catholicism. They also enjoyed the confidence of their suppliers because they acquired a reputation for honesty and also as good payers. This allowed them to obtain sufficient initial stocks without having the resources at first to purchase them. Between 1850 and 1864, the Barcelonnettes' fabric stores grew from five to twelve in Mexico City, and they had established around twenty more in other states. By 1864, there were around forty-five companies in different sectors, employing four hundred Barcelonnettes around the country.[40] However, one should not exaggerate the importance of the Barcelonnettes' stores in the mid-1860s. In 1864, their stores were still simple retail shops that sold fabrics at low prices to the lower classes.

The French intervention in Mexico, which began in 1862, also favored the Barcelonnettes. First, their French ancestry allowed them to supply the French army with uniforms during the war of intervention. As a result, many large fortunes were made at this point. Following the war, the Barcelonnettes had no problems with the Mexican government because they declared themselves to be friends of liberalism and because they opposed their own country's intervention in Mexico. In fact, "French consuls consistently complained about the immigrants from the town of Barcelonnette to Mexico. They were perceived as narrowly self-interested and unpatriotic toward France. The immigrant merchants seemed to have allegiance only to other people from the village of Barcelonnette."[41] In this way, a seemingly anti-French attitude favored them.

The French intervention also resulted in the creation of a sea route between St. Nazaire, a city on the west coast of France, and Veracruz in 1863, which was complemented by the 1873 inauguration of a railroad line that connected the coast of Veracruz and Mexico City. This radical change in transport conditions would become a powerful catalyst for the development of the Barcelonnettes in Mexico, since their dependence on intermediaries stopped. Beginning in 1863, the French gradually eliminated the English, German, and Spanish wholesale houses in Mexico, buying merchandise directly from Paris and Manchester. This represented the beginning of the Barcelonnette colony's real success in Mexico.

The phase of capital accumulation by the Barcelonnettes in Mexico also began during the 1870s. They began to build up the funds that enabled them to finance a successful expansion. This can be seen as part of the consolidation of the Porfirian government in Mexico. The state was becoming stronger; the power of the central government was continually increasing. Stephen Haber writes, "The engine driving this whole process of political and economic transformation [included] the inflow of capital from Europe and the United States. After 1870, capital and capitalists flowed into the nation, draining and retimbering the mines, spurring the growth of *haciendas* and plantations and financing the whirlwind construction of a national railway system."[42] This process enabled the Barcelonnettes to accumulate capital, as they could now count on a better distribution system, due in part to the better transportation system.

The special treatment given to foreign capital and migration and the access that foreign entrepreneurs subsequently obtained to negotiate directly with Porfirian government officials, build companies together, and share profits represent the foundation of early crony capitalism in independent Mexico, which are analyzed in detail in chapter 2. The very nature of migration (and Mexican migration policies) was critical in undermining the long-term establishment of strong institutions, and it contributed to crony capitalism. That is, since the state encouraged migration with privileges and few controls and from a point of weakness, it exacerbated the obstacles to the construction of functional national and state institutions rather than contributing to their development and strengthening. The way of doing business in Mexico is rooted in informal practices that, over time, became difficult to control without affecting the economy. Nor have the individual economic interests of different business participants generated incentives for change.

As stated by Paul Garner, the promotion of Mexico's abundant natural resources and huge economic potential successfully helped persuade foreign business owners and financiers to invest in the country. According to the Díaz administration, Mexico needed the resources and technology developed in the United States and European countries to modernize Mexico's infrastructure and factories. To this was added the high appreciation that various Mexican administrations had given to foreign tastes, values, and race. The Díaz government assigned substantial resources to promote Mexico's international image as a nation fully committed to material progress and science. Among other actions, the regime spent almost $1 million USD on the country's representation at the world's fair in Chicago in 1893 and almost half a million USD in Paris in 1889. The promotional catalogs distributed there described Mexico as a model of stability and prosperity and as a haven of legality for foreign businessmen.

For its part, diverse codes and laws promulgated throughout the Porfiriato, beginning with the 1884 commercial code, also encouraged foreign investment in Mexico without limiting local investment. Both local and foreign investment benefited from clearer rules established in those codes and laws and the emergence of modern business figures, such as the limited company. Also, Limantour's European origin and the macroeconomic stability this gave Mexico after he was appointed minister of finance in 1893 presented a very attractive environment for foreign investment during the Porfiriato. Limantour battled with the balance between US and European investment, favoring, as far as possible, the latter.[43]

The prerogatives that the Mexican government specifically granted to foreign investors, for example, included specific agreements established with some foreign companies allowing them to introduce construction materials for the establishment of factories and other buildings free of all taxes and duties. In addition, other necessary investments for operation and the shares of those companies were also exempt from any tax contribution.

These foreign companies were also protected against competition because the Mexican government agreed in writing not to grant greater or comparable franchises to individuals or similar companies. But the most important aid the government offered to foreign investors was the high tariff protection it imposed, creating a captive market for industries established in Mexico. In addition to the prerogatives granted by the federal government, the states of the republic eliminated taxes and provided concessions to foreign investors for the same reasons.[44]

The Evolution of Barcelonnette Economic Activity in Mexico: General Practices

Barcelonnettes who prospered in Mexico began with small commercial concerns in the 1860s. They later became one of the dominant forces in commerce, founding most of the country's main department stores, and in the textile industry in a significant area of Mexico. They also became a powerful force in the banking sector, through their participation in important banks such as Banamex and the Banco de Londres y México (BLM), among others.

In the manufacturing sector, they not only acquired or founded textile mills but also developed interests in paper, soap, canned goods, beer, tobacco, and energy production, to name a few. However, the overall success of ventures by Barcelonnette entrepreneurs led to a persistent myth that all French immigrants from the region of Barcelonnette became rich and prosperous in Mexico, discounting the fact that a significant part of them were unable to found companies and remained as employees.

In addition, the prominence of an important percentage of the successful Barcelonnette families decreased following the Mexican Revolution, WWI, and the economic crisis of 1929. Nonetheless, other families who migrated later, such as the Jean family studied in this book, created and consolidated their wealth in the first half of the twentieth century. That is, those families that had come from Barcelonnette by the end of the nineteenth century not only inherited the privileges that being European gave them but also some of the business practices of their compatriots, particularly that of encouraging relationships and sharing profits with public servants. This eventually strengthened crony capitalism in the Mexican economy, thus saddling the Barcelonnettes with a negative legacy that has proven to be lasting and difficult to control even today.

Commerce

Prior to 1870, the French colony in Mexico was made up of small merchants, craftsmen, employees, cooks, seamstresses, and restaurant owners, like almost all French colonies around the world. They were not involved in wholesale commerce, finance, or industry. As to what is normally understood by "commerce," the English and Germans monopolized the wool, cotton, silk, iron, steel, and wholesale jewelry industries in Mexico. The Spanish focused on the commerce of wines, liquors, preserved foods, and grocery items.

A modest, fragmented, and underdeveloped market existed in Mexico prior to 1870. It had a limited and incomplete communication range, which had led to the prevalence of small, generally disconnected local markets—we cannot speak of a national market. However, the political, social, and economic environment started to stabilize, which led to important advances in the construction of infrastructure. For example, the railway tracks that covered 640 km in 1876 had grown to 19,280 km by 1911.[45]

It was within this context that French commerce flourished in Mexico, severely hindering its European rivals. The Franco-Prussian War of 1870–71 also contributed to French investors taking over not only retail sales in the textile sector but the textile business as a whole. This happened throughout most of Mexico with the exception of the northern states, which had created its own market centered in the city of Monterrey.[46] The French retailers that still used German wholesale warehouses as intermediates to distribute their products in Mexico started to use French intermediates instead. This situation also affected the English, to the point that they ceased to serve as commercial intermediates. Some of the Barcelonnettes who had been their main clients now established their own companies to obtain products directly from Europe. A few even opened offices in England and France to manage the export of goods to Mexico. The commercial business of the Barcelonnettes in Mexico grew to include much of the distribution of both wholesale and retail sales of those products, which were sold to other retailers established in the country.

In summary, the 1870s and 1880s were crucial years for the commercial growth of the Barcelonnettes in Mexico. Of eighty houses importing German goods in 1870, two-thirds had already disappeared by 1889. The last German fabric house established in Mexico closed in 1892.[47] In that same year, the French possessed 150 fabric houses, of which 30 were wholesalers and 118 belonged to the Barcelonnettes. By 1910, the total number had reached 200, and 150 of these belonged to the Barcelonnettes.[48]

In addition, the Barcelonnettes imported and sold high-quality products in their shops, with the primary objective being to satisfy the tastes of an affluent and sophisticated clientele. Importation did not occur with standard articles, for which the Mexican industry was both sufficient and cheaper. To ensure a stable supply of cloth in the national market, by the mid-1870s some

Barcelonnettes had signed annual contracts with Mexican fabricants from places like Puebla—for example, Ciriaco and Marrón y Carballo.[49]

Between 1870 and 1880, the Barcelonnettes' economic activities centered on commerce and the consolidation of clothing distribution. They also ventured into the textile industry, with the goal being production control. The French already had a history of producing textiles in Mexico; for example, the Cocolapan mill in Orizaba, Veracruz, was the largest factory before 1850 and had French investment.[50] Prior to the full incorporation of the Barcelonnettes in the textile industry, the French had also become involved in the Mexican financial sector.

The Banking Sector

As wholesalers, the Barcelonnettes needed to provide credit to their customers in order to facilitate their purchases. Offering credit conditions to retailers was necessary at the beginning of the 1880s since Mexico had nothing more than a rudimentary banking system at that time. The first commercial bank in Mexico City was the Banco de Londres, México y Sudamérica, a branch of an English bank, founded in 1864. This branch remained the only commercial bank in the city until the early 1880s, but there were also small local banks located mainly in the northern states of the country, such as Chihuahua and Nuevo León. As a result, the Barcelonnettes progressively made up for the lack of a formal banking system starting in the early 1870s. An informal credit system developed, which grew as businesses grew. American capitalists also participated in this system; some of the Americans had accumulated capital from other economic activities such as the construction of railways.[51]

The entry of French banks into the formal banking system in Mexico took place in 1881. Edouard Noetzlin, president of the French-Egyptian Bank, obtained a concession and created the Banco Nacional Mexicano (BNM), mainly with French and Mexican capital (8 million pesos). The leading partner in the BNM was the French-Egyptian Bank, with 16,500 out of a total of 80,000 shares. The French owned a total of 59,116 shares, and the rest were distributed among businessmen from New York and representatives of the Mexican political and economic elites, for whom 20 percent of the capital had been reserved. The BNM opened its doors in February 1882. This was a bank for deposit, discount, circulation, and issuing currency. While it was not a state bank, the government could control the issuing of particular bills through this bank. At the time of its inauguration, the BNM offered the federal government a credit line of 4 million pesos.[52]

Shortly after the creation of the BNM in 1882, the Banco Mercantil Mexicano (BMM) was founded. It had only half as much capital invested as the BNM, and this capital came predominantly from Spanish and Mexican merchants who resided in Mexico. The two banks merged in 1884, creating the Banco Nacional de México, or Banamex.[53] The capital for Banamex came from French investors (both from Europe and from the French colony established in Mexico), as well as Mexican and Spanish investors. Its operational model was based on the French banking model, which combined public and private functions.[54]

Big Spanish capitalists, originally from the Iberian Peninsula but established in Mexico, dominated Banamex at first. Capital participation by the Barcelonnettes, although present, was scarce at the beginning. The first Barcelonnette to invest in a Mexican bank was Sébastien Robert, who invested a small amount of money in the BNM.[55] The importance of French capital in the banking sector in Mexico grew as time passed, and 70 percent of the 20 million pesos of capital that Banamex held by 1910 belonged to the French.[56] Since no new currency-issuing banks could be established after Congress ushered in a new commerce law in 1884, Banamex enjoyed a guaranteed monopoly and came to be the most powerful Mexican bank. By 1896, it controlled more than 60 percent of the capital held in banks in the country. In practice, this meant that "the State renounced to create a public banking system, like the one in England or in France, to confide Banamex privileges that made it not only a private quasi-monopoly but practically the only referee in the financial operations of the country."[57] In this sense, Banamex played a dual role in the Mexican economy as both a public and private bank, with specific central bank-like functions such as the production of coins and bills.

As far as the banking sector is concerned, the Barcelonnettes also had a great deal of vision. Exactly as had happened when they came into possession of the wholesale market, there was a major shift from being merchants to being financial partners.[58] The Barcelonnettes invested massively in what was the second most important bank in the country, the Banco de Londres y México (BLM), with the purpose of taking it over. This bank was the direct descendant of the Banco de Londres, México y Sudamérica, which was renamed BLM in 1889.

The BLM became more focused on economic activities such as private investing rather than becoming more involved in public funding. Beginning in 1896, a number of Barcelonnettes invested heavily in the BLM. In that year, the capital of the bank doubled from 5 to 10 million pesos, and the board of directors increased from five to twelve partners.[59] Most of the new partners were the owners and associates of the main Barcelonnette stores and businesses: Joseph Ollivier; Leon Signoret; Leon Honnorat; the Tron brothers, who had created El Palacio de Hierro (a department store that still exists); and Alphonse Michel, managing partner of the Puerto de Liverpool. The latter is in fact the only Barcelonnette-owned department store still under the control of a Barcelonnette family in the present day. El Palacio de Hierro and Liverpool, well-known Mexican chains today, were fundamental to the formation of the Mexican middle class from a sociological perspective. The BLM also had Spanish partners, such as the wealthy entrepreneur Antonio Basagoiti; political figures like Senators Rafael Dondé and Rosendo Pineda; and a financier who was Díaz's son-in-law, Ignacio de la Torre y Mier. English investment was still present in the BLM's capital; however, this participation dropped from 90 percent to 50 percent after 1896.[60]

By 1899, the Barcelonnettes had taken almost complete control of the BLM. The BLM actively participated in its partners' activities, funding large textile consortia like the Compañía Industrial de Orizaba S.A. (CIDOSA) and the Compañía Industrial Veracruzana S.A. (CIVSA); funding the biggest department stores like El Palacio de Hierro, El Centro Mercantil, and El Puerto de Veracruz; and funding mining, agricultural, and other manufacturing projects, such as beer factories and cigar companies.

The French also participated in other banks, such as the Banco Central Mexicano. This was a fixed-asset bank, meaning that it was established to fund real estate, agriculture, and mines. It also funded industries, albeit to a smaller extent.[61] This bank's capital came to be 60 percent French, as French participation in the bank grew to 18 million of the total 30 million pesos of capital. Sébastien Robert became an important shareholder in the Banco Central Mexicano upon its creation in March 1897.

The Barcelonnettes also participated in other banking projects, such as the Sociedad Financiera para la Industria en México (SFIM). Created in 1898, the SFIM turned into an important intermediary for obtaining funds in Europe. Its main task became to provide small capital contributions to different companies that were generally owned by the SFIM's own partners. In 1909, Compañía Bancaria de París y México (CBPM) was founded with a significant sum of capital: 10 million pesos.[62] Half of this capital came from the Barcelonnettes who were living in Mexico, including members of the Jean family, while the other half came from shareholders established in France, like the Rouvier Bank.[63] For its operation, a consulting and surveillance committee was created in France. Unlike the SFIM, which concentrated mainly on long- to medium-term loans, CBPM solved the liquidity problems of its own owners by focusing on short-term operations.[64]

Total French investment in the banking sector in Mexico had grown to 100 million pesos by the end of the nineteenth century. This was distributed among commercial banks in Mexico City (51 percent); commercial banks in other states (8.5 percent); mortgages, real estate, and other financial companies (35.5 percent); and other investments (5 percent). France was by far the largest investor, with around 60 percent of the total capital in the banking sector.[65] Bank investments made by the United States in Mexico were smaller, at 34 million pesos, while investments made by England and Germany totaled 17 million pesos and 12 million pesos, respectively. However, it is important to mention that the Mexican banking system was still in its infancy at the beginning of the twentieth century. Even though the Mexican banking sector grew, it was still limited to fewer than twenty firms in 1910.[66] Additionally, banking regulations were limited by the interests of the federal government and banks' partners, which the banks mainly served to fulfill.

The Manufacturing Sector—Cotton Textiles

In 1875, the textile factories in Mexico were still small units that satisfied only regional necessities, even though their growth had been rapid. In 1853, forty-seven manufacturers worked in the cotton sector; by 1878, ninety-nine had ventured into it. However, the productivity of each manufacturer was weak, and its products in general were of low quality.[67]

During the first years of the Porfiriato, between 1877 and 1889, the growing internal demand for national textiles was primarily satisfied by increasing the number of factory workers, not by adding new textile mills. Additionally, even though the Mexican economic model was supposedly liberal, protectionist tariffs increased steadily, tripling the value of imported fabrics from England. This trend continued during the rest of the Porfiriato, with important tariff increases in 1892, 1893, 1896, and 1906. The textile and paper industries were probably the best protected.[68] The fall of the price of silver after 1884 exacerbated this phenomenon, making textile imports in Mexico more expensive.

One of the consequences of protectionism—and of the considerable depreciation of the Mexican peso—was that textile importers in Mexico (like the Barcelonnettes) were forced to substitute part of the production they had been importing from England and France with domestic textiles. As a result, they ventured into new investment projects that included the founding of new textile mills with modern installations. The creation in 1889 of the CIDOSA stands out. The CIDOSA gradually added four textile mills to its business: Cerritos, San Lorenzo, Río Blanco, and Cocolapan. All of them were located in or near Orizaba, in the state of Veracruz (fig. 1.8). Río Blanco, founded in 1892, still best known even now because of a violent strike that occurred in 1907, was the largest and perhaps most modern mill in Latin America with somewhere between two and three thousand workers. The mill was equipped with tax-exempt machinery and facilities, a measure supported by both the federal and local governments to help achieve industrialization in Mexico. Three-quarters of the textiles produced by the CIDOSA mills were basic articles destined for

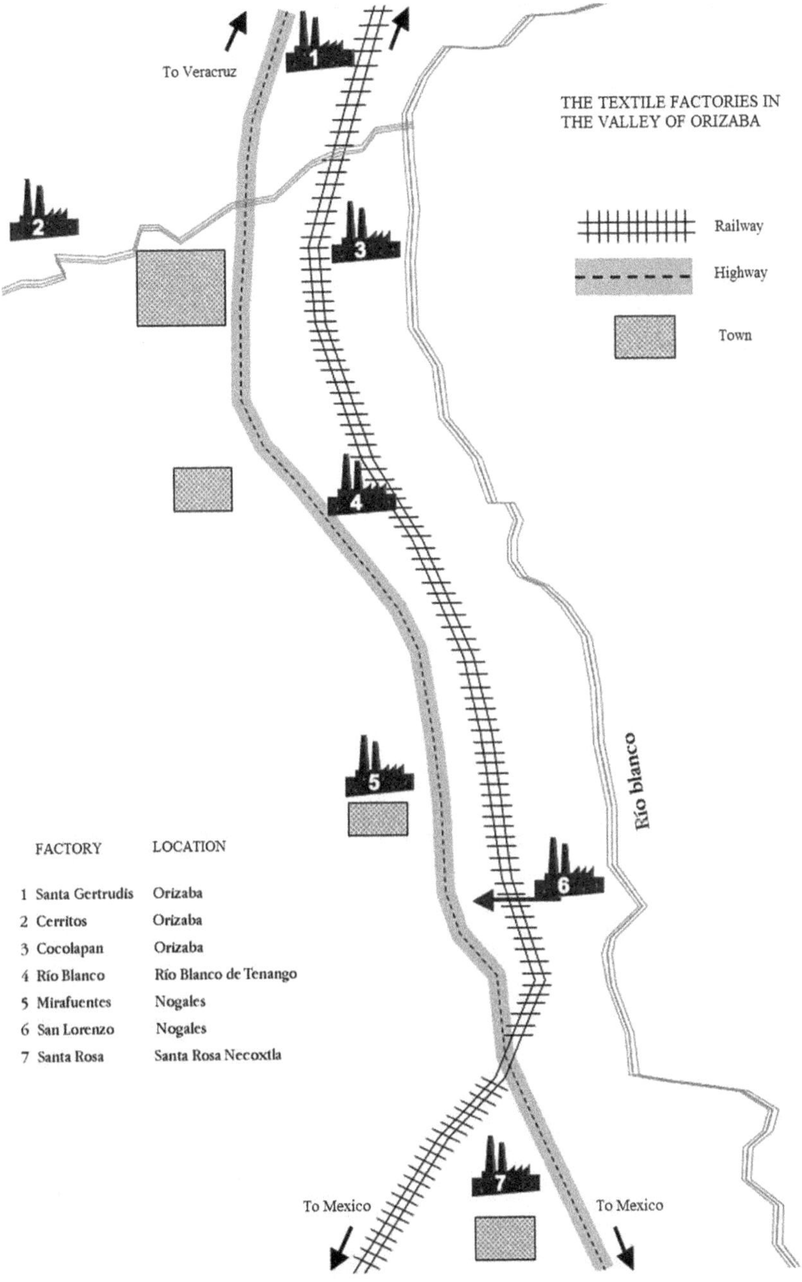

Figure 1.8. Textile factories in the valley of Orizaba. Based on data from Gómez-Galvarriato Freer and García Díaz, "El escenario industrial." (José Galindo)

the masses. The rest were high-quality products that mainly Río Blanco began producing to substitute the textiles that were still being imported.

Other Barcelonnettes began to emulate this model, buying old factories and creating new ones. Some of the oldest textile factories had been founded during the first wave of industrialization in the country in the 1830s, when figures like Esteban de Antuñano in Puebla played a key role.[69] In a short time, the Barcelonnettes had passed from being retailers to becoming wholesalers, bankers, and industrialists.

However, as a result of the new investments in textile mills, Mexico now faced an overproduction of textiles. This overproduction led to attempts to export textile products to other markets, including South America. These projects were generally unsuccessful because of high transportation costs and the high protectionist tariffs that usually each country had, which made domestic prices of imported goods more expensive. As was the case with Mexico, most countries were protecting their industries in this period.[70]

The Barcelonnettes made other important investments in the textile industry in the 1890s:

> The Compañía Industrial de San Antonio Abad (CISAASA), founded in 1892, which managed the Miraflores and La Colmena

Figure 1.9. Part of the building and chimney of Santa Rosa factory, 1900. (Instituto Nacional de Antropología e Historia, Consejo Nacional para la Cultura y las Artes, Mexico)

> mills in the state of México, as well as the San Antonio Abad mill south of the capital.
>
> The Compañía Industrial de Atlixco (CIASA), founded in 1899, held one of the largest mills in the country, the Metepec mill.
>
> The CIVSA, founded in 1896, built another enormous factory in 1898—Santa Rosa (fig. 1.9 and fig. 1.10)—that was capable of competing with Río Blanco and was located around 11 km away (see fig. 1.8). Their leaders were two well-known Barcelonnettes: Alexandre Reynaud and Sébastien Robert.

In 1907, the CIDOSA, the CIVSA, the CISAASA, and the CIASA accounted for 35 percent of the total Mexican cotton textile industry. The Río Blanco and Santa Rosa mills dominated Mexican production of high-quality textiles.[71]

Other Sectors

The Barcelonnettes expanded their activities to the production of wool textiles and to other manufacturing sectors. The favorable economic environment after 1893, combined with the presence of the Barcelonnettes in the banking system, contributed to this diversification of economic activities. Some Barcelonnettes also had access to substantial credit lines from Europe, which allowed them to increase their levels of investment. Some of the important wool textile factories with French investment included the San Ildefonso factory, where

Figure 1.10. Santa Rosa factory label, 1900. (Archivo General de la Nación, Mexico)

the CIVSA and the CIDOSA participated, and La Victoria S.A., which a group of Basque-Asturian businessmen controlled in conjunction with the Barcelonnette Augustin Garcin. Paper production also became an important manufacturing sector. The San Rafael y Anexas company was opened in the mid-1890s by a group of Barcelonnettes, along with Thomas Braniff, an important US investor who had also participated in the CIDOSA. This company established a monopoly in paper production in Mexico.[72]

Other large companies with significant Barcelonnette capital investment included the cigarette factory El Buen Tono; Clemente Jacques, a preserved food factory still in operation; glasswork companies, like Calpulalpan; and dynamite and explosives companies, like the Compañía Nacional Mexicana de Dinamita y Explosivos.[73]

The Barcelonnettes also provided energy to different regions of southern Mexico City, including San Ángel, Mixcoac, Tlalpan, and Coyoacán. In 1904, Sébastien Robert, along with other Barcelonnettes, founded the electric light company La Luz Eléctrica. Additionally, his company S. Robert y Compañía Sucesores partnered with Veyán, Jean y Compañía, the original company owned by first-generation Jean family members at the time, and with Noriega y Compañía, to create the Compañía Hidroeléctrica del Río de la Alameda S.A. in 1909.[74]

Figure 1.11. Las Fábricas Universales, Mexico City, 1909. (American Book and Printing)

Figure 1.12. Main stairs in Las Fábricas de Francia, Guadalajara, Jalisco, 1907. (C. H. Barrière, Photography)

By 1910, 55 percent of the foreign investment in Mexican industry was French.[75] This growth allowed them to construct new, more luxurious buildings for their department stores, beginning in the second half of the previous decade. For example, the construction of a new Ciudad de Londres began in 1907, El Palacio de Hierro introduced a new store in 1907, Las Fábricas Universales opened in 1909 (fig. 1.11), and Liverpool inaugurated a new store in 1911. La Ciudad de México opened in the state of Puebla in 1910.[76] The construction of luxury department stores (fig. 1.12) continued even after the end of the Porfiriato and the Mexican Revolution. For example, Liverpool, the only one of these department stores still managed by Barcelonnettes today, was remodeled, and a new, modern building opened by 1936. Liverpool was characterized by being the only department store with electric escalators, a soda fountain, and a beauty salon, among other great novelties for customers.[77]

At the same time of Díaz's ouster, a group of great department stores comparable to the most important department stores in the world had just been installed. Their operations were innovative and modern, and they provided an image of luxury, power, and beauty.

Although the Barcelonnettes were primarily urban industrialists, some also ventured into agroindustry. Mexico was not an exception to the pattern that many underdeveloped economies followed in this period: the economy relied on the development of primary goods for internal consumption and for export, as part of the export-led growth model. To this end, Mexico produced agave in Hidalgo, henequen in Yucatán, and tobacco and sugar in other regions including Veracruz, among other agricultural products. As a result, Joseph Ollivier and other Barcelonnettes founded the sugar company Compañía Azucarera del Pánuco S.A. in 1898.

However, this company never had the success the partners had anticipated.

TABLE 1.2. Foreign investment in Mexico by countries and sectors, 1911

	France	%	United States	%	Great Britain	%
Public Debt	328,132	65.89	59,322	11.91	82,760	16.62
%	36.1		4.6		8.3	
Mines and metallurgy	179,552	21.97	499,000	61.06	116,887	14.31
%	19.8		38.6		11.8	
Railways	116,240	10.29	534,683	47.29	401,396	35.5
%	12.8		41.4		40.6	
Banks	99,994	60.28	34,328	20.69	17,558	10.59
%	11.0		2.7		1.8	
Commerce	80,000	65.5	8,960	7.34	280	0.23
%	8.8		0.7		0	
Industry	71,932	54.9	21,200	16.2	10,856	8.3
%	7.9		1.6		1.1	
Real estate	16,000	8.2	81,420	41.9	90,990	46.8
%	1.8		6.3		9.2	
Public services	10,040	4.22	13,473	5.68	211,558	89
%	1.1		1.0		21.4	
Oil	6,800	6.54	40,000	38.46	57,200	55
%	0.7		3.1		5.8	
Total	908,690	26.72	1,292,386	38	989,485	29.1
%	100		100		100	

Source: Data from various sources such as Turlington, *Foreign Investments*; The Economist, "Our Crony-Capitalism Index"; Liste Approximative des Intérets Francais Engagés au Mexique.

Note: Figures are expressed in thousands of pesos. Percentages are calculated with the information available.

The quality of the sugar was poor, and consumers preferred the sugar produced at Paraíso Novillero, which belonged to other French investors who were not from the region of Barcelonnette. The sugar and agricultural industries were outside of the Barcelonnettes' expertise, and, as a result, they were unable to successfully manage these businesses.[78]

The distribution of foreign investment in Mexico by country and sectors at the height of Barcelonnette development can be observed in table 1.2. The countries with the highest levels of investment in Mexico were the United

Germany	%	Other countries	%	Total per sector	% Total
2,000	0.4	25,800	5.18	498,014	100
3.0		17.8		14.6	
—	—	21,760	2.66	817,199	100
—		15.1		24.0	
18,720	1.65	59,506	5.27	1,130,545	100
28.5		41.2		33.2	
12,000	7.24	2,000	1.2	165,880	100
18.3		1.4		4.9	
—	—	32,890	26.93	122,130	100
—		22.7		3.6	
26,960	20.6	—	—	130,948	100
41.1		—		3.9	
6,000	3.1	—	—	194,410	100
9.1		—		5.7	
—	—	2,640	1.1	237,711	100
—		1.8		7.0	
—	—	—	—	104,000	100
—		—		3.1	
65,680	1.94	144,596	4.24	3,400,837	100
100		100		100	

States, Great Britain, and France. The United States and Great Britain were both leaders and competitors in key sectors, such as railways, real estate, and oil. Paul Garner's recent study of the British investor Weetman Pearson explains in detail how Pearson became not only the most influential British businessman in Mexico between 1889 and 1919 but also one of the most successful British investors in countries outside of Britain.[79]

The Myth of the Success of the Entire Barcelonnette Community in Mexico

A persistent myth is the idea that the entire Barcelonnette community in Mexico succeeded economically. As Pérez Siller points out, once the first Barcelonnettes returned to France with great capital, "the idea that in Mexico it was possible to make a fortune easily was repeated from mouth to mouth; it penetrated the collective beliefs and situated itself in the imaginary." It was believed that "for the simple fact of belonging to the group and taking the trouble to emigrate," everyone would become rich.[80] However, in reality, even though most of the French immigrants could easily access the Mexican middle-class, only some of the Barcelonnettes became rich out of the two to three thousand men who had arrived throughout the nineteenth century and up until the Mexican Revolution. For others, becoming rich in Mexico was not easy. In fact, it was necessary to undergo a lengthy process to reach the level of capital required for a large company. Normally, the employees' situations progressed as their responsibilities increased. There were no bosses who had not first been employees, and many of the employees never rose through the ranks.

However, the focus on success stories has helped to spread a vision of triumph for the community as a whole. For example, in 1908 the *Journal de Barcelonnette* (March 29, 1908), an important source of information for the Barcelonnette population, reproduced an article published by *Le Temps de Jalisco*, a newspaper for the French colony in Guadalajara. It assured readers that the French merchants in Mexico were "all originally from Barcelonnette" and "managed all the cloths commerce in the [Mexican] Republic. . . . Thanks to the efforts and starting from insignificant commercial relations," these men could "create the magnificent establishments" that existed in all the Mexican state capitals and that were "the cause of a legitimate pride and source of important benefits."[81]

The most influential Barcelonnettes spread their triumphs but hid the destiny of those that were unsuccessful.[82] It is difficult to estimate the percentage of Barcelonnettes who became successful, since the studies available have distorted the reality. Additionally, there have only been a few studies about the experiences of average Barcelonnettes. Gamboa Ojeda studied these aspects in more detail for the state of Puebla in the period between 1845 and 1928. She concluded that only 44 of the 174 Barcelonnettes established in the city of Puebla came to be partners of a company (25 percent); even then, not all of them achieved the same status as there were different partnership levels.[83]

Finally, it is useful to recognize other factors favorable to the Barcelonnette community in Mexico. First of all, the French were particularly welcome in Mexico during the Porfiriato, since they practiced the only tolerated religion (Catholicism), they were white men of Latin origin, and they came from a country with material and cultural progress, which was a cause of admiration and imitation. The French also benefited from other elements of colonial heritage; in addition to religious intolerance and racism, the Spanish colonies established in the region that became Latin America were classist and hierarchical. This not only gave the French established in Mexico a privileged social status but also kept the vast majority of Mexicans out of the capitalist arena, saving the French from other competition.

Additionally, French immigration in Mexico in this period was small compared to French immigration elsewhere and to migration from other countries to Mexico. In that sense, it did not represent demographic colonization. That is, French immigration in Mexico was qualitative and not quantitative. In Argentina, for example, the French were far more numerous, not to mention the Spanish and Italians.

For some Barcelonnette families who were prominent during the Porfiriato, success was short-lived and their fortunes declined as a result of the effects of the Mexican Revolution, WWI, and the economic crisis of 1929. Some of these businessmen were also simply incapable of successfully transitioning control of their companies to the next generations of their family. Other Barcelonnettes, such as the Jean family, began the process of constructing their wealth later and built a different and contrasting story of success, which we will study next.

This chapter analyzes the context that will allow a historical case study of the Jean family. It delves into key points to help us understand the different waves of French migration to various regions of Mexico throughout the nineteenth century, which then relocated and adapted. This makes it possible to clearly locate the Barcelonnette wave of migration, which the Jean family belonged to.

The chapter also presents the evolution of occupations of French migrants in Mexico and the importance of their contribution to the Mexican economy.

Focusing on the Barcelonnette group, whose expansion occurred in a period when French values and tastes had become particularly influential in Mexican culture, helps us understand the weight of French migration compared to migration to Mexico from other countries. French migration in Mexico in the nineteenth century was small in numerical terms; nevertheless, its contribution to the development of certain economic sectors, such as the manufacturing industry, wholesale and retail trade, and banking, was substantial. That is, the French became the leaders in those sectors and held assets and created companies at a level disproportionate to their size. The very nature of migration and Mexico's lax migration policies toward certain ethnic groups, together with the exceptional policies that discretionally favored foreign investment from specific countries, boosted French investment in Mexico, undermining attempts to establish strong institutions in the long term, which contributed to crony capitalism.

The next chapter presents elements of the theory of social networks, crony capitalism, and the persistence of the economic elite over time. Together with the historical background introduced in this first chapter, it will allow a deeper analysis of the case study of the Jean family in chapters 3 and 4.

CHAPTER TWO

Crony Capitalism in the Late Nineteenth and Early Twentieth Centuries

General and Theoretical Considerations

Mexico is a country of weak formal institutions. This has led to the creation of informal business networks to compensate for this lack of institutional solidity. These networks, however, operate today in favor of small, corrupt power groups composed of a few politicians and business elites. In protecting their individual interests, these groups have also contributed to maintaining weak institutional development over the years, thus generating a vicious circle.

These characteristics, although present from colonial times, have prevailed since the implementation of capitalism during the Porfiriato (1876–1911). This chapter describes the early evolution of capitalism in Mexico, leading to the creation of power elites and crony capitalism in the country, which persists to this day. I analyze different definitions of "elite" and present my own definition of "power elite" to better fit the Mexican case. I also address the persistence of the Mexican economic elite, dividing the study into industrialists and landowners. I then discuss crony capitalism and address the following questions: Why do crony economic systems come into being? Why do these systems have negative effects on economic growth? What is the role of social networks in overcoming the weaknesses of institutional frameworks, in particular weak contract enforcement and restricted capital markets? What general conclusions have been reached in the case of Mexico?

The last section of this chapter specifically relates to the French community in Mexico and the networks they developed to conduct their businesses. Here, I clarify what is known about social networks and crony capitalism with regard to the Barcelonnettes.

CONSIDERATIONS OF THE PERSISTENCE OF THE MEXICAN ECONOMIC ELITE IN THE LATE NINETEENTH AND EARLY TWENTIETH CENTURIES

In Mexico, the power elite is composed of economic, political, military, and social actors with the capacity to consistently and substantially affect a great variety of national and regional issues. It is notable that, despite the political instability that arose from the revolution (1910–20), no significant changes took place among individuals who had controlled the industrial sector during the Porfiriato. Many of the same industrialists continued to enjoy favorable conditions for several decades. For example, after the Great Depression of 1929, traditional industrial elites recovered in the 1930s and thrived during and after the Second World War (WWII), despite the eventual participation of new actors in the Mexican economy, including the so-called New Group.

Furthermore, in rural areas, despite aggressive land reform after the revolution and during the Lázaro Cárdenas administration (1934–40) in particular, a number of landowners managed to protect themselves and their wealth using a range of strategies. This suggests that the Mexican Revolution did not represent an important change in the composition of Mexico's economic elite.

The evolution of the behavior of economic and business elites in an environment characterized by political instability and institutional uncertainty has been a concern for many scholars. After briefly explaining my own definition of the power elite, this section analyzes some of the measures taken by members of the economic elite, particularly industrialists and landowners from the Porfiriato when faced with the aftereffects of the Mexican Revolution. It primarily examines industrial activities and landownership but does not focus on the analysis of specific individuals, although sometimes names appear. The goal is to investigate how and to what extent industrialists and landowners were able to adapt to the new political, economic, and social conditions that arose after the Madero movement of 1910, successive armed conflicts involving different revolutionary factions, and the subsequent reconstruction process that took place over the following two decades. This period of reconstruction is important because new rules were established. This new structure allowed the regime that rose to power following the Mexican Revolution, the PRI, to remain in power for over half a century.

Definition of Power Elite

During the second half of the twentieth century, experts on elites began a debate about the importance of correctly defining this concept. Researchers face certain difficulties when constructing a definition of elite. The main problem lies in the selection of elements to consider in a definition.[1] Recently, a number of renowned researchers have conducted empirical studies of the elite, taking ideas from different theoretical studies to understand the elites of a country or region.

William Domhoff affirms that the role of social class, which is an element of analysis of Marxist theory, and the role of institutions, which authors such as C. Wright Mills emphasize, are important considerations when understanding the power elite.[2] As Domhoff explains, the "ruling class could not exist without the institutions, but the institutions are infused with class (elite) values."[3]

However, some authors find that neither Marxist theory nor the theory of classical elites, developed by Pareto and Mosca, can be applied appropriately to Mexico. Classical theorists divide society into two groups: the ruling class, or the elite, and the governed. For Marx, the elite control the means of production. However, in Mexico, during the period considered in this study, class identification shifted, especially as a result of the changes produced by the revolution.[4] These shifts in that period, which certainly occurred in the political elite, make it difficult to divide Mexican society neatly in two and to directly associate rulers with control of the means of production.

I propose a definition of power elite for Mexico: "The power elite, a concept made popular by C. Wright Mills (1956), will be defined in general terms as economic actors (in this case, mainly landowners, industrialists, and bankers) as well as political, military, and social actors (i.e., labor leaders) with the capacity to consistently and substantially affect a great variety of national and regional issues (e.g., economic, religious, military)."[5]

This definition borrows elements from others, including Mills, but especially from the analysis offered by Field, Higley, and Burton.[6] These authors originally sought to define political elites, but their definitions can be extended to other groups of actors that influence a society. Additionally, I included the regional aspect in the proposed definition, since Mexico was a remarkably fragmented country during most of the nineteenth and part of the twentieth centuries, which complicates discussing it in terms of a single national elite, at least not in the economic and political spheres.[7] In the present day, the leaders of the power elite in Mexico do not share power in multiple spheres of influence; with a few exceptions, the political, economic, social, and military elites are separated.[8] This is important to note since the economic, political, and military elites overlapped across several spheres during the Porfiriato.[9]

When political and economic elites overlap, they affect a variety of national and regional issues, generally in a negative way. The regulatory capacity of a government in the economy is reduced, and businesses and large estates (haciendas in the Porfirian period) are incentivized to operate outside the law because of increased privilege to do so. This often leads to the creation of monopolies and to the exaggerated growth of rural properties, to the detriment of other economic agents.[10] The greater the percentage of government officials on corporate boards, the more likely it is that the government will share the policy preferences of economic actors, leading to crony capitalism.[11]

Industrialists

Here I focus on the analysis of key aspects that allowed an important percentage of the traditional industrial oligarchy of the Porfiriato to persist as part of the economic elite until at least the 1980s, surviving specific events such as the revolution and the institutional "innovations" it brought about. I also analyze how the interests of that oligarchy hampered new, smaller firms that emerged in Mexico after the revolution.

Although agriculture and mining had been the traditional economic activities in the country since the colonial era, many other economic activities emerged before the Porfiriato. One of these activities was manufacturing, which allowed the formation of new economic elites. Most late nineteenth-century Mexican businessmen had come out of trade sectors that had been established fifty years earlier. Their accumulated capital was reinvested in other sectors, allowing large modern manufacturing companies to proliferate between 1870 and 1910. These manufacturers produced cotton fabrics, shoes, cigarettes, dynamite, beer, paper, cement, steel, glass, soap, and other products.

In the period under study, the development of the manufacturing industry was concentrated geographically in defined areas and was urban as opposed to rural. At the end of the 1860s, the cities of Puebla and Mexico were home to the majority of manufacturers; their products were primarily cotton textiles. During the Porfiriato, cities like Orizaba, Monterrey, and Guadalajara also underwent significant industrial development. By 1930, distribution of manufacturing production by zone, in terms of total value of production, was as follows: Federal District, 27 percent; central region (excluding the Federal District), 25 percent; northern region, 23 percent; gulf, 14 percent; north Pacific, 8 percent; and south Pacific, 3 percent.[12]

Some of the merchants who had accumulated capital from commercial activities also invested in agriculture and cattle farming during the Porfiriato, which turned them into new landowners. Similarly, traditional landowners had begun to transfer resources to other activities, such as commerce, mining, banking, and manufacturing, but not in the same proportion as the merchants.[13] In this sense, traditional landowners proved to be more risk averse.

Foreign investment also played a very important role during the Díaz administration, and foreign investors occasionally settled in Mexico to handle their new projects; in this way, these immigrants also began to form part of the Mexican economic elite. This was the case for the Barcelonnette community.

In 1987, John Womack published an article criticizing the traditional historiography of the revolution, noting that the economic impact of this process was not homogeneous nor did it take place in either particular sectors or regions. Since the publication of that article, the once predominant idea that "everything changed" was discredited. In recent decades, it has been argued that, in fact, the revolutionary movement had little or no effect on the economy, based on the evidence of the "physical permanence of the industrial bourgeoisie."[14] However, this may also be considered an extreme view, similar to the one that maintains that everything changed. It is important to clarify that the permanence of the bourgeoisie, as a class and/or as individuals, and of a considerable portion of the Porfirian industrial plants does not necessarily mean there was little change in the economy. Change varied depending on the economic sector and the actions taken by business groups and individual entrepreneurs producing within them. In addition, as explained in the following section, the changes brought by the revolution were more pronounced in the rural sector, independently of the fact that some landowners found ways of subsisting.

Reflecting Womack's argument, other studies indicate that no major changes took place in private investment and industrialists continued to enjoy favorable conditions, despite the political instability that arose from the revolution, which extended beyond 1920, and the constitutional reforms of Articles 27 and 123 in 1917.[15] According to these studies, mostly elaborated by neo-institutionalists, the traditional industrial elite enjoyed favors from the government during the Porfiriato and the revolutionary years through such mechanisms as vertical political integration (VPI). This allowed them to survive and even grow under the new conditions of uncertainty in the institutional framework (both formal and informal).

In addition, companies related to banks had reduced risks of bankruptcy and fewer changes in ownership. Bankers lent each other money (insider lending), and banks provided long-term loans to individuals and companies associated with members of their boards of directors. In Maurer's words: "The fastest-growing firms were not the best firms; they were the best-connected firms."[16] This is one of the main characteristics of crony capitalism, which will be discussed later in this chapter.

Musacchio and Read have shown the great influence held by the entrepreneurial interest networks during the industrialization of the country in the late Porfiriato. The links that entrepreneurs established with politicians were highly important to this group; politicians also formed part of corporate boards. However, this close-knit network of interests unraveled in some cases with the growing political and social tensions that led to the revolution.[17] One example of this is the case of some members of the Barcelonnette group, who lost much of their network, as Porfirian politicians lost power, and were unable to maintain the wealth gained during the Porfiriato and their status as economic elites as the revolution, WWI, and the Great Depression progressed. The Jean family, which inspired this book, was an exception to this trend.

The general case of the Barcelonnettes, as well as of other economic elite groups, has divided opinion among specialists regarding the continuance of industrial elites during and after the revolution. Carmen Collado, for example, states that the economic elite's political and economic power had been significantly weakened by the time the *sonorenses* rose to power in 1920, even though it was virtually unchanged from the Porfiriato. The elites were found to be divided. According to Collado, industrialists in particular saw few benefits under the various new administrations, and they struggled to solve a pressing labor problem, as well as to secure the enactment of a protectionist policy. These industrialists, some of whom clearly identified with the Porfirian regime, were also forced to lobby strongly when the government implemented an income tax in 1921.[18]

In addition, the founding of some formal institutions in Mexico during the 1920s affected the economic interests of members of the economic elite. For example, Mexico's central bank, Banco de México (Banxico), was founded in 1925. The creation of this bank had been planned since the revolutionary period, during Pres. Venustiano Carranza's term, but had faced delays due to a lack of resources. The bank initially faced hostility and mistrust from the general public, international creditors, and commercial banks.[19] The latter, which were just beginning to regain their oligopolistic power after the revolution, lost some of their prerogatives and faculties and began to see Banxico as another competitor.

The strengthening or weakening of the industrialists of the Porfiriato during and after the revolution, therefore, depends on which economic sector, specific group of entrepreneurs, or individual entrepreneur is analyzed. The Jean family, for example, used different strategies from most of the other Barcelonnettes. These included forging new relationships with revolutionary politicians (crony capitalism), exploring new economic sectors, and changing the network business strategy to a more individual one. This not only enabled them to survive the revolution and its institutional consequences, such as the strengthening labor movement, agrarian reform, and the foundation of the central bank, but also to start building their wealth while some of their compatriots were weakened.

Like the Jeans, other entrepreneurs strengthened during the Porfiriato were capable of subsisting in the following years. For example, although Mexican industry suffered greatly from the effects of the Great Depression, which led to a reduction in new investments between 1926 and 1932, there were exceptions to this, like the steel and cement sectors—two sectors headed by Porfirian entrepreneurs. This was the result of the strong growth of public infrastructure projects during those years.

In fact, these same Porfirian-era industries headed the recovery of the Mexican economy after 1932. This allowed Porfirian entrepreneurs running those sectors to remain strong despite the Depression. Although the 1920s saw new entrepreneurs investing in the cement industry, the old oligarchy still managed both the cement and the steel industry.[20] In steel making, the traditional Monterrey elite, which constituted the Grupo Monterrey, faced ideological conflicts with the postrevolutionary state, and particularly with the Cárdenas administration (1934–40). However, postrevolutionary politicos like Aarón Sáenz and Juan Andreu Almazán, who were linked to right-wing groups, played an important role in mediating these disputes. This mediation and the internal cohesion of the Grupo allowed it to remain strong within the Mexican business structure.[21]

The consumer goods industry also recovered in the 1930s, and, as in other sectors, old industrialists led the recovery process with two industries: beer and textiles. Some studies indicate that an important number of smaller companies were created within the textile industry that were able to compete successfully with the Porfiriato giants.[22] This was also the case in the tobacco industry, where the old Porfiriato giants' success increased competition in the sector.

In the beer industry, the Modelo brewery was founded in 1922. By 1930 it claimed a significant percentage of the market formerly held by the established industrialists. By that year, Modelo had also created a new market share in the central part of the country. However, Modelo was not founded by underfunded new entrepreneurs—it was a large new venture created by industrialists, mostly of Spanish descent, who came from other traditional sectors of the economy, such as flour and bread production, milk, rubber, and oil. Some of them had built strong political ties with the new revolutionary governments, which was a common tendency among the "new" entrepreneurs (those who founded successful new businesses during and after the revolutionary period). They basically replicated some of the business patterns of the Porfiriato.[23]

However, in all these cases, traditional entrepreneurs were still the leaders in the different sectors where they participated (textiles, beer, tobacco), and they sought to block new small businesses whenever possible. For example, small businesses were not allowed to send representatives to a general industry convention held in Mexico City in 1917.[24] In addition, as a result of that convention, an organization that represented the interests of the Porfirian business leaders was created in 1918—the Confederación de Cámaras Industriales de los Estados Unidos Mexicanos (CONCAMIN)—which integrated formerly separated industrial chambers. CONCAMIN marginalized small participants over time, leading to the creation of some small, industry-specific organizations, and the Cámara Nacional de la Industria de la Transformación (CANACINTRA) in 1941, which was a more general organization.

Newer and smaller entrepreneurs used CANACINTRA as an instrument to express their point of view and to influence government policy. According to Shadlen, "this organization exploited opportunities made available by the nature of the Mexican political regime (which was an executive-dominated authoritarian political system where interests of different groups were channeled through corporatist institutions such as this) and economic policy to seek the state as an ally. . . . [However,] CANACINTRA exchanged autonomy (which implied avoiding political activism, outspoken criticism of the political regime and its economic policy, and bypassing alliances outside the state) for organizational stability . . . to gain . . . a . . . role in the postwar Mexican political economy."[25] However, over time, smaller entrepreneurs faced different situations that continued to limit their ability to compete with the traditional oligarchy, such as a lack of credit.

It is important to mention that during the Cárdenas period, before the creation of the CANACINTRA, contrary to what some studies assert, industrial development was not limited. Cárdenas's economic policies were certainly more focused on rural areas, however. Between 1935 and 1939, more than six thousand industries were established in Mexico's national territory.[26] Investment by entrepreneurs of Jewish, Lebanese, and Syrian origin was of particular importance and was concentrated in industries that produced textiles, including rayon, silk, high-quality cotton, and clothing.[27] Immigrants coming as refugees from Spain after 1937 also contributed to the industrial development of chemicals, as well as to the cinematography and publishing businesses. Consequently, this was a period in which new companies, different from the traditional ones, began to share the market with the old industrialists in specific sectors of the economy.

WWII also had a great impact on Mexico's economy and on industrialization. The country became a strategic provider of raw materials for the United States, and US pullback on providing manufactured goods during WWII fostered industrialization in Mexico even though the United States continued to provide these goods to a limited extent.[28] At the same time, Mexico received production goods used by industrial firms in the manufacture of their finished products from its northern neighbor, which also allowed industrialization. So WWII stimulated import substitution in a natural way; that is, it emerged naturally due to external constraints.

The war also changed the government's vision of the country's economic development. Industrialization became a priority until the mid-1980s through the explicit implementation of the import substitution industrialization (ISI) model. This implied the adoption of new formal and informal institutions, such as a series of public policy strategies, and increasing the role of the state in the economy. In addition, "a new class of technocrats appeared, with skills in economics, planning, management and engineering. . . . They were instrumental in drawing up strategic plans for infrastructure development, and for setting up developmental agencies and financial institutions."[29] This model and its consequences are studied in more detail in chapter 5.

Throughout this long period from the 1940s through the 1980s, old industrialists and their heirs continually faced the emergence of new investors. An example that stands out is that of the so-called New Group (NG), identified by Mosk in a book published in 1950. This group emerged during WWII but included smaller entrepreneurs that appeared in the 1920s and 1930s. For example, it included the numerous entrepreneurs of Arab and Jewish origin that came to Mexico in those decades.[30] The NG used the CANACINTRA as an instrument to represent its interests. The NG was comprised of proprietors of small manufacturing industries created to provide the Mexican market with goods that were no longer available from foreign markets because of the war.[31]

According to Mosk, the NG strengthened the Mexican economy and gained influence within it. However, this is questionable. Traditional industrialists considered the NG to be a threat to their interests, one that limited their expansion options. In fact, Porfirian entrepreneurs again blocked their proposals in the Third National Congress of Industrialists, which took place in Mexico City in 1946. This was possible because "large firms [were] better able to organize independently of state-imposed regulations on interest associations."[32] In other words, large firms could act with more autonomy, independently of state guidelines. They "became integrated into a loose network of sector-specific industrial chambers and associations" that allowed them greater flexibility.[33] In addition, they had more economic power and political connections and shared more economic interests with politicians, which were sufficient to limit and control smaller firms. Even though Mosk affirmed in 1950 that the NG would take over leadership of industrialization in the country, displacing the old economic elite, evidence proves the opposite.

Pres. Miguel Alemán (1946–52) was not supportive of the economic nationalism and excessive protection demanded by the NG, despite the fact that protectionist tariffs were raised during his administration due to the sudden increase in imports and the reduction of exports after WWII. Alemán, like his predecessor Manuel Ávila Camacho (1940–46), invited US capitalists to participate in Mexican industry during his time in office.

In 1942, the company Altos Hornos de México was launched as a joint venture with Mexican and foreign capital in the iron and steel sectors. In 1944 in the textile industry, the company Celanese Mexicana emerged from a joint investment of private capital, public funds, and US capital. US investment also became more prevalent in other industries, such as the electricity, aluminum, and heat-resistant materials industries. This investment gradually eliminated the potential for NG hegemony in the long term, as the private national capital that participated in these large ventures generally came from traditional sectors operated by the old guard. According to Niblo, the following Mexican governments of the golden age of the PRI and the United States also opposed the NG as a result of its nationalist position.[34] In fact, tremendous pressure was generated against any politics that excluded US entrepreneurs from Mexican finances, resources, and markets.

It is important to mention that more recent studies, perhaps influenced by Mosk's ideas, assert that the NG held a greater influence in the Mexican economy, maintaining it from the 1940s until the 1980s. For instance, Medina Peña writes that "the New Group, in close alliance with the State . . . , would serve for many years as a counterbalance to traditional industrialists and conservative merchants and would provide strong support for a nationalist economic policy and the government's intervention in the economy."[35]

Although this influence may have been present ever since the CANACINTRA obtained prerogatives for small firms and participation in the national political economy, it is also true that important obstacles hindered the growth of the NG.[36] Aside from the post-Cardenista government support for US investments, an important barrier to credit limited the participation of new entrepreneurs as commercial banks still held strong links to the old industrialists. This credit barrier caused the new industrialists to seek other forms of funding, including large commercial companies and other individual lenders that offered lines of credit with higher interest rates than those offered by commercial banks.

Even Nacional Financiera (Nafinsa), a development banking institution founded in 1934 that promoted savings and investment through project management, did not support small industrial projects. This institution primarily benefited the old industrialists because it was more involved in financing large new industrial projects. As a result, Nacional Financiera acted as a partner of the old guard on many occasions, for instance, in the Industria Eléctrica de México, an electrical equipment company established in 1945.

The entire analysis constructed in this section shows how the traditional industrial elite of the Porfiriato was able to survive for many years after the revolutionary movement, a situation that would change during and after the 1980s. The way in which some elements of the traditional elite were weakened after the 1980s represents a complex process that is analyzed in chapter 5. Briefly, there was a process of substitution of individuals from the privileged economic groups through the implementation of neoliberal policies that began in the 1980s.

Landowners

Throughout the history of Mexico, agriculture has been one of the most important economic activities. Although its history as a productive unit dated from colonial times, the hacienda played a crucial role in agricultural production in the country during the government of Díaz, allowing the enrichment of multiple landowners in this period. The haciendas have been widely studied from different perspectives and in different regions of the country. This section analyzes how the traditional landowners of the Porfiriato were threatened by various rural policies that emerged in Mexico following the revolution, particularly agrarian reform. It also analyzes how a significant percentage of landowners in many regions persisted as part of the Mexican economic elite throughout most of the twentieth century, even though they were severely affected.

Two of the first studies about the Mexican Revolution, by Molina in 1909 and Tannenbaum in 1929, focus on the problem of land concentration by the haciendas and land-surveying companies and consider these aspects to be the leitmotif of the revolution. A law passed in 1883 authorized the president to contract land-surveying companies to examine vacant lands in exchange for a percentage of those lands.

Later works, especially those written after the 1970s, have considered the complexity of this process, emphasizing the heterogeneity of the hacienda structure and of its labor system.[37] Katz also emphasizes that "the Revolution was not driven mainly by *peones* [a type of hacienda worker] nor do the historical facts confirm the idea that the Revolution originated where the spiritual and material deprivations of the *peones* were greater."[38] Additionally, Nickel considers that "any simple definition of peonage is insufficient . . . [as there are] particular circumstances and variables found in every region and every time."[39] More recently, Antonio Escobar Ohmstede and Matthew Butler's collection of essays, *Mexico in Transition*, makes some important contributions to the "new" agrarian history of Mexico and its inherent complexities.[40] Nevertheless, for most of the twentieth century, a significant number of studies on the Porfiriato held the idea that a small group of landowners completely dominated agricultural lands, with workers living in haciendas representing the majority of agricultural workers.[41]

Land concentration in Mexico during the second half of nineteenth century, which in fact existed, can be in part associated with laws discussed and enacted by liberal administrations that were meant to modify land property rights to foster private landownership by individuals. Although this was the expected result, the confiscation of goods, the claiming of vacant lands, the development of land-surveying companies, and the construction of railways instead permitted the concentration of large expanses of land belonging to just a few owners.[42] However, the transfer of lands during the Porfiriato cannot be generalized. There were considerable differences between regions, between state governments, and even between cities and towns. For example, there were exceptions to this process in the states of San Luis Potosí, Tlaxcala, and Oaxaca, among others.[43]

In addition to the concentration of landownership during the Porfiriato, economic and political elites were closely linked in many regions. In fact, in many states, economic and political elites were one and the same. Two prime examples are the Terrazas-Creel clan in Chihuahua and the Molina-Montes clique in Yucatán. Díaz tried to separate political power from economic power several times in many regions to avoid threats to his government, even fostering opposition between rival groups. However, a significant proportion of economic oligarchies were also able to monopolize political resources in the long term.[44] Some exceptions to this trend can be found in the states of Puebla, Tlaxcala, and Veracruz, among others, where there was no marked predominance by families.

The political elite certainly changed with the Mexican Revolution, as mentioned above, and came to include elements of a younger middle class; however, a significant fraction of the landowner elite survived the event. Wasserman provides a remarkable contribution to the understanding of the survival of landowners throughout the revolution. He does so by analyzing the elements of change and continuity in old landowner elites established in the Porfiriato, arguing that their survival was in part ensured through a system of alliances with the new elite that emerged from the revolutionary movement. Illustrating this point, Wasserman cites the Terrazas-Creel clan, whose family includes politicians, farmers, bankers, miners, and industrial and commercial entrepreneurs.

The Terrazas-Creel family implemented a wide range of strategies to maintain control over its possessions during and after the revolution. These ranged from open warfare and direct negotiations with revolutionary groups for the sale, division, and repurchase of its properties to direct partnerships with new local and national political leaders, taking advantage of their weaknesses and needs to enable politicians to implement some of their revolutionary strategies while largely retaining the family's privileged position.[45] Thus, Wasserman argues that the landowner elite in Chihuahua could not ultimately be destroyed, despite the severe impact of the revolution.

Similarly, Wasserman summarizes several regional studies and concludes that the more diversified the economic activities of the members of the old oligarchy were, the more likely they were to survive the revolution. However, the more dependent the elites were on their lands, the more vulnerable they turned out to be.[46] For example, the revolution virtually destroyed their power in the state of Morelos, where the bourgeoisie consisted mainly of landowners. However, most survived the revolution in Monterrey, where the elite diversified its assets. During this period, old and new elites made many alliances. Knight argues that marriage played an important role in the merger.[47]

The revolution affected landowners in different ways in its different stages. In the first stage of the revolution, from 1910 to 1913, Pres. Francisco Madero was careful not to upset the oligarchy with the government's policies. Madero himself came from a family of landowners. He faced some violent opposition from leaders such as Emiliano Zapata, who formally condemned the president and proclaimed a national campaign to return hacienda lands to the people with his Plan de Ayala.[48] Between 1914 and 1917, the political situation changed. It was a period characterized by intense armed conflict, during which many lands were expropriated. Additionally, the economic crisis of those years affected many landowners, some of whom abandoned their properties to pursue other economic activities. Some of these owners had commercial and financial businesses in large cities or abroad, all of which they began to manage directly.

During these years, land expropriation varied depending on the region of the country but was concentrated mainly in the states where Francisco Villa and Zapata were most influential: Morelos, Guerrero, Michoacán, Puebla, Tamaulipas, Nuevo León, Chihuahua, Durango, Zacatecas, and San Luis Potosí. Nevertheless, there were several successful attempts by landowners to adapt to their region's changed political climate, seeking arrangements with revolutionary leaders in which they would exchange part of their harvest for protection. Other landowners left the haciendas in the hands of managers, who struck agreements with leaders from different sides to balance their alliances.

After 1917, the movement led by Carranza did not significantly affect landowners. He only seized haciendas on a few occasions; in fact, he returned lands to several hacendados. This returning of haciendas also took place during part of the period led by the sonorenses, which started in 1920; however, this topic has rarely been discussed by scholars, and these land returns are difficult to quantify. The sonorenses took actions that sometimes endangered and sometimes helped consolidate the influence of the old landowning oligarchy.

These new revolutionary governments pursued the modernization of the economy more aggressively than land distribution. Therefore, the agrarian law of January 1915, which is considered the beginning of the agrarian reform in Mexico, and Article 27 of the 1917 constitution, which allowed for the seizure of lands for their redistribution, were not applied fully until the Cárdenas administration (1934–40). In fact, when the government needed support from the rural population to address conflicts, such as in the Adolfo de la Huerta rebellion of 1923 and the Escobar insurgency of 1929, the government turned to land redistribution. This policy was initiated to pacify Zapata's peasant followers in Morelos, Puebla, Tlaxcala, and the state of México as early as 1920, and the government resorted to this same action in the years that followed, whenever it deemed it to be appropriate. Before Cárdenas, land distribution was limited to ten million hectares. Most of this land was public; when it was not, distribution generally did not affect the main buildings within haciendas.

Haber, Razo, and Maurer argue that, between 1910 and 1920, the major landowners in the Porfiriato mitigated some of the effects of political instability and institutional change by building VPI coalitions with the federal government and generals. The latter played the role of a third party, providing protection in exchange for revenue.[49] Through these coalitions, land reforms regressed between 1914 and 1917. This mechanism also worked in later years, especially in the north, and even Pres. Álvaro Obregón and Pres. Plutarco Elías Calles participated in these alliances.[50]

The trial by fire for the former landowners from the Porfiriato would be the land reform program implemented by Cárdenas during his administration. Cárdenas's program was different in essence from the land reform projects of previous governments. Before him, land reform had mainly been used for short-term political purposes; however, Cárdenas had a genuine desire to transform Mexican rural areas, so his program focused on economic and institution-building objectives.[51] In addition, his agrarian reform was much more extensive. During his presidency, he redistributed about twenty million hectares. Even though landowners used different methods to try to retain their land—such as dividing, selling, or using a straw man—this time the methods generally proved to be fallible. Expropriations, in fact, usually affected the landowning class. For example, in the states of Coahuila, Michoacán, Sonora, Baja California, Yucatán, and Chiapas, among others, the vast number of expropriations left many families with almost no land. This period of expropriations coincided with a period in which the power and influence of most of the revolutionary generals had weakened considerably.[52] Coalitions between the generals and the landowners also weakened or disappeared.[53]

Landowners in Mexico certainly suffered much more than industrialists during this period. However, one cannot conclude that all these families lost their economic power. Diversification played a major role once again. Although the economically active segment of the country's population was still primarily employed in agriculture in 1940, manufacturing came to lead the Mexican economy by the mid-1930s. According to Josué Sáenz's figures, calculated in those years, manufacturing even surpassed all other economic activities in its contribution to the gross domestic product in 1937.[54] This change is important given that, at the time Cárdenas's agrarian reform took place, there were many opportunities to invest in other sectors the resources obtained from the sale of land. For example, Diane Davis shows in *Urban Leviathan* how real estate prices in the Federal District soared in the late 1930s as landowners decapitalized their holdings in rural areas out of fear of Cardenista expropriation and sank their capital into urban real estate.[55] Indeed, the elites' preference for urban (not rural) real estate, which was clear in this period, is an important and long-ignored feature of Mexican economic history.

To conclude, even though landowners were weakened between 1910 and 1940—and in some states, such as Morelos, their economic power was almost eliminated—some landowners found different methods to protect themselves from these negative conditions. Their approaches, though fallible, were effective at times. In the north and parts of the south of the country, landowners divided their lands among relatives to comply with the legal requirements or they sold or simply leased their lands. They also used other legal means, such as the writ of *amparo*, or else they bribed local authorities to be able to maintain their holdings and took advantage of the fact that some opposed the agrarian reform.[56] Some VPI coalitions were also formed to deal with the effects of political instability and the formal institutional changes. The most important element that emerges from this analysis is the role the diversification of assets and economic activities, together with family and social networks, played in maintaining the old elite.

As Buve notes, the differences in local conditions and the revolutionary process in the center of the country make it difficult to draft a general outline of the situation, particularly for the more turbulent years of the revolution between 1914 and 1920.[57] Many decisions were based on the conditions of the haciendas, the mindset of the hacienda owner, and the weight and power of local revolutionaries. Some landowners abandoned their haciendas, while others defended their property with armed dependents or made arrangements with various revolutionary leaders.

We can say that the Mexican Revolution did not represent an important change in the composition of Mexico's economic elite. Virtually all of the industrial plants owned by the traditional entrepreneurs remained intact. Additionally, even though the hacendado class was more affected than the industrialists, it has been shown that a significant number of them also survived the period. As a result, the old economic elites and new politicians created a new coalition.

It is also true that some entrepreneurs who had been close to Díaz could not persist as part of the power elite. For example, part of the Barcelonnette elite was affected by events that occurred between 1910 and 1940. However, many Barcelonnettes were also capable of surviving the changes brought about by these episodes. Descendants of Porfirian entrepreneurs were prevalent in every postrevolutionary government until the 1980s.[58] In addition, many elements of Mexican business culture were kept intact. For example, politicians and entrepreneurs reproduced the same types of arrangements between them, keeping business and political power in the hands of a few.

Despite the fact that formal institutions in Mexico began to strengthen after the revolution, especially since the 1920s, the force of the shared economic interests between politicians and businessmen that addressed institutional weaknesses during the Porfiriato proved to be stronger than law enforcement after that period. The details of and theory behind crony capitalism will be studied in the following section.

While there was a great deal of continuity in the pre- and postrevolutionary periods, one major change brought about by the revolution was that the political power of Mexico's workers became stronger after the armed revolution. In fact, after the 1920s, every government in Mexico integrated organized labor into the ruling coalition through confederations of labor unions, such as the Confederación Regional Obrera Mexicana (CROM) and the Confederación de Trabajadores de México (CTM). The result was an equilibrium in which the rest of Mexican society served as a source of rents for the government, a subset of manufacturers, and a subset of their workforces.[59]

DEFINING AND EXPLAINING CRONY CAPITALISM

Mexican industrialization during the Porfiriato was accompanied by what is described as crony capitalism, in which the interests of economic and political elites (elements of the power elite) are intermingled. In this section, I construct an argument about what crony capitalism was in Mexico during the Porfiriato. Crony capitalism in that period lies in between the Haber-Razo-Maurer (neo-institutionalists) explanations of crony capitalism as a result of VPI and Edward Beatty's analysis of Porfirian capitalism, which stresses that there were many more formal institutions operating in business during the Porfiriato than those neo-institutionalists recognize.[60]

While the Porfiriato in Mexico exhibited aspects of crony capitalism, there was also an institutional, legal, and political framework of constraints on Díaz. Nonetheless, it cannot be denied that the formulation of laws and policies in this period was often the product of mixed interests of the political and business elites. This combination of mixed interests—which includes the creation of laws or manipulation of those already established or the exemption of them for the benefit of a few—is what characterizes crony capitalism in the Porfiriato.

Broadly speaking, *crony capitalism* is a term used to describe an economy in which success in business depends on the relationships or links between business leaders and government officials. The term *crony capitalism* itself dates from the late 1990s. It has been used to contrast the virtues of American-style capitalism with the economic model of countries that allow close links between government and businesses. However, crony capitalism exists in most of the countries of the world to differing degrees.[61] For example, several scandals have come to light in recent years showing that the United States has a considerable degree of crony capitalism in the operation of its economy. Nomi Prins's book *All the Presidents' Bankers*, for example, shows the links between US presidents and the powerful bankers in the country, such as JPMorgan Chase and National City Bank.[62] The author argues and demonstrates that Wall Street and the White House collaborated to shape national policy through the Great Depression of 1929, the World Wars, the establishment of the World Bank and the IMF, the Cold War, and the financial and military expansion of the United States. Additionally, the author stresses that alliances between bankers and presidents and their cabinets continue to define the policies and laws that direct the economy in the United States in the present day.

Stephen Haber, exploring this topic for Latin America, defined crony capitalism as a system "in which those close to the political authorities who make and enforce policies receive favors that have large economic value."[63] In other words, those connected with political or economic agents usually receive cheap credit, tax exemptions, and protection from international competition by tariffs, among other conditions, which allow them to earn higher profits than in a competitive market where all participants start from the same set of conditions.[64] Furthermore, within the established system, government officials get part of those extranormal profits from private businesses in return.

On the purely economic side, favored entrepreneurs can operate their businesses as monopolies or near monopolies under a system of crony capitalism. Monopolies generally have two negative consequences for the economy: They produce less than would be produced in a competitive market, and products are sold at higher prices than they would be in a competitive market. This creates a loss to society that, as a consumer, transfers resources to the privileged actors. This has an effect on income distribution. Even if production is not reduced within certain markets, the existence of protected sectors of national and international competition allows privileged businesses to manipulate their prices to be higher than those that would exist in a more competitive market, which is reflected in profits similar to those that monopolies would obtain.

Society also loses on the supply side. That is, a producer's ability to supply is limited in the economic sectors in which privileged "friends" operate. In that sense, we can say that crony capitalist systems distort economic incentives, negatively affecting the growth rates of various sectors of the economy because under crony capitalism "industries will exist that would not exist otherwise . . . and opportunities will be denied to entrepreneurs who have the required skills and assets but not the political access or protection required."[65]

Analyzing the six main requirements for modern capitalism that Max Weber identified, there are two fundamental differences between capitalism and crony capitalism. The first relates to the rule of law, and the second relates to property rights. With regard to the rule of law, in crony capitalism, "application of the law becomes arbitrary, unpredictable, and dependent on informal relations and factors other than universal rules."[66] In short, the law does not apply equally to all social and economic actors. Second, in these systems, property rights are weak and transient. Crony capitalism is a system that ensures the property rights of selected economic actors.

Cronyism dates back to the origin of capitalism itself. Various authors have studied the integration of government and economic groups during very different time periods, such as prerevolutionary France, prerevolutionary Mexico, Eastern Europe under communism, and Eastern Europe today. Even so, it is difficult to determine a specific period in which crony capitalism first appeared. The need to obtain financial capital was one of the main features that stimulated the formation of social networks in general and among entrepreneurs and government officials in particular. Bureaucrats have long used their power to help enrich their friends and networks outside the government. When relations between government officials and economic actors dominate policy making, cronyism becomes crony capitalism.[67]

It is also true that the construction, bolstering, and quality maintenance of formal institutions have varied markedly over the years. This, in turn, has had an effect on limiting the use of "crony" strategies in different economies. That is, these strategies, while necessary at the beginning of the construction of capitalist nations—in part, due to the lack of financial capital mentioned above—were either controlled to a certain degree in developed countries over the years or transformed into strategies that were deeply rooted in business practices, as is the case in Mexico and most developing nations. In that sense, the arbitrary application of law and the weakness of property rights vary in degree among countries, depending on the existing level of crony capitalism.

The specific reasons why some countries have been able to control crony capitalism more than others are multiple and complex. However, they are related to the proper functioning of legal processes, supervised through a system of checks and balances on each formal institution participating in the control of this type of corrupt practice. A newly created legal structure in Mexico seeking to deal with this sort of corruption is the National Anti-Corruption System, created in 2015. This system includes several formal institutions and laws and regulations that document each step in a given corruption process from the beginning and act in a coordinated manner to combat it. However, there has been great resistance to its implementation and the appointments of its heads have been rigged. This brings us to a second reason why some countries have been more successful in controlling crony capitalism than others. This reflects a more abstract aspect related to the vision that society as a whole has on the value of the common good, to which each individual contributes in some way with their actions.

The Debate on Crony Capitalism in Mexico in the Porfiriato

Here, I describe how the academic debate over the level of crony capitalism existing in Mexico during the Porfiriato has been constructed. In the introduction to the compilation *Crony Capitalism and Economic Growth in Latin America*, Stephen Haber asks why crony capitalism systems arise if they are not ideal for an economy to produce what it needs or to be competitive. He responds by saying that crony capitalism is the second-best solution to a problem—the problem of commitment: "Any government strong enough to protect and arbitrate property rights is also strong enough to abrogate them."[68]

Haber ponders how a government can create a credible commitment that does not abuse this power: simply promising that it will not do it is not enough because the government can always break its promise at some later time.[69]

Haber argues that members of the government itself or members of their families should share the revenue generated by entrepreneurs in economic activities: "The intermingling of economic and political elites means that it is extremely difficult to break the implicit contract between government and the privileged asset holders."[70] In 2003, Haber, Armando Razo, and Noel Maurer published the book *The Politics of Property Rights*, which attempts to theorize and formalize the study of crony capitalism in Mexico, explaining it through the VPI model.

Gulnaz Sharafutdinova goes further and categorizes different explanations of the phenomenon of crony capitalism into three approaches: cultural, historical institutionalism, and new institutionalism (or neo-institutionalism).[71] She states that cronyism and the importance of informal relationships at various levels of society are the results of old cultural patterns of behavior under the cultural approach: "Corruption and patronage based on personal relationships are therefore culturally embedded practices."[72]

With regard to historical institutionalism, which is the approach that the author adopts in her book on Russia, she mentions that different types of limited access orders (those in which "the political system manipulates the economy to create rents as a means of solving the problem of violence"[73]) require careful historical examination. In fact, historical institutionalists focus on the lasting effects on institutions and political patterns, which appeared in response to key challenges faced by political actors and societies at particular moments in time.[74] The author notes that different historical and cultural contexts have led to different manifestations of the phenomenon we are studying.[75]

Instead, for Sharafutdinova, the neo-institutionalist approach that Haber and others adopted for studying crony capitalism in Latin America "provides a solid starting point, but it does not address the issue of the origins of cronyism."[76] Coatsworth makes a similar criticism.[77] He says that the model used by Haber, Razo, and Maurer does not address time horizons. In addition, neo-institutionalist models cannot explain the existence of some characteristics of crony capitalism in developed countries, which have supposedly solved the commitment problem of governments by setting limits to governments: those that respect due process and are bound to respect individual and universal political and economic rights through formal institutions. In this sense, neo-institutionalist models operate with a high level of generalization, one that cannot distinguish between specific versions of crony capitalism or systems with some degree of limited access.

Razo acknowledges the lack of time horizons in his analysis performed with Haber and Maurer, which he says does not theorize about the factors behind the prolonged existence of informal arrangements. In his book, *Social Foundations of Limited Dictatorship*, published in 2008, he seeks to explain the durability of informal agreements and to specify the political and social bases that extended beyond the Porfiriato to the kind of informal arrangements between Díaz and entrepreneurs. According to Razo, *Politics of Property Rights* accurately shows that economic and political actors during the Porfiriato found it to be in their interest to collaborate, but microlevel mechanisms that enabled cooperation and integration are not explained in this work.[78]

Díaz, according to this author, protected a limited set of entrepreneurs rather than providing universal protection. He points out that the government granted variable concessions to private companies, even to companies in the same industry. For example, "firms with higher expected rents were more likely to obtain better concession terms."[79] Razo concludes that "the network structure of special privileges that Díaz awarded created a critical mass of actors with the incentive to defend the system against predation."[80] The central players in Díaz's network were powerful enough to keep him in check, even though this network was not particularly dense. This argument shows the significant neo-institutionalist influence on Razo's ideas.

A clear criticism of Razo's book is central to Aurora Gómez-Galvarriato Freer's published review. In it, she states that the dictatorship described in Razo's model did not resemble that of the Porfiriato to the degree Razo would like because "recent historiography has shown . . . that Porfirian Mexico's institutional framework was more complex and that there existed stronger legal and political constraints to the dictator's power, than the author acknowledges."[81] The reason public officials were prevalent in Razo's network is due to the sources used, according to Gómez. These sources showed a bias toward large companies where foreign investment was prevalent and where the law required at least one public official on their boards.

In Edward Beatty's book *Institutions and Investment*, there is an implicit notion that the Porfiriato was not necessarily a case of crony capitalism. Beatty notes that by planning and administering a series of laws and policies such as an intellectual property law (patents), trade policy (tariffs on imports), and providing tax incentives to employers who established new industries, among others, Díaz's government pushed for and developed a national industrial sector. He argues that the formation and investment practices in Mexico owed their existence to these formal laws and policies. Following these arguments, Sergio Valerio Ulloa affirms that there were a number of small and medium enterprises that did not have special privileges during the Porfiriato and that were subject to the laws.[82] Sandra Kuntz also sustains that the nature of laws doubtless improved during the Porfiriato and mentions that "going backwards in the history of nineteenth century independent Mexico, we can better appreciate the institutional progress of the Porfiriato."[83]

However, the reality of crony capitalism in Mexico falls somewhere between the position of neo-institutionalists and that of Beatty, Valerio Ulloa, and Kuntz.[84] This implies that the term *crony capitalism* should be understood for Mexico as a hybrid model or a nuanced version of what the neo-institutionalists—the proponents of the term for Latin America—consider. That is, crony capitalism was not as prevalent as the neo-institutionalists maintain, but other authors seldom acknowledge just how prevalent and persistent it was. For example, if federal law required public officials to be on the boards of certain companies, as is Gómez's contention, the economic incentives in these sectors were distorted and profits very likely shared in many cases. In addition, there were many other cases where companies' boards included politicians or individuals directly related to them without the law necessarily requiring it. While this conclusion can be found in most neo-institutionalist studies, it should not be exaggerated because politicians were not involved in companies in all economic sectors nor in most small and medium companies established in Mexico, which were subject to laws.

In addition, whether or not the law in the Porfiriato had a greater impact than that recognized by neo-institutionalists, it was political and business elites who formulated most laws and policies that affected them—a major distinction between crony capitalism and cronyism, as noted previously. The government's creation of the General Law of Credit Institutions of 1897 in conjunction with the few existing banks at the time provides a clear example. This law limited the entrance of new participants into the banking arena, which led to a highly concentrated banking sector with monopolistic characteristics. This is a particularly important point because the lack of financial capital was the crucial element that gave rise to crony capitalism in the origins of capitalism. In other words, the need for governments to have access to financial resources led to the formation of social networks between politicians and bankers, which in turn gave monetary benefits to individuals on both sides. As a result of this law, which institutionalized previous practices, bankers continued to enjoy monopolistic profits due to the limitation on participants in the sector; government officials, who decided who would receive a bank charter, usually exchanged this "for a sit on a board and substantial quantities of stock."[85] The concentration of industries was the result of the multiple firms connected to banks, which received credit via insider lending practices. That is, banks lent to their own partners as a result of the weak banking regulations and controls that existed in that period.

SOCIAL NETWORKS AND CRONY CAPITALISM IN THE FRENCH BUSINESS COMMUNITY IN MEXICO

Social networks played a particularly relevant role in Mexico's business activity, especially during the Porfiriato. The Barcelonnettes represent a clear example of a tightly interwoven social network of entrepreneurs, which allowed for the expansion of their businesses, insider lending, and exploitation of key political connections during the Porfiriato.

The Monopolistic Structure of the Mexican Economy

Before the Porfiriato, independent Mexico was generally defined by the little control it had over productive forces, social disorder, political chaos, and marked regionalization. In addition, the independent country inherited a highly hierarchical and segmented society. As a result, the formation of a solid and productive economic infrastructure was to be a complicated and fraught process. The increasing creation of new industrial plants did not take place until the Porfiriato established control over the country's territory, setting up a basis for economic action. Part of this control was the result of creating alliances and networks with local strongmen.

Díaz's ability to keep the interests of powerful men limited to local ambitions, in a country with strong regionalism, distinguishes the Mexico of this period as a state led effectively by a strong executive, able to promote agreements with the various caciques of those times. Political power within the country, after a long process, became subordinated to Díaz. Those backing the dictatorship were put in strategic positions within the federal government or in key positions in different regions, which is clear evidence of the control that was being exercised by the president. Strongmen loyal to Díaz remained powerful throughout most of the Porfiriato, including such individuals as Bernardo Reyes in Nuevo León; Francisco Cañedo in Sinaloa; Jesús Aréchiga in Zacatecas; Teodoro Dehesa in Veracruz; Aristeo Mercado in Michoacán; Francisco González de Cosío in Querétaro; Mucio Martínez in Puebla; Alejandro Vázquez del Mercado in Aguascalientes; José Vicente Villada in the state of México; the Meixueiros in Oaxaca; and Luis Terrazas, Enrique Creel, and Miguel Ahumada in Chihuahua.

Some of them became governors of their respective states for over fifteen years. They also enjoyed the economic privileges of being part of Díaz's network.

For example, after passage of the 1897 banking law, they could decide who would obtain each of the severely restricted federal banking charters permitted outside Mexico City. As a result, they also got seats on the boards of and stocks in banks established locally and, consequently, the power to use these banks to fund their own economic interests.

This concentration of banks and firms controlled by closed business networks across the country allowed the formation of monopolies, typical of the Porfiriato. Trade, finance, land, and manufacturing were concentrated in a few hands. The people who controlled the economy also controlled the political system, so there was no incentive to break the monopolies. In addition, the concentration of manufacturing industries among a small number of producers was supported by the excess production capacity of the Mexican industrial apparatus, which made investment in new plants unnecessary in some sectors. Haber shows that the cement industry reached an average of 47 percent utilization of its installed capacity between 1906 and 1910. In the case of the steel industry, this figure is even smaller: only 30 percent in the same period.[86]

This considerable industrial capacity was the result of a process that mainly occurred during the Porfiriato. In some sectors, there was a transformation from family-run companies producing for local and regional markets to large, vertically integrated, and capital-intensive firms producing for the national market. In glass, paper, soap, steel, and dynamite production, one big company in each of them held a monopoly or quasi-monopoly. Two firms controlled cigarette production, and in cement and beer, three companies carved up each market. The cotton textile industry had a different kind of industrial organization; there were many companies operating in the local, regional, and national markets, and some of them kept the characteristics of small family-run firms, while others grew more and became large consortia comprising individual companies. However, even in this more competitive market, two consortia (the CIVSA and the CIDOSA) claimed almost all the production of high-quality goods and around 20 percent of all other national production.[87]

Mexico was not the only country fostering a monopolistic structure in its economy. By the early twentieth century, the economies of many countries worldwide, including the United States, were characterized by a marked trend toward a monopolistic organization of industry, despite the fact that this period also saw the earliest efforts to implement antitrust legislation. The first attempt to regulate this type of activity in the United States was the Sherman Act of 1890, which aimed to stop anticompetitive behaviors and promote economic development; however, it was insufficient, given the ease with which businessmen were able to violate the law through various tactics. These included cooperation between businessmen and the political sector and legal evasions using technicalities and loopholes to enable them to continue unimpeded. In Mexico, Article 28 of the 1857 constitution prohibited monopolistic practices.[88] In both countries, however, the close relationship or social networks between politicians and entrepreneurs, which led to crony capitalism, were key to the development of monopolies.

Social Networks

Before discussing the particular case of social networks in the French business community in Mexico, it is important to first identify the role of social networks in overcoming the limits of institutional frameworks. These limits were examined earlier and can be summarized in the arbitrary application of the law, the limitations and gaps in the legal system, and the weakness of property rights—an aspect always discussed due to its importance in a functioning capitalist system. The consensus among scholars is that social networks in general (not necessarily including government officials) were instrumental in economic success beyond the Porfirian period in Mexico, although this period stands out. What is the reason for this?

It has been argued that "businessmen can use networks to monitor one another, and negotiate within a system that relies more on convention than on publicly declared rules to function."[89] In fact, the Mexican business network of the early twentieth century facilitated the exchange of information between companies. Again, the banking sector is a clear example of this. The extensive insider lending that occurred in Mexico throughout the Porfiriato and several decades beyond resulted from the use of networks to compensate for information asymmetries.

In sociological terms, there are two types of entrepreneur: individual entrepreneurs and network entrepreneurs. Individual entrepreneurs are more common in societies in which trust prevails. Without trust, which affects transparency in economic transactions, entrepreneurs predominantly operate in networks. Individuals that conform to the network must have personal attributes considered to be acceptable, as well as the support of the other members of the network, which is based on shared values. But, more importantly, network entrepreneurs should have the proper connections to develop productive businesses and to exploit market niches.[90] Additionally, when circumstances are uncertain and the institutional framework offers only a weak legal apparatus and little protection of property rights, shared goals, attitudes, and aspirations may replace external rules and regulations.[91]

Some authors agree with Gómez who argues that, contrary to the belief of most neo-institutionalists studying early industrialization in Mexico, "it is impossible to conclude from the existing literature whether the importance of networks in Mexico was the result of weak institutions; however, it is undeniable that networks played an especially relevant role in the country's business activity,"[92] which certainly they did. However, as we will see in chapter 5, something that can also be affirmed about networks in Mexico is that they are a key factor in explaining why formal institutions have remained weak over the years.

The Barcelonnette Social Network and Political Ties

The Barcelonnettes are a clear example of network entrepreneurs. In the Barcelonnette business network, which was relatively dense and tightly interwoven, 86 percent of the partners had French surnames. Some functions of the Barcelonnette network meant that they hired and trained personnel almost exclusively from within their community. Additionally, "those who came later would take advantage of the early network and use their entrepreneurial abilities, not only to expand their businesses, but also to increase the network itself, and, in so doing, to give their compatriots' firms the opportunity to expand."[93]

Aurora Gómez finds no evidence of links between public officials and the Barcelonnette network beyond the banking sector. However, even if true, the consequences of the banking link were more profound than Gómez acknowledges. As has been analyzed before, the connections with capital providers explain the distortion and concentration of multiple markets in the hands of few suppliers, strengthening the monopolistic structure of the productive apparatus and crony capitalism.

Additionally, even though some banking companies managed by the Barcelonnettes in the late Porfiriato and during the revolution boasted of not having had any relationship with Díaz, many of their board members had close relations with Porfirian public servants. José Yves Limantour, minister of finance for an extended period during the Porfiriato, was a partner and close friend of Joseph Ollivier, who had created the bank CBPM in 1909 with other Barcelonnettes, including members of the Jean family. This Barcelonnette entrepreneur took advantage of his relationships by asking for concessions from the federal government. For example, in 1900, J. Ollivier and Company successfully asked Limantour to annul a fine for 212 packages that were at Tampico customs house. Similarly, Limantour constantly requested that Ollivier send him objects from Paris. They were usually personal items (shoes, clothing, etc.) or items for his home (chandeliers, tapestries, furniture, etc.). In 1908, Limantour required that he be sent French trees to plant in the Chapultepec forest, velvet fabrics, accessories for his car, and a chassis for Porfirio Díaz's wife's car.[94]

Another common Barcelonnette practice was insider lending. This practice, as mentioned earlier, served as a way to compensate for information asymmetries in a period where information about possible trustworthy bank clients was poor and banking regulation was weak. The Barcelonnettes took advantage of these weaknesses and used their banks to fund their own companies and those of their friends. This situation goes far beyond the Porfirian period. A review of the loan portfolios of banks managed by the Barcelonnettes, such as Banamex, confirmed that the company primarily financed its partners. In addition to their partners, they supported the friends of clients—customers related either directly or indirectly to members of the same bank. In fact, according to Haber, 100 percent of all nongovernmental loans made by Banamex between 1888 and 1901 went to members of the institution.[95] Banamex also granted loans to politicians linked to the production and distribution of certain products. For example, in 1901, the credit line of Pablo Macedo's Compañía Industrial Manufacturera was increased to 380,000 pesos, which was given as a mortgage jointly with the BLM.[96]

Employing insider lending practices, Banamex financed, for example, the CIDOSA; in 1891, it authorized a loan of 200,000 to 250,000 pesos to the Compañía Manufacturera de Cerritos S.A.[97] In 1921, it opened a current account credit to J. Ollivier y Cía. Sucesores of 100,000 pesos, with a guarantee of 2,000 CIDOSA shares.[98] In 1928, it gave the same firm a loan of 60,000 pesos with a guarantee of CIDOSA and CIVSA shares.[99] Likewise, in 1922, Banamex approved the opening of a commercial loan for 75,000 pesos for the Bank of Montreal, which members of the CIDOSA had requested.[100] The Barcelonnettes originally created all these companies, and a significant percentage of the ownership of Banamex was also in the hands of these French investors by that time.

In the next chapter, we examine the Jean family's story of wealth creation and consolidation and contrast the specific characteristics of their business development with the general analysis presented here and in chapter 1. The members of the Jean family arrived late (by the end of the nineteenth century) compared to the bulk of the Barcelonnette community in Mexico. While they benefited from their ties to the Barcelonnettes in Mexico, they built different and more individualistic business strategies that allowed them to create their wealth in a period when the relative importance of these French emigrants had decreased (1910–40).

The Jean brothers who were the first generation in Mexico and their descendants were also able to diversify their assets in new economic sectors, such as housing construction. They also built networks with new businessmen from France and other countries, as well as with politicians born out of the revolution.

CHAPTER THREE

The Expansion of a Successful French Business Family in Mexico

The Jean family prospered in Mexico throughout the twentieth century because they networked socially but remained economically independent from their peers. This allowed them to be flexible when dealing with black swan events like the Mexican Revolution, as well as diversify into fields that most Franco-Mexican investors had not discovered, like real estate. The Jeans also profited from relationships with politicians who emerged from the revolution through links established between different administrations, such as Madero's, and companies managed by the Jean family, such as the banking company, the CBPM. They also benefited through relationships with prominent partners of Banamex, like the Legorretas. This allowed the Jeans to obtain key positions in this bank, which was strongly connected to various governments, and in other companies. These crucial events and others, such as the marriage of a member of the third generation of the Jean family with the daughter of El Tigre Azcárraga, owner of Televisa—the most important media company in Latin America—have sustained the prominence of individuals of this family until today.

This chapter analyzes the Jean family's experience in Mexico after their emigration from Meyronnes, a town near Barcelonnette, to this country in the late nineteenth century and their accomplishments in banking and business. I relate how the Jean family members became established and constructed their wealth. To this end, I explain their start in the textile industry and how they diversified into many other businesses, mainly in central Mexico. I trace their trajectory with attention to the particular circumstances and strategies the family used to preserve and increase its wealth and position, which allowed them to persist as part of the economic elite in central Mexico. I also discuss the effects of the Mexican Revolution (1910–20) and the agrarian reform programs of the 1920s and 1930s on their expansion and properties.

This chapter is significant to the understanding of crony capitalism and institutional solidity in Mexico. It shows how the Jean family established direct or indirect relationships with government officials to build and preserve its riches. These relationships evolved both qualitatively and in terms of economic sectors. That is, through the banking sector, the Jeans first established mutually beneficial relationships with the government in the early twentieth century, which helped the family to consolidate their economic power in an environment of institutional weakness and lack of information. These relationships continued through Banamex until the banks in Mexico were nationalized in 1982. In addition, from the 1920s onward, the Jeans maintained close ties with government officials and eventually associated with families also strongly connected with politicians in the housing sector. This allowed them to expand their housing business, sometimes obtaining land illegally through invasions permitted by those same public servants.

The relationship of the Jeans with the Azcárragas through marriage was also important in strengthening their ties of the Jean family with the government. From its origins in the 1950s, Televisa has been known for establishing agreements with all Mexican governments of all political parties. These agreements allowed Televisa to maintain quasi-economic profits while actively censoring and manipulating the information presented through television, radio, and periodicals according to the interests of successive governments and in accordance with the company's business interests. This even led Televisa and the government of the state of México to establish the presidential couple who governed Mexico between 2012 and 2018: Peña Nieto and the Televisa actress Angélica Rivera. This marriage ended in divorce in May 2019, a few months after the end of the six-year term.

It is clear that the nature of the connections between members of the Jean family and politicians changed over the years. In the early twentieth century, relations with the government strengthened the Jean family economically in an environment of institutional uncertainty. Later, by constructing alliances with members of different governments to facilitate the implementation of different businesses, and through their participation in companies like Televisa, they contributed to keeping institutions weak, as some of the members of the family continued strengthening their economic interests through privileges like tax exemptions and few legal restrictions at least until the change of administration in 2018.

INDUSTRY

At the beginning of the Porfiriato, Mexico was challenged by economic stagnation and political disorder, and the government was continually broke. As a solution, President Díaz supported the creation of financial institutions to provide the government with financial resources. However, the owners of the banking system became the main owners of the manufacturing industry, leading to monopolies and concentration of power, supported by a protectionist structure. In this context, the Jean family entered the textile and paper industry in the mid-1890s by becoming partners of a company near Mexico City. They gained greater prominence and importance in the early 1900s when other families left the firm. Unlike many other companies, the Jean company grew during and after the revolution, expanding to other states. The Jean family also began to participate in other sectors of the economy, such as energy—through hydroelectric plants—and construction and housing, which was an area not many of the Barcelonnettes were involved in.

The Jean family distinguished itself from other Barcelonnettes by gradually acquiring almost the entire capital of the enterprises in which they had originally been secondary partners, thereby expanding their influence and the companies' activities. Moreover, whereas Barcelonnettes typically created large consortia comprising individual companies, the Jeans ensured that company partnership was restricted to individuals, usually family members.

Though never central to the Barcelonnette social networks in Mexico, the Jeans did benefit from them and the various associations and social clubs the community founded, which facilitated networking with the business elite.

The Structure of the Manufacturing Industry in Late Nineteenth- and Early Twentieth-Century Mexico

When Díaz took power in 1876, he faced several hurdles. Formal institutions were weak, and the governments that preceded him had utilized strategies outside the law to compensate their supporters and to weaken their enemies. In general, nineteenth-century Mexico was characterized by the struggle for power among different factions across different regions. Additionally, Díaz's government faced severe political and financial constraints due to the economic stagnation and political disorder that existed when he took office. As Bortz and Haber note, "the Mexican government was continually broke. . . . It did not have the resources to buy off the regional warlords or cow them into submission. In the short run, Díaz could not solve the problem by raising taxes because the government did not have the administrative structure necessary to carry out effective taxation. In addition, the economy was simply too small to provide much in the way of taxes. Nor was foreign borrowing an option: Mexico had a long history of reneging on its foreign debts. Thus, Díaz had to find a way to begin a virtuous cycle of economic growth, tax revenues, and political order."[1]

Part of Díaz's solution was to create Banamex, which was able to provide the government with financial resources. This helped the government restore its credibility with international lenders. However, in part as a result of the 1897 General Credit Institutions and Banking Act, the main owners of the banking system became the main owners of the manufacturing industry in Mexico. Additionally, the tendency in Mexico to form groups based on ethnic background facilitated the concentration of industry into a few hands.

Monopolies in Mexico arose in part as a result of the barriers to entry to its banking system. In some cases, monopolies were created through tax exemptions for specific firms or through patent laws. In addition, the government provided Mexico's local manufacturing monopolies with trade protection. This protectionism increased over the years and, due to the lack of competition, it eventually led the Mexican industry to produce low-quality goods at higher prices than those paid internationally. This situation became unsustainable toward the second half of the twentieth century.

The Development of the Jean Family Textile Industry

Within this context, three French investors—Leon and José Meyran and Antonio Donnadieu—created the company Meyran Hermanos in 1891. This company owned a store in downtown Mexico City named La Francia Marítima, where it sold clothes of both domestic and foreign origin. When Donnadieu grew more influential within the company through the acquisition of shares, the partners changed the name of the company to Meyran Donnadieu y Compañía (MDC) in 1895. From 1895 to 1898, they initiated production ventures while maintaining their commercial businesses.

La Magdalena, Santa Teresa, and Other Mills in Mexico City

One of these ventures began in 1897, with the acquisition of the paper mill Santa Teresa. Nine months later, the partners bought three ranches in the southwest region of Mexico City (Anzaldo, Contreras, and El Molinito) and the textile factories established there, La Magdalena and El Águila, from the Spanish entrepreneur Pio Bermejillo.

La Magdalena became these investors' most important asset for many years. The new owners made significant changes to La Magdalena after acquiring it in 1898. For instance, the factory started using hydroelectric power. At the same time, they increased the number of looms (from 304 to 1,767), spindles (from 7,768 to 17,128), and laborers (from 320 to 1,000), as well as its output (from 400,000 kg to 852,706 kg of cotton goods) in the period between 1898 and 1912.[2]

In 1898, the owners of the company invited Adrián Jean to join them as a partner.[3] Adrián, a native of Meyronnes, arrived in Mexico in the mid-1880s and initially worked on the ranch of a cousin near the city of Pachuca, Hidalgo. He stayed there for approximately three years and then traveled to Mexico City, where he met the Meyran family. Adrián worked for this family for about six years as an employee in their dry-goods store, La Francia Marítima, until the Meyrans invited him to become a secondary partner.[4]

When Adrián arrived, MDC began the process of transforming into a firm managed entirely by members of the Jean family. The owners restructured the new company to include Adrián and to focus on the production of paper, yarn, woven fabrics, coarse cloth, and cotton prints in its two factories, La Magdalena and Santa Teresa. The company continued to sell its goods at La Francia Marítima in Mexico City and in its branches, located in the cities of Pachuca and Durango. Soon they began producing wool fabric in a mill named El Águila, located in the town of Contreras.[5]

By 1903, the Veyans and the Donnadieus had become the main capital holders in MDC, with 400,000 and 235,000 pesos, respectively, and the company's name changed accordingly to Donnadieu Veyan y Compañía Sociedad en Comandita. Luis Veyan, who was the head of his family, was from Marseille (a city located in the French Mediterranean coast, 227 km southwest of Barcelonnette), and at that point also owned manufacturing businesses in Michoacán, Jalisco, and Durango. The Meyran family's importance diminished accordingly. Leon Meyran, the most important original founder, acted as a silent partner for the first time, allowing younger partners to take over direct responsibility for the firm.

Table 3.1 shows the distribution of the centrality (importance within a network) among each of the shareholders of the companies in which at least one member of the Jean family participated. Thus, when Adrián Jean first partnered with these companies between 1891 and 1907, it can be observed that he did not play a central role. At that time, the Jeans possessed little capital. Adrián and his brother Camilo had only 65,000 pesos combined.[6] Camilo had arrived from France by the turn of the century at Adrián's invitation. He followed a similar path to his brother and became a partner in the company in 1903.

The enterprise reported strong profits in the last decade of the Porfiriato, particularly between 1900 and 1903. These profits generated an increase in the

TABLE 3.1. Centrality of entrepreneurs in the firms in which the Jeans participated, 1891–1907

Entrepreneur	nEigenvec
Antonio Donnadieu	53.165
Leon Meyran	53.165
Sebastian Donnadieu	38.469
Luis Veyan	27.342
José Meyran	14.696
Adrián Jean	14.555
Luis Veyan Jr.	14.555

Note: This centrality measurement (Eigenvector centrality, nEigenvec), calculated using UCINET (software for social network analysis), includes the number of connections of a given member of a network and the connections of those to whom that member is connected. Eigenvector centrality is a measurement of the influence of a node on a network. It assigns relative values to all nodes in the network, based on the idea that connections to high-scoring nodes contribute more to the score of a particular node than similar connections to low-scoring nodes. (For a more complete explanation, see Borgatti, "Centrality and Network Flow.")

company's capital of around 200 percent.[7] A large percentage of the profits came from textile production at La Magdalena, which was the second-largest cotton textile mill in the Federal District at that time, after the San Antonio mill. Between 1903 and 1908, the Jean brothers' contribution to the company's capital grew precipitously, from 7.2 percent to 32.6 percent. In 1908, Leon Meyran returned to France and the Donnadieus left Donnadieu Veyan y Compañía.[8] These movements led to some important changes in the company.[9] The trading name changed to Veyan Jean y Compañía Sociedad en Comandita (VJC), highlighting the importance of the Jeans' role in the company.

Additionally, although the Veyans were still the primary partners, Camilo and Adrián Jean served as managers. By 1908, total capital reached 1,550,000 pesos, an increase of 72 percent over the previous company. VJC also experienced several changes in its production. The Santa Teresa factory no longer produced paper; the mill switched to exclusively producing wool textiles. At the same time, the El Águila wool factory closed.

Contrary to the situation experienced by other Barcelonnette companies, VJC grew during this period. In 1913, it acquired new lands around La Magdalena to provide its mills direct access to the railway station. Now they could transport textiles more easily to Mexico City and other commercial centers. In 1914, three years after the Mexican Revolution began, Luis Veyan Sr., the head of the Veyan family, died. That same year, Alfonso Jean became a partner.[10]

By 1914, the Jean brothers had purchased the largest proportion of capital at VJC, and the company continued to grow. Between 1914 and 1920, it made 5,361,601.36 pesos in profit.[11] Half of its profits came in 1919, following the most violent years of the revolution. This growth during the revolutionary period can be attributed in part to the company's link with the banking company CBPM, which in those years provided working capital to its partners, including VJC.

The last member of the first generation of the Jean family, José Jean, became a partner in 1920.[12] The 1920s brought important changes to the textile industry in Mexico, some of which affected the Federal District. A number of small companies entered the playing field, many of which had Arab or Jewish owners. These small mills began to grow in the next decades, generating true competition for the French and other investors in the textile sector by the 1940s. However, the Jean family continued to expand their cotton textile business during the 1920s, which generated greater profits.[13] By 1929, La Magdalena alone manufactured approximately 3 percent of all cotton textiles in the country, which is discussed in the section on the effects of the Mexican Revolution on the Jean family.[14] Table 3.2 shows that members of the Jean family constructed a family front, participating in many ventures simultaneously. In addition, we can see other collaborators in this family emporium, some of whom would secure greater participation within the family's business

TABLE 3.2. Centrality of entrepreneurs in the firms in which the Jeans participated, 1908–1931

Entrepreneur	nEigenvec
Adrián Jean	43.054
Camilo Jean	42.197
Alfonso Jean	32.772
José Jean	27.105
Camilo Reynaud	26.737
Luis Vernier	23.883
Pedro Guzzy	23.883
Leon Meyran	14.813
Luis Veyan	8.778
Luis Veyan Jr.	4.155
Pedro Fortoul	4.001

Note: See table 3.1 for an explanation of Eigenvector centrality (nEigenvec).

structure in the 1930s. This can be observed in table 3.3, which also shows the incorporation of members of a new generation of the Jean family.

The Expansion of the Family's Textile Business to the States of Puebla and México

Since the Jean brothers had been very successful in the expansion of their textile business during the 1920s and had also gained control of companies where they were once second-level partners, they decided to expand their business to other places in central Mexico. Thus, they would gain control of cotton textiles in the center of the country, notwithstanding the possible risks they faced in some states such as Puebla.

As a result, in 1929, the Jean family acquired the El Carmen factory in Atlixco, Puebla, from the Díaz Rubín brothers. According to José Conde Cervantes, a direct descendant of the Díaz Rubín family, his relatives sold their factory to the Jeans because they were young and inexperienced.[15] Alfonso Jean was chosen as the new president of the board of directors.[16] The Jean family made other acquisitions during the 1920s and 1930s, showing themselves to be more flexible and less risk averse in their period of expansion than other economic elites.

In the 1920s and 1930s, Puebla experienced a lot of violence and presumably some members of the economic elites decided to rid themselves of properties,

TABLE 3.3. Centrality of entrepreneurs in the firms in which the Jeans participated, 1931–1938

Entrepreneur	nEigenvec
Camilo Jean	38.938
Alfonso Jean	38.446
Pedro Guzzy	38.446
Camilo Reynaud	38.446
Luis Vernier	35.442
Casimiro Jean	26.961
Adrián Jean	25.165
Pedro Fortoul	20.618
Camilo Alfonso Jean	16.589
Heriberto Faudrin	16.465
Pablo Jean	13.281

Note: See table 3.1 for an explanation of Eigenvector centrality (nEigenvec).

even selling them at a steep discount. In addition, the structure of business creation in Puebla was centralized among very few players and controlled by entrepreneurs with links to political authorities. As a result, it was almost impossible to do business there without an understanding with Maximino Ávila Camacho and his friends.[17] In this case, trying to capitalize on seldom-seen business opportunities in places ignored by most participants, the Jeans used their own networks to do business in Puebla. Those connections came mainly from the broad portfolio of clients in Puebla held by the bank they owned, the CBPM.[18]

How the Jeans and their partners obtained La Constancia Mexicana factory in 1924, which was also in Puebla, involves a complicated story. Francisco M. Conde, a member of a prominent Spanish family, made a significant part of his fortune in textiles.[19] However, like the Díaz Rubíns, the Condes faced problems continuing in the textile industry. In the 1920s, Conde's widow accumulated considerable debt and thus transferred the textile mill she had inherited, La Constancia Mexicana, to her primarily French creditors, a common way of obtaining properties in that period. [20] Bank creditors got loan guarantees such as these without payment from debtors, who used their properties as collateral. One of these creditors was the CBPM and, soon, the four French creditor companies appointed Camilo Jean to create a partnership to operate the mill.[21] However, in this case the Jeans shared the property with their French partners.

The state of México became another area of expansion for the Jean family businesses. One of the last cotton textile mills that the Jeans bought was La Industria Nacional in Toluca. This mill was larger than the Río Hondo factory, previously acquired in the same region in 1923. Table 3.4 provides an overview of the mills owned by the Jeans in 1938, with mill size indicated by numbers of spindles and looms.

By 1938 the Jeans contributed at least 6 percent of the country's total textile production. That year, there were 221 operating mills, 865,626 active spindles, 34,987 active looms, and 43,299 workers employed in the cotton textile industry in Mexico, and 50,809 metric tons of cotton were consumed.[22] Santa Teresa was the largest active wool textile mill that year.[23] In addition, by that time, the Jeans controlled a widespread commercial network of textiles throughout Mexico.[24]

The Jean Family's Business Diversification

Energy

VJC's partners decided to exploit water concessions they had obtained to generate electricity. In 1909, VJC partnered with another Barcelonnette company, S. Robert y Compañía Sucesores, and a Spanish investor to establish the

TABLE 3.4. Overview of Jean family textile mills, 1938

Mill	Location	Year of acquisition	Spindles	Looms
La Magdalena	Distrito Federal	1897	18,820	743
La Constancia Mexicana*	Puebla, Puebla	1924	10,824	590
La Industria Nacional	Toluca, México	1931	7,512	236
Santa Teresa (wool factory)	Distrito Federal	1898	7,070	150
Río Hondo	Naucalpan, México	1923	5,860	214
La Carolina	Atlixco, Puebla	—	2,960	112

Source: Data from the Archivo de la Secretaría de Hacienda y Crédito Público, *Directorio de las Fabricas de Hilados y Tejidos Registradas en 1938.*

*The Jeans shared ownership of this mill with other partners who were external to their central clique and sold it in 1930.

Compañía Hidroeléctrica del Río de la Alameda S.A., which developed three Alameda River concessions in the state of México.[25] VJC subsequently began to supply electrical power to its own mills and other factories, such as La Hormiga, La Alpina, and the Loreto paper factory. To do so, they developed water concessions they had obtained on the Magdalena River.[26] In addition, since the Río Hondo mill was located near the Hondo River, in 1929 VJC obtained the rights to generate hydroelectricity there too.[27]

VJC was not the only company that vertically integrated their own hydroelectric power. By the nineteenth century, other companies, such as the CIDOSA in Veracruz, San Ildefonso in Mexico City, and the Compañía Industrial de Atlixco in Puebla, built their own hydroelectric plants to supply their mills. However, the provision of electricity to other factories represented important additional business for VJC—one that set it apart from other Barcelonnette companies.

Housing

After many years of working primarily in textiles and finance, the Jean family created a completely new business in the construction and housing sector. The size of two properties VJC held in the mid-1920s, approximately eight hundred hectares,[28] permitted them to start this business in Mexico City, which would then expand overall. The family also used lands surrounding the Río Hondo mill in the state of México to construct and sell housing estates.[29] The Jean brothers additionally received land to settle debts in Atlixco, Puebla, and sold this land or built housing on it.[30]

In 1925, the Jean family started a housing estate known as La Concepción, located in southwest Mexico City on the Anzaldo and Contreras ranches, which were divided into various blocks and lots.[31] In the late 1920s, they created two new companies in Mexico City—La Compañía Explotadora y Realizadora de Bienes Raíces S.A. (1927) and La Inmobiliaria Comercial S.A. (1929)—with the primary objective of expanding their real estate business.[32] La Compañía Explotadora was in charge of subdividing and selling land obtained as payment for debts and "[also] exploit[ed] two power plants, which produced light, established in the city of Atlixco, Puebla."[33]

Both companies soon began to grow. Camilo became president of La Compañía Explotadora, and José became the first president of the board of directors of La Inmobiliaria; however, José died two weeks after La Inmobiliaria was formed.[34] By the end of 1930, the Jeans had constructed three new housing estates in the same region of Mexico City: the fraccionamientos Padierna, El Molinito, and Guadalupe.[35]

In the period between 1920 and 1940, it was difficult to invest in the building of new neighborhoods in Mexico City without political connections, and the Jean family could not have been an exception in view of their dynamism in this sector.[36] The laws that regulated urbanization in the Federal District evolved in this direction at the time. In fact, the Ley de Planificación y Zonificación—which was published in the official gazette, the *Diario Oficial*, in 1936—incorporated the private sector into urban planning in the Federal District, "seeking to solve the problems, until then exclusive to the administration."[37] The law intended to address housing problems that emerged as a result of the city's tremendous population growth. In addition, this law created a Planning Commission of the Federal District, supported by a Mixed Commission that included distinguished businessmen and members of the banking sector who would contribute to financing construction.[38] Banamex was among those banking companies, and the Jeans had become partners in its operations since it had acquired the CBPM in 1930.

After 1945, as textiles became less profitable, the housing business became an important income stream for the Jean family. In 1950, the Jeans built a number of housing estates. La Magdalena S.A., which had been in charge of the operation of La Magdalena factory, built a new block of houses known as Colonia Plazuela del Pedregal. In this development, they sold small flats through private individual contracts. La Concepción, El Molinito, Guadalupe, and Padierna may have been built for similar purposes because they were all located in the same area and were very likely directed at the same type of buyers: the lower-middle-income population. The region of Contreras (located within the area of Magdalena), which separated from the municipality of San Ángel in 1927, maintained its rural character until the 1950s when Mexico City began expanding southward. Until that decade, its population was devoted to the production of vegetables and fruits and/or textiles.

In addition to the construction of Colonia Plazuela del Pedregal in 1950, the family sold some of its southern Mexico City ranches to another business group, the Rivera Torres family, in 1953. The Rivera Torres family built new housing estates in this area through the company Jardines del Sur del Pedregal S.A.,[39] and the Jean family participated in their construction. The Rivera Torres family, partners of the Jean family and well-known for their connections to various governmental administrations, subsequently claimed ownership of several plots of land adjacent to Rancho Anzaldo. They used notarial deeds issued by public notaries close to the regime for this purpose. For example, the real estate company El Encino S.A. de C.V., owned by the Rivera Torres family, "fraudulently claimed ownership of a 71-hectare plot . . . arguing that it is part of another larger plot," referring to Rancho Anzaldo. "The operation was endorsed by the notary 116 of the Federal District, Ignacio Morales Lechuga, who served as Attorney General of the Republic and ambassador of Mexico to France during the government of Carlos Salinas de Gortari." This expropriation affected small landowners and *comuneros*, who engaged in judicial complaints against the companies owned by the Rivera Torres family for more than thirty years.[40]

Although information about this is sparse, Minouche Suberville, the founder and former president of the association Raíces Francesas en México (French roots in Mexico), confirmed that the Jean family was associated with prestigious architects at that time and constructed part of the upscale neighborhood of Pedregal de San Ángel in Mexico City. The latest document found relating to the Jean family in housing dates from 1964, when Casimiro Jean used the land surrounding the Río Hondo mill to construct low-income housing.[41]

Throughout the years, the Jeans had managed risk in an interesting way: diversifying their holdings geographically to avoid being vulnerable to a single, unpredictable regional strongman; making risky investments when other capitalists were selling off assets at a discount, as was the case in Puebla in the 1920s and 1930s; and diversifying their business activities, not only into different regions but also into different economic sectors. For example, they were one of the few French families to make a "very Mexican" choice to invest in real estate. Although other Barcelonnettes ventured into real estate, doing so was uncommon so the Jeans set themselves apart from the rest of the group. The only other example that the author is aware of parallel to the Jeans in the capital is Enrique Tron and Leon Signoret. In 1891, Tron and Signoret built a block of houses in Mexico City, originally planned for the middle and upper-middle classes in arrangement with other investors. This development, known as Colonia San Rafael, is located in southwest Mexico City.

Sergio Valerio Ulloa found that the Barcelonnettes got involved in the housing sector at an earlier period in Guadalajara. They began splitting and selling lands and building housing by the turn of the twentieth century, founding firms such as La Compañía Jalisciense de Construcciones in 1898 and the Compañía de Fomento y Bienes Raíces en Guadalajara in 1910.[42] However, it is not clear from the information provided in his work if companies in this sector grew successfully in this city.

Specific Business Strategies of the Jean Family

Analysis of the Composition of the Boards of Directors of the Companies in Which the Jeans Participated

By 1931, the three families that founded the original company in the late nineteenth century—the Meyrans, the Donnadieus, and the Veyans—had all departed. As evidenced by the eventual name change from VJC to Jean Hermanos, the Jean family had complete control of the company.[43]

Between 1891 and 1940, the Jean family participated in at least twenty-three companies and most were reconstituted at least once (table 3.5). Some of these companies were new incarnations of previous companies. For example, the first two companies in table 3.5 were reconstituted several times, ultimately to become Jean Hermanos in 1932. There were other similar cases, like La Inmobiliaria that became the Inmobiliaria Comercial. The Jeans had a total of eighty-one direct partners in these companies (individuals and roughly ten partner companies), although not all the partners participated in every business. The one constant in the twenty-three companies analyzed is the presence of at least one member of the Jean family, although each company had five members on the board of directors on average.

The whole process of evolution of the Jean family's main company, Jean Hermanos (which consisted of several textile factories), began with a company that had many different partners and only one member of the Jean family was on the board of directors. This figure grew to four family members by 1920, in a gradual incorporation process. By that year, the company had become wholly owned by the family, although there was still a significant external partner: Luis Veyan. By 1932, Veyan had left the business.

At that point, the company's board of directors became entirely composed of members of the first generation of the Jean family. The company continued to incorporate members of the second generation and eventually added other external partners so that the operation became decentralized again. That is, the composition of partners within the boards of directors of companies managed by the Jean family changed over the years to include individuals with different last names, such as Vernier and Reynaud, who eventually acquired

TABLE 3.5. Business diversification of the Jean Family, 1891–1934

Company	Economic sector
Meyran Hermanos	1891—commercial business
Meyran Donnadieu y Compañía	1895—commercial business and textile mills
Compañía Industrial de Atlixco	1902—textile mills
Donnadieu Veyan y Compañía	1903—commercial business and textile mills
Compañía Bancaria de Paris y México	1908—financial sector
Compañía Hidroeléctrica del Rio de la Alameda	1909—electric power generation
Compañía Industrial de Toluca	1915—textile mills and electric power generation
El Universal	1916—newspaper
La Constancia Mexicana	1924—textile mills
Veyan Jean y Compañía Sucesores	1926—textile mills, commercial business, and electric power generation
Compañía Explotadora y Realizadora de Bienes Raíces	1927—real estate
Santa Teresa	1927—textile mills (wool) and real estate
A. Martel, Sociedad en Comandita Simple	1928—commercial business (clothing)
El Carmen	1929—textile mills
Edificio Cogordan	1929—real estate
La Inmobiliaria	1929—real estate
La Magdalena	1929—textile mills and real estate
La Inmobiliaria Comercial	1930—real estate
La Industria Nacional	1931—textile mills
Jean Hermanos	1932—textile mills, commercial business, and electric power generation
San José de Río Hondo	1932—textile mills, electric power generation, and real estate
Cogordan y Compañía	1934—real estate

Source: Data from Archivo General de la Nación, Registro Público de la Propiedad, and *Mexican Yearbooks*.

more representation on these boards and, as a result, in the companies' decisions. This was also the case with members of new generations of the Jean family, who gained representation throughout the years; as a result, they amassed more power within the business structure created by the first generation of Jean brothers.

Figure 3.1 shows the restructuring of internal power among partners within the Jean family's entire business empire (including all the companies where they participated) between 1891 and 1940. This chart offers a visualization of the centralization of power in the hands of first-generation Jean family members in the companies where they were partners and how this power was decentralized again once partners with other last names and members of subsequent generations of the Jean family gained influence.

Table 3.6 allows us to observe the interconnections of individual companies where the Jeans participated as partners within the family's general network (represented in fig. 3.2). This same table allows us to see how connected the boards of directors were in the companies where the Jeans participated. The less central companies in the table generally had fewer members of the Jean family on their board of directors and were associated with

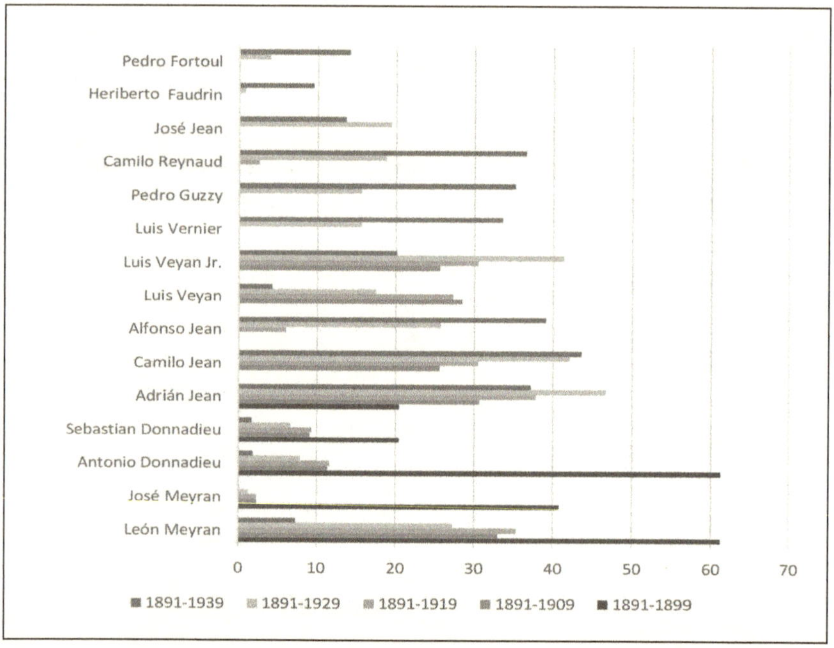

Figure 3.1. Change in the composition of partners within the Jean family's companies, 1891–1939. (José Galindo)

lesser-known partners than those prominent in other companies where the Jeans participated.

There were no politicians on the board of directors of companies managed by the Jeans. The only politician involved was a federal deputy, Carlos Romero, who was linked to the La Magdalena textile factory—the Jean brothers' largest factory. However, the Jeans used political connections to operate their businesses, directly or indirectly. These connections were evident in the banking sector, within the Compañía Bancaria de Paris y Mexico, where managers and several politicians planned projects together during the period of Francisco I. Madero (1911–13) for example. This will be explained later in the chapter, in the section on the Jean family's activity in the banking sector. Also, the CBPM's broad client portfolio in various Mexican states allowed the Jeans to establish companies in states where only individuals with strong political connections could do business at that time, such as Puebla. The Jeans' political connections are also evident in sectors such as housing, where their partners,

TABLE 3.6. Centrality of enterprises

Company	nEigenvec
Santa Teresa	38.765
Jean Hermanos	37.852
Compañía Explotadora y Realizadora de Bienes Raíces	34.064
Compañía Industrial de Toluca	32.883
La Magdalena	31.557
La Inmobiliaria Comercial	30.764
El Carmen	29.083
La Industria Nacional Mexicana	28.552
San José de Río Hondo	22.996
Compañía Bancaria de París y México	20.857
Compañía Hidroeléctrica del Río de la Alameda	13.654
El Universal	4.765
Compañía Industrial de Atlixco	4.631
Martel, Sociedad en Comandita Simple	4.151
Cogordan y Compañía	2.736
La Constancia Mexicana	0.602

Note: Centrality measures the preponderance of each enterprise within the web. See table 3.1 for an explanation of Eigenvector centrality (nEigenvec).

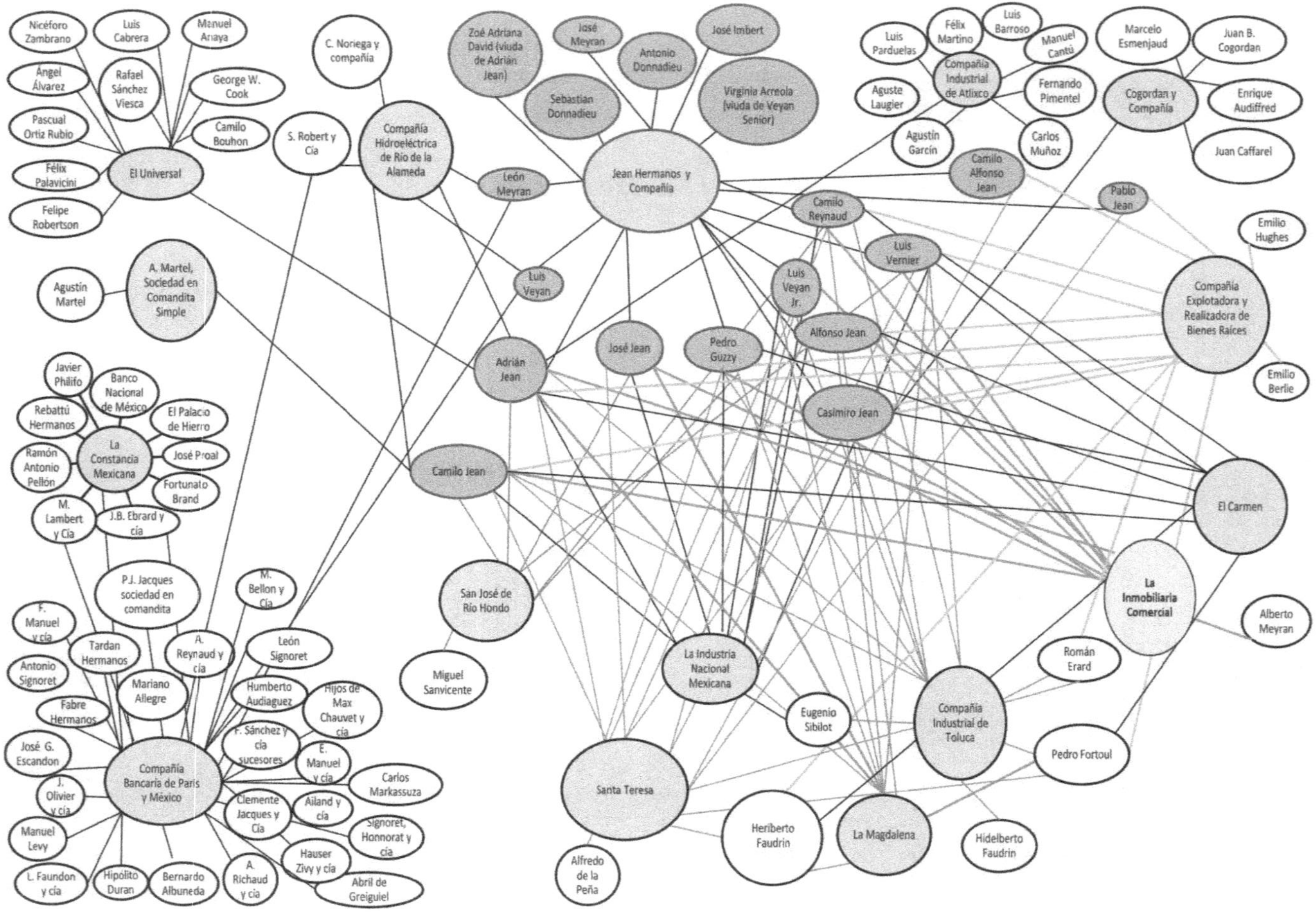

Figure 3.2. Jean family general social network. (José Galindo)

like the Rivera Torres family, had close connections with political regimes from the golden age of the PRI and used them to illegally obtain more land neighboring areas that had previously been obtained legally, such as the Ranchos Anzaldo and Contreras.

The Inverse Transformation of the Jean Family's Companies

The Jean family distinguished itself from other Barcelonnettes in the textile industry by gradually acquiring almost the entire capital of the company in which they had originally been secondary partners. They expanded their influence in VJC, their main company, which eventually changed its name to Jean Hermanos, while this company swiftly expanded its activities. Once the Jeans acquired the firm, they continued to purchase other textile mills and established different joint-stock companies to manage them. At the same time, using the same legal association (joint-stock company), they separated those mills that were still managed by the central company for their individual operation. The family supplied almost all the capital needed for the creation of these companies, except at La Constancia Mexicana.

Other Barcelonnettes had initially expanded by creating family companies, at least in the center of the country, and over the years, they began associating their companies with other companies, and in some cases also with individual partners, to create large consortia. These associations facilitated their control of many textile mills and shops at the same time, as can be observed in table 3.7. The original composition of these big companies, made up of French and occasionally Spanish partners, was typically maintained over the years. Additionally, in only 24 percent of the textile firms, half or more of the partners had the same family name. That is, most of these textile firms were not family firms.[44] In the Jean companies, however, the partners were mostly Jean family members. In addition, in the textile sector, the Jeans usually associated with other individuals not companies (see Veyan Jean y Cía [VJC] in table 3.7). This confirms how exceptional and unique the Jeans' business strategy and firms were compared to those of other textile producers.

Large corporate consortia composed of several companies, owned by various Barcelonnette partners, aggregated many textile factories and department stores simultaneously. The significance of this analysis is that the Jeans did not associate with these consortia, contrary to what is generally said about the successful operation of the Barcelonnettes in Mexico. The Jean family, however, maintained multiple family businesses that varied in their member composition but always had a strong family presence. Under this family structure, they managed to build an economic empire in Mexico equal in size to their countrymen's.

TABLE 3.7. Overview of large textile companies in Mexico in 1912

Company	Year founded	Textile mills
Compañía Industrial de Orizaba S.A. (CIDOSA)	1889	Cerritos, Cocolapan, San Lorenzo, Río Blanco
Compañía Industrial Veracruzana S.A. (CIVSA)	1896	Santa Rosa, El León
Compañía Industrial de San Antonio Abad S.A.	1892	San Antonio Abad, La Colmena, Barrón Miraflores
Compañía Industrial de Atlixco S.A.	1902	Metepec
Compañía Industrial Manufacturera S.A.	—	Hércules, San Antonio, La Purísima, La Sultana, La Teja, Río Grande
Compañía Industrial de Jalisco/ Compañía Industrial de Guadalajara S.A.	1899	Río Blanco (Jalisco), Atemajac, La Escoba
Compañía Industrial de San Ildelfonso S.A.	—	San Ildelfonso
Veyan Jean y Cía (VJC)	1898	La Magdalena, Santa Teresa

Source: Based on data from notaries public from Mexico City and Gómez-Galvarriato Freer, *Los Barcelonnettes*, 210.

Analysis of the Jean Family's Social Network

Social Associations

Although we have seen certain peculiarities within the Jean family's business strategies, it is important to explain the general conditions that affected the whole Barcelonnette community in Mexico. The community's cohesion was strengthened by its association with, or founding of, charitable organizations, schools, and pantheons. These included the creation of the Asociación Franco Mexicana, Suiza y Belga de Beneficencia (AFMSB) in 1841, El Panteón Francés

Stores	Partners
El Palacio de Hierro, El Puerto de Liverpool, La Ciudad de Londres, El Gran Oriental, El Puerto de Veracruz, El Correo Francés	Tomás Braniff, J. Ollivier y Cía., J.B. Ebrard y Cía., J. Tron y Cía., Signoret, Honnorat y Cía.; Lambert, Reynaud y Cía., Garcín, Faudon y Cía., and Juan Quinn
Las Fábricas Universales, La Ciudad de México, El Centro Mercantil, La Reforma del Comercio	A. Reynaud y Cía., S. Robert y Cía., F. Manuel y Cía., P. y J. Jacques y Cía., and Paulino Richaud
La Reforma del Comercio	Íñigo Noriega, Adolfo Prieto, Agustín Garcín, Enrique Mojardín
La Reforma del Comercio	B. Rovés y Cía., A. Richaud y Cía., S. de Juanbelz y Cía., Solana Barreneche Cía., Antonio Basagoiti, Luis Barroso Arias, Agustín Garcín, Leopoldo Gavito, Félix Manino, Benjamín Oncins, Íñigo y Constantino Noriega, Sotero de Juanbelz, Emilio André, Eduardo Vega y Santiago Aréchaga
Las Fábricas Universales, La Reforma del Comercio, La Ciudad de Londres (Guad.)	Agustín Garcín, Joseph Signoret, Brun, Lerdo de Tejada, Cuzin, Fortuol Bec, E. Lèbre y Cía.
La Ciudad de Londres (Guad.), Las Fábricas de Francia (Guad.)	Fortoul Chapuy y Cía., Gas y Cía., Laurens Brun y Cía., Bellon Agorreca y Cía., E. Lèbre y Cía.
El Puerto de Liverpool	J. B. Ebrard, H. Reynaud y E. Pugibet
La Francia Marítima	Partners in 1912: Luis Veyan, Adrián Jean, Camilo Jean, Alfonso Jean, Leon Meyran (silent partner)

cemetery in 1864, and the Liceo Franco Mexicano in 1937—a school where most of the French community in Mexico studied up to high school.

The Barcelonnettes also created social clubs: the Club France (a sports club) and the Club Hípico Francés (an equestrian club). The rise of associations and social clubs was not, however, exclusive to the French community in Mexico. Most immigrant groups from other countries built associations, largely beginning in the 1840s, with those of US and Spanish origin remaining the most common in Mexico City today.

However, the composition of these associations has varied over time. At first, they were primarily established to gather and assist migrants from the members' country of origin. They were mutualist societies that provided social security in a period when it had not been institutionalized as part of the functions of the state. For example, the Hospital Francés, founded in Mexico soon after the creation of AFMSB, provided health services to the population of French origin in Mexico. Like the Panteón Francés, the hospital was also under the administrative structure of the AFMSB. The latter was sold in the second half of the twentieth century and demolished in the 1970s.

Just as the AFMSB and Club France acted as social security organizations prior to the emergence of state social security, the Barcelonnettes provided assistance for the construction of housing for their workers in the areas surrounding their factories and for the creation of sports teams when the labor movement became stronger in Mexico during the 1920s. Although they were tough bosses,[45] they were innovative with different methods of increasing productivity.[46]

These associations eventually opened up membership to people of other nationalities so as to strengthen links between particular foreign communities, Mexicans, and individuals of other nationalities. This was always done while maintaining the traditions and cultural practices of the association's country of origin.[47] In the case of the AFMSB, they only accepted French members at first; however, they subsequently opened their doors to the Swiss community in Mexico, then to Belgians, and finally to Mexicans and others.[48] This association has continued with its altruistic work in the present day. For example, it has opened rest homes for the elderly in Coyoacán and Cuernavaca, has a 6,000-meter^2 dormitory, and is building another home for one hundred girls.[49]

In Mexico City, the Panteón Francés de la Piedad cemetery was founded on an 80,000-meter^2 plot in 1864. It was full by 1940, so the AFMSB obtained a 315,000-meter^2 field and founded the Panteón Francés de San Joaquin in 1942. Nowadays, the two Panteón Francés cemeteries are perhaps among the most beautiful in Mexico, as well as the most expensive. Several notable people are interred there, including Carmen Romero Rubio—the wife of Porfirio Díaz.

The origins of Club France date from 1870, when the French Circle of Mexico was founded by a group of seven French families in downtown Mexico City. This circle was exclusive to those of French origin in its aim to encourage and bolster relationships among employees at all levels. The association underwent a change in 1928, as it moved to southern Mexico City as a new sports club called Club France. By that time, the club's policy accepted members of other nationalities. "The main goal of the club was to provide the French and Mexican communities with a large area in which they could enjoy sports, as well as a place where families and young people from both countries could meet and better know each other."[50]

The Jeans were not among the founding families, since they came to Mexico more than twenty-five years after its inauguration. However, they had become active members in this social club by the 1920s, when the circle changed its location and name. Camilo Jean became president of Club France in the mid-1930s and held the position until the end of the 1940s. Another member of the Jean family and grandson of Adrián, Emilio Jean, became the director of the club in the 1960s. Thierry Jean is one of approximately forty members of the club's board of directors today. The membership of the club has changed over the years. These days, the club comprises around 80 percent Mexicans and 20 percent French, some of whom work in companies of French origin, such as Peugeot and Renault.[51]

The Club Hípico Francés was founded in 1933, near Chapultepec and Reforma in Mexico City. Although perhaps not linked to Club France, members of the Jean family had become involved in its management by the mid-1940s. Casimiro Jean was president of the club during this period and the owner of Arete, a horse trained at the Hípico and ridden by Humberto Mariles in the London Olympic Games of 1948, where he won two gold medals.

In the mid-1940s, top members of the business elite in Mexico frequented Club France and the Club Hípico Francés. This allowed the Jeans to increase their network. Notable members who attended the Club Hípico Francés over the years were the architect Luis Barragán; the intellectual Elena Poniatowska; the media entrepreneur Emilio Azcárraga, owner of Televisa; the banker Agustín Legorreta; the owner of the department store Liverpool, Max Michel; Diego Creel, a member of the prominent Creel family from Chihuahua, who governed the state for many years during the Porfiriato; and many other prominent figures, including politicians, artists, and entrepreneurs.[52]

Many of these figures were very close to Jean family members. Agustín Legorreta, for example, allowed the Jean family to continue in the banking sector through Banamex, which had been the most important and connected bank in Mexico since its foundation. In addition, the president of the Club Hípico Francés in the 1960s was Pablo Jean, a second-generation member of the Jean family.[53] Pablo's daughter Nadine met and married Emilio Azcárraga Milmo at this club in 1965; Emilio's father founded the most influential media company in Latin America, Televisa, known for its strong connections with the governments of the golden age of the PRI as well as with subsequent governments to the present day. Their son, Emilio Azcárraga Jean, is the primary partner of Televisa today. An association between the Jeans and the Azcárragas ensued and was to be fundamental to the continuing presence of the Jean family within the Mexican economic elite, following their declining fortunes in the textile industry.

Emilio Azcárraga Jean, who became the CEO of Televisa in 1997, followed exactly the same strategies as his father and grandfather, manipulating the information presented on TV to protect government interests. His company obtained privileges in exchange, some of which related to the prerogative of maintaining Televisa as a near-monopoly within the Mexican media sector. Through Televisa, Azcárraga Jean contributed to the construction and public image of the presidential couple who governed Mexico between 2012 and 2018, pairing Televisa actress Angélica Rivera with the former governor of the state of México Enrique Peña Nieto.[54]

This is convincing proof that the social networks established between entrepreneurs and politicians, at first necessary instruments for the takeoff of capitalism in Mexico in an environment of weak institutions and lack of information, were transformed over the years into instruments for maintaining the privileges of a few. Consequently, the incentives for these privileged groups to strengthen formal institutions were nonexistent. This allowed monopolies to flourish, as in the case of Televisa, where government officials celebrated their control over disseminating the latest information while television entrepreneurs enjoyed the possibility of securing stratospheric profits without a real threat of direct competition, among other concessions.

The Centrality and Significance of the General French Social Network to the Economic Development of the Jean Family

One notable fact about the Jean family was that it was not central in the Barcelonnette social network in Mexico (the measure of centrality used, as mentioned earlier, takes into account not only the number of connections that a member of a network has but also the connections of those to whom that member is connected). However, they were nonetheless partners in two central companies, a banking company and a hydroelectric company: the CBPM and the Compañía Hidroeléctrica del Río de la Alameda (table 3.8).

As can be deduced easily from these outcomes, the core business of the Jean family, the textile companies, operated separately from the Barcelonnette network as a whole. That is, they created their independent textile business with individuals who were not central to the French grid. In particular, the Jeans had a group of partners, or a constant clique, in several companies in the 1930s. This clique comprised four French individuals: Pedro Guzzy, Camilo Reynaud, Luis Vernier, and José Imbert.

Another individual who acquired substantial power in the Jean family companies was Pedro Fortoul, who was also of French origin (fig. 3.3). According

TABLE 3.8. Centrality of Barcelonnette companies and entrepreneurs

Number of times connected to other network member	Company/entrepreneur	Number of connections	nEigenvec
1	La Abeja	56	49.58
2	Cía. Industrial Veracruzana S.A. (CIVSA)	56	42.41
3	Robert Tron y Cía.	36	36.45
4	Cía. Industrial de Orizaba S.A. (CIDOSA)	60	32.66
5	El León Fabrica de H. y T. S.C.	29	20.50
6	Cía. Industrial de S. Antonio Abad S.A.	22	19.11
7	Cía. Eléctrica Robert S.A.	18	17.18
8	Cía. Hidroeléctrica del Río de la Alameda S.A. (CHRA)	22	17.13
9	Robert S. Y Cía.	12	15.31
10	Cía. Bancaria de París y México (CBPM)	28	11.68
1	Ollivier, José	25	25.53
2	Signoret, José	17	20.41
3	Robert, Sebastián	15	19.38
4	Robert, Deslderio	11	17.50
5	Abad, Pedro	10	17.22
6	Caire, Fermín	10	17.22
7	Chaix, Pedro A.	8	17.02
8	Honnorat, Leon	9	15.98
9	Signoret, Leon	14	15.84
10	Barbaroux, Fernando	8	14.81

Source: Based on data from Gomez-Galvarriato Freer, "Networks and Entrepreneurship."
Note: See table 3.1 for an explanation of Eigenvector centrality (nEigenvec).

to Minouche Suberville, former president of the association Raíces Francesas en Mexico, Fortoul had humble origins: he began as a waiter. However, as time passed, he became one of the family's right-hand men and perhaps benefited the most of anyone in the entire Jean clique, in terms of the assets he kept when members of the first generation of the Jean family passed away.[55]

Neither the Jeans, as previously mentioned, nor any of the four French partners who composed the Jean family clique, belonged to the large textile corporations founded by other Barcelonnettes, such as the CIVSA or the CIDOSA. In an interview, Minouche Suberville confirmed that "the Jean family always moved apart from the other Barcelonnettes."[56] However, the Jean family associated with various core members of the French business network with regard to obtaining funding or providing electricity for their businesses or selling electricity to others. Consequently, the specific companies dedicated to those activities were decentralized in their general social network, as shown in fig. 3.2.

In addition, since family members created individual companies to operate specific businesses, their network was further decentralized. Jean Hermanos and Santa Teresa were focal companies in the network because all members of the Jean family had connections to them. Finally, fig. 3.2 allows us to see the individual connections of each member of the Jean family, as well as the importance of CBPM, to which many leading members of the general Barcelonnette network were also connected.

This strategy gave the Jean family greater adaptability and flexibility in business decision making, while at the same time enjoying the benefits of belonging

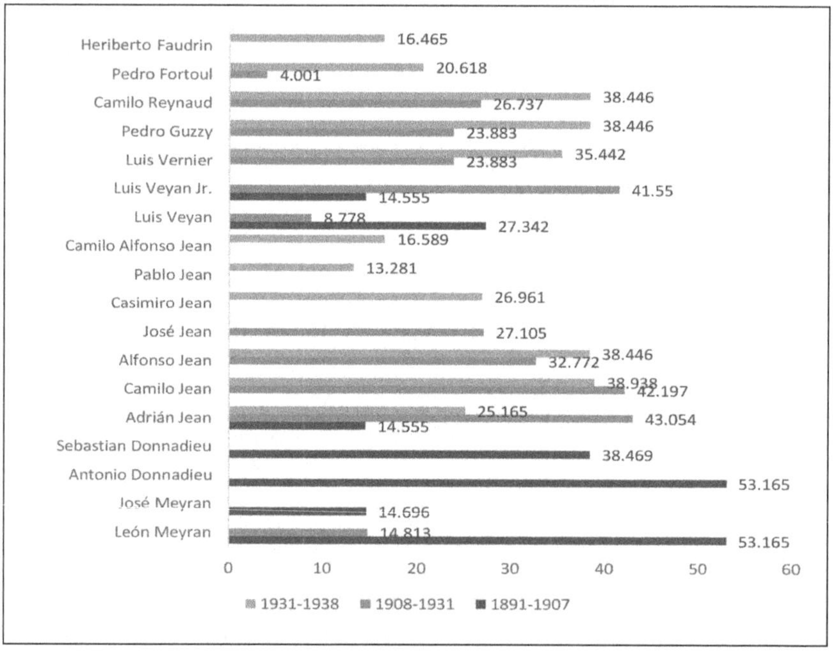

Figure 3.3. Importance of individual partners per period within the Jean family's companies. (José Galindo)

to a large social network. These benefits were evident, for example, in the possibility of doing business in places where it was difficult to make headway, such as in Puebla, and in the way the family obtained credit while participating in the banking system. Research on organizational structure, evolution, and change in firms, as summarized by Sharma, Chrisman, and Chua, suggests that companies kept under family control are "less horizontally differentiated and more reliant on informal controls. . . . As a result, the family firm can be more successful in businesses that require a lean and responsive structure."[57] In my view, this characteristic helped the Jeans to better deal with the informal institutional environment they faced when they started. It gave them the capacity to grow at or above their competitors' rates and to respond effectively to external events, like the Mexican Revolution.

The Jean family and their mills have not attracted as much scholarly research as the CIDOSA and the CIVSA, the largest French consortia, in part because they expanded more discreetly than the other Barcelonnette producers—this explains why they escaped the predations of revolutionary politicians. That is, the Jean family took over a smaller company that initially operated two mills and started acquiring other textile mills, founding family joint-stock companies for the mills' management. Throughout this process, the family also became involved in other sectors of the economy.

Effects of the Mexican Revolution and Agrarian Reforms on the Jeans' Economic Activities

Some studies have found that most of Mexico's manufacturing plants emerged intact from the Mexican Revolution, and the Jean family's mills were no exception.[58] That said, La Magdalena and Santa Teresa suffered several incursions when the Zapatistas invaded the region of Contreras in March 1912. These two mills represented a source of raw materials (including cotton) and fuels (including coal), which the revolutionaries needed to run trains. The Zapatistas also took blankets and other textile products from the mills for their survival. However, although textile production was interrupted during these invasions, the owners negotiated with the invaders to maintain the integrity of factories and employees in exchange for providing them with the raw materials and products demanded.[59]

The situation ended by December 1913 because the government dispatched several detachments of *rurales* to protect the region of Contreras and many other regions around the Federal District. Because of its importance, La Magdalena became one of the most protected mills in the region.[60] After that, violence and disruption of communications only occasionally affected the mills throughout the course of the revolution up to 1920, obstructing the distribution of textile products to the rest of the country and delaying raw materials' arrival for processing.[61]

An important consequence of the revolution was land reform.[62] During the 1920s, after the agrarian reform program had come into force, many towns near the industrial area of San Ángel asked the governor of the Federal District to allocate lands for their communities. As a result, the owner of the neighboring Hacienda La Cañada, for example, lost more than 500 hectares from 1920 to 1924 as a consequence of the resolution passed by the governor; 373.5 hectares were transferred to the communities of the town of San Bernabé Ocotepec and 135 to those of La Magdalena Contreras.[63] A parallel process happened in the case of Hacienda La Eslava. The owner lost 1,300 hectares, which were transferred to the town of San Nicolas Totolapan in 1924.[64] VJC was no exception and one year earlier, on August 1923, after two years of struggle with the neighbors of the town of San Jerónimo Aculco, the local agrarian commission expropriated 201 hectares from the Rancho Anzaldo belonging to the company.[65] This represented more than a third of the Anzaldo and Contreras ranches, which together covered 517 hectares. Around the same time, many residents demanded the expropriation of other lands owned by the same company. However, the Jean family successfully defended themselves, arguing that those properties could not be appropriated due to their small size.

Following these expropriations, agrarian reform in this region lessened, and it was not until the Cárdenas period that many of the local towns attempted to increase their *ejidos*.[66] In May 1938, the residents of San Jerónimo Aculco asked for an extension of their ejidos. While this petition was accepted, it did not affect the Jeans' properties; instead, 205 hectares were expropriated from the neighboring hacienda, Hacienda de Copilco, owned by Sra. Margáin.[67]

The trend that agrarian reform followed in the region of San Ángel is applicable to the whole Federal District. Table 3.9 shows that three-quarters of the total land distribution within the Federal District had already taken place before 1935. In addition, it shows that there were more ejido extensions than the creation of new ejidos in the capital city during the Cárdenas period (1934–40), when many regions of the country were severely affected by his land redistribution program.

VJC lost almost half of the Rancho Anzaldo with the expropriation that they suffered in 1923. Even though they could demand compensation for the losses using the terms established by the law, the situation obviously caused discontent to the Jean family.[68] When, in 1930, they sold a large section of the two ranches, they indicated their displeasure by writing a clause on the selling deed in which Camilo Jean declared that "despite the fact that VJC makes

TABLE 3.9. Agrarian reform in the Federal District

Years	*Ejidos* (common lands)	Extensions	Hectares	% (accumulated)
1915–20	6	0	2,567.59	8.8
1921–29	47	1	17,144.25	67.9
1930–34	13	1	1,842.79	74.2
1935–40	8	23	6,819.95	97.6
1941–61	7	2	667.24	99.9
Total	81	27	29,041.82	99.9

Source: Based on data from Archivo General Agrario and Cruz Rodríguez, *Crecimiento urbano*.

reference [in the deed] to the ejidos of the town of San Gerónimo to describe the limits of VJC properties, that does not mean that the company agrees with the expropriation."[69]

However, in an indirect way, the owners of the mills of San Ángel promoted agrarian reform among their workers. By doing so, they could maintain lower salaries without facing the protests that would have taken place if the employees had performed only textile work.[70] For example, when the Hacienda La Cañada was expropriated in 1924, benefiting the population of San Bernabé Ocotepec, nineteen of the beneficiaries worked in La Magdalena. One of these beneficiaries, Raymundo Calleja, recounts that he worked in the ejido in the afternoon after working for the mill in the morning, since the 1.5-peso daily wage that he received in the factory was a mere pittance.[71]

Perhaps a more significant loss for the Jeans may have occurred in their nascent housing business as land expropriation to VJC took place near the area where they were planning to construct housing estates. However, this loss is not clear since they sold land in that area that could have been used for building housing when this business was consolidating. For example, in September 1930, seven years after the expropriation of the Rancho Anzaldo, the Jeans sold a large part of the Anzaldo and Contreras ranches to the Martínez Alemán family.[72]

Thus, it cannot be affirmed that the land expropriation from VJC in 1923 affected the Jeans' housing business in the center of the country. This may not have been the case in other states of the Mexican Republic where the Jean family had been working to expand their construction business. For example, in 1934 the Jeans acquired a 420-hectare property in the state of Oaxaca very inexpensively. They had planned to build houses there; however, three years later, the property had been reduced by more than half to 115 hectares due to "ejidal affectations."[73]

To conclude, I argue that agrarian reform did not necessarily represent any significant threat to the economic expansion of the Jean family's core businesses in Mexico City, the states of México and Puebla. The expropriations in those states did not affect their factories and in some cases the expropriations occurred in neighboring haciendas, something that may have even been advantageous for them as mentioned earlier. However, the expropriations that took place during the Cárdenas administration could have hindered the expansion of the Jeans' housing business to other regions of Mexico such as in the state of Oaxaca.

Table 3.10 shows how the percentage of total production of the top ten companies in the cotton textile industry in Mexico evolved between 1910 and 1929. In the years of armed revolution in Mexico (1910–20) and of subsequent agrarian reform in the 1920s that saw greater expropriation of lands in the Federal District, the Jean family's 3.2 percent contribution to Mexico's total textile production remained more or less stable. However, we also know that the Jean family invested in many other cotton textile companies in this period, so their percentage of participation within the national production of cotton textiles certainly grew in those turbulent years.

TABLE 3.10. Top ten companies in the Mexican cotton textile industry in 1910 and changes in the top twenty positions, 1910–1929

Owner	% of total output (1910)	Rank in 1910	% of total output (1915)	Rank in 1915
CIDOSA	9.1	1	12.3	1
CIVSA	6.8	2	5.7	3
Cía. Ind. Atlixco S.A.	5.5	3	—	—
Cía. Ind. Sn. Antonio Abad S.A.	4.1	4	2.7	9
Cía. Ind. Manufacturera S.A.	3.2	5	3.2	8
Hijos de Angel Díaz Rubín	3.2	6	—	—
VJC	3.2	7	2.3	10
Eusebio González S en C.	2.9	8	1.5	19
Cía La Hormiga S.A.	2.7	9	—	—
C. Noriega y Cía. Sucrs	2.7	10	2.2	11

Source: From data presented in Haber, Razo, and Maurer, "Political Instability."

*This figure is for the La Magdalena textile mill. The percentage of the Jeans' total production in 1929 was much larger because they were the owners of other cotton textile mills. After 1930, they acquired more factories.

BANKING

The French community in Mexico participated broadly in the banking sector, holding three-fifths of all foreign investment in Mexican banking by 1911. The Jeans, together with other members of the French community, founded the commercial bank the CBPM; Adrián Jean (and later Camilo) served on the board of directors and then as president. The CBPM performed credit operations in Mexico and other countries and lent money to federal and local governments, as well as providing funding for various corporations and expanding its activities throughout Mexico.

The CBPM was used by shareholders to finance their own companies in keeping with the common practice of insider lending at the time, which continued in Mexico well into the twentieth century through a concentrated banking structure. The CBPM had links with Porfirian politicians and later with the Madero government through the funding of various projects. This close relationship with the government continued after Banamex acquired the CBPM in the 1930s. Banamex had been expanding its participation in this banking company since the early 1920s, as a result of liquidity problems the CBPM faced. Finally, Banamex fully absorbed the CBPM at the beginning of the following decade.

% of total output (1920)	Rank in 1920	% of total output (1925)	Rank in 1925	% of total output (1929)	Rank in 1929
13.4	1	12.9	1	11.8	1
5.6	2	8.2	2	7.9	2
4.0	4	3.8	5	3.2	8
2.8	7	2.8	10	—	—
5.5	3	4.2	4	4.7	3
—	—	1.8	13	—	—
3.4	6	3.9	6	3.0*	10*
—	—	—	—	1.3	19
2.5	9	3.3	9	3.3	6
3.9	5	4.4	3	3.7	4

Even though the Mexican Revolution and the first revolutionary governments had a genuine intention to change the status quo in Mexico, some business practices remained unchanged. The revolution certainly brought about institutional changes—some of which had begun in the Porfirian period—and new forces and practices over the years, such as organized labor and agrarian reform. It also weakened influence of some foreign nationals and countries over Mexico's economy and caused other significant repercussions. However, the construction of networks between entrepreneurs and politicians, with elements from both groups obtaining individual benefits, is a practice that endures even today, independently of formal institutions that have supposedly tried to control these practices. Even Madero's government, the first revolutionary government, supported the status quo by emulating its predecessor's techniques, associating with members of the old business elite, for example. In this section, we will explain how this occurred by examining the links this bank established with revolutionary politicians and how it funded and planned different projects.

Creation of the CBPM

VJC followed the general trend of French participation in the Mexican banking system, and a group of individuals, mainly from the French community, founded the commercial bank the CBPM in October 1909.[74] The firm's capital investment totaled 10 million pesos. In 1921, Auguste Génin, who was close to the Porfirian financial circles, regarded the bank to be one of the nation's most important financial institutions, considering that most of the old issuing banks remained closed or subject to close government supervision.[75] However, the historiography of the period barely mentions the company.

The two main Barcelonnette firms that invested in this bank were J. Ollivier y Compañía and S. Robert y Compañía Sucesores, with 9,770 shares each. Other major investors included Carlos Markassuza, who held 8,140 shares. Markassuza, the most important individual investor, became the first president of the board of directors. A third group, which included VJC, held 3,260 shares each. Finally, a group of small investors acquired between 650 and 1,650 shares each. In total, there were thirty investors. Although VJC was an average-sized investor, Adrián Jean always played an important role on the board of directors. After serving as a member on the first board of directors, he took over the presidency of the company from Markassuza in 1914 and held the position for more than five years in a period that represents a clear increase of VJC profits as previously explained.[76] Table 3.11 shows the partners who subscribed to the CBPM, their shares, and their ownership percentages.

TABLE 3.11. Major investors in the Compañía Bancaria de París y México (CBPM), 1909

CBPM partners	Number of shares	Percentage of shares
J. Ollivier y Cía.	9,770	9.8
S. Robert y Cía.	9,770	9.8
Carlos Markassuza	8,140	8.1
Hauser Zivy y Cía.	6,510	6.5
Clemente Jacques y Cía.	4,890	4.9
Fabre Hermanos	4,230	4.2
P. J. Jacques Sociedad en Comandita	4,230	4.2
A. Reynaud y Cía.	3,260	3.3
A. Richaud y Cía.	3,260	3.3
Humberto Audiaguez	3,260	3.3
J. B. Ebrard y Cía.	3,260	3.3
Leon Signoret	3,260	3.3
M. Bellon y Cía.	3,260	3.3
M. Lambert y Cía.	3,260	3.3
Signoret, Honnorat y Cía.	3,260	3.3
Tardan Hermanos	3,260	3.3
Veyan, Jean y Cía.	3,260	3.3
Abril de Greiguiel	1,630	1.6
Hijos de Max Chauvet y Cía.	1,630	1.6
Jose G. Escandon	1,630	1.6
Mariano Allegre	1,630	1.6
F. Manuel y Cía.	1,300	1.3
F. Sánchez y Cía. Sucesores	1,140	1.1
Bernardo Albuneda	970	1.0
Hipolito Duran	980	1.0
Ailland y Cía.	810	0.8
E. Manuel y Cía.	650	0.7
L. Faudon y Cía.	650	0.7
Manuel Levy	330	0.3

Source: Data from Notary Bernardo Cornejo, 1909, vol. 51.

The Branches and Operation of the CBPM

The CBPM carried out the normal operations of a commercial bank. It received demand deposits and long-term deposits and opened current accounts. It performed credit operations, and it lent money to the federal and local governments.[77] The bank became increasingly involved in financing manufacturing companies. For instance, it provided substantial funding for important companies, such as the Compañía Fundidora de Hierro y Acero in Monterrey and the Manufacturera La Teja in Jalisco. It subsequently expanded its activities throughout Mexico. Two very important branches that it established included one in Veracruz and one in Torreón; the latter financed cotton producers in La Laguna in Coahuila. By 1920, the CBPM had invested approximately 4 million pesos in credit in Coahuila. In Veracruz, an important share of its portfolio was in credit for imports.[78] The CBPM also operated directly with other financial institutions: "Initially, their most important transactions were with the BLM, where this bank granted preferential credits to the 'French' institution. However, as the years of the Revolution passed, Banamex acquired importance in the Bancaria's capital."[79]

Lending by the CBPM

Insider lending

The CBPM, in which members of the Jean family were involved as partners and direct administrators, was undoubtedly used by its shareholders to finance their own manufacturing companies. Insider lending like this was commonplace in various countries in the early decades of capitalism. For example, insider lending was common in the United States between the 1830s and the 1870s.[80] As had been the case in the United States, insider lending in Mexico initially solved an information problem. Bankers did not have precise information about possible clients' default risk, so they preferred to lend other people's money to themselves.

According to Noel Maurer, several observers have demonized insider lending practices in Mexico, considering it as "an outright fraud perpetuated on the Mexican people by the Porfirian financial elite." However, he considers these interpretations to be incorrect, since banks in Mexico in this period "served as the means by which kinship networks channeled impersonal capital into their businesses," which in the end served as "engines of economic development."[81]

Even so, it is important to clarify that these banking resources did not benefit other groups of society by providing them with opportunities to invest and that the authorities had no real will to change this situation. This was independent of the existence of banking client information problems during the years of the modern banking sector boom in Mexico. Insider lending in Mexico was filtered through a concentrated banking structure that persisted well into the twentieth century, when other countries had made important institutional advances to both limit insider lending and increase competition in the banking sector. Thus, insider lending proved to be very resistant to oversight in Mexico, even when there were sufficient conditions to control it, as formal institutions in the banking sector grew throughout the country in the 1920s. Gustavo del Ángel shows that private banks in Mexico between 1940 and 1982 (the year when they were nationalized) maintained high profit levels in large part as a result of insider lending.[82]

Unlike SFIM, a long-term financing bank founded in 1898 where some Barcelonnettes participated, the CBPM was used for commercial purposes and shorter-term financing. That is, the CBPM portfolio shows that it served mainly as petty cash for its partners. It was dedicated to the issuing of promissory notes and loans to trade and industry, managing the movement of capital and credit orders and acting as an agent in commercial transactions. It was a classic financing bank aimed at strengthening the treasuries of its clients and helping them manage their finances and cash flows.

However, many of the CBPM's customers were directly or indirectly related to its partners. The only volume of the CBPM's administrative books found in the Archivo Histórico de Banamex recounts in detail renewals of promissory notes and new loans obtained by the CBPM's partners and clients related to them.[83] Some examples are a renewal of 30,000 pesos to Julio Barbaroux, a relative of Fernando Barbaroux (a member of the bank's Paris Committee and of Compañía Industrial de Atlixco, where Adrián Jean was also a partner); a renewal to the Compañía Deshinadora S.A. (linked to M. Bellon & Co., a bank's partner company); and a renewal to Julian Tron (related to El Palacio de Hierro, the CIDOSA, and M. A. Lacaud). In addition, the CBPM made a loan of 300,000 pesos to the Compañía Cervecera de Toluca y México (CCTM) in March 1911. The CCTM had connections with many companies and partners of French origin, as well as shareholder companies associated with the bank, such as M. Lambert y Co., and other individual shareholders related to the bank, including Carlos Markassuza, Mariano Allegre, Pascual Roux, and José Fabre.

CCTM shareholders also included Antonio Donnadieu, who until 1908 had been the Jeans' partner in Donnadieu Veyan y Compañía. In May 1911, the Compañía Manufacturera La Teja S.A., which had several French partners, obtained a loan for 250,000 pesos from the CBPM. Moreover, Adrián

Jean received a personal loan for 1,100 pesos in August 1911 on the occasion of a trip to Europe, and Luis Courl (a relative of the director Agustín Courl) also received a loan of 10,000 pesos at around the same time.

Leon Signoret, a CBPM individual shareholder, received a loan of 49,000 pesos in April 1911. During that same year, a loan of 15,000 pesos was given to Leopoldo Gout, a partner in the Compañía Industrial de Atlixco, and another to Damasco Melero, a partner of the same company. A. Richaud y Cía., a direct partner of the bank, received a renewal for 30,000 pesos in May 1911 and C. Jacques y Compañía, also a founding member of the CBPM, received a renewal of 50,000 later that same year.[84]

The Links with and Funding of Governments and Government Officials

Although the CBPM boasted having had no relationship with the government of Díaz (which was due to its creation in 1909), many of its partners had close relations with Porfirian politicians. José Yves Limantour was a partner and a close friend of Joseph Ollivier, the CBPM's most important partner.[85] Ollivier took advantage of this relationship to ask the government for certain concessions, and members of the government also asked favors of him.

In addition, once the revolution was underway, the CBPM funded the cotton production and distribution of La Laguna, Coahuila, under the Madero government. It made a loan of 40,000 pesos to A. Zirión Saravia Compañía, guaranteed by Francisco Madero Sr. in December 1911, and a loan of 9,721.04 pesos, linked to José Madero in March 1912. These loans were fully associated with the production and distribution of cotton in La Laguna, Coahuila—a business managed by the Madero family, who were the major producers at that time. In that year, the Madero family exported more than eighty thousand bales of cotton to Europe. In addition, the Torreón branch of the CBPM had invested about 4 million pesos in loans to fund cotton production in La Laguna by 1920.[86]

Francisco León de la Barra, interim president of Mexico, was also linked to the CBPM in the second half of 1911. The CBPM enjoyed sufficient public credit, and this allowed León de la Barra to participate in it during his brief time in office. In addition, after failed attempts to finance his personal businesses through Banamex, León de la Barra also switched his personal investments to the CBPM.[87] The León de la Barra family co-owned two important mining companies in conjunction with other private partners: the Queensland and Australia and El Barreno.[88]

The CBPM also funded some state governments. For example, in the Banamex board of directors meeting on March 20, 1930, when the bank was acquiring the CBPM, it was mentioned that the CBPM had lent the government of Guanajuato 500,000 pesos during the Madero administration. However, there is little information on the CBPM to corroborate whether this type of loan was recurrent.[89]

Funding the Madero Administration (1911–13)

The CBPM's ability to maintain a clean image to President Madero, supposedly without contact with government officials associated with Díaz (there were no government officials on the CBPM's board of directors), enabled them to become one of Madero's favorite banking companies. In a letter dated January 26, 1912, Scherer informs Limantour, who was in exile in France, about the new government's intention to create a construction company to carry out the contracts of almost all public works planned in the country, in conjunction with the CBPM: "This week I've been looking for subscriptions for a new Compañía Nacional Mexicana de Construcciones, which is currently being formed with a capital of two million, and whose board is composed of: Gustavo Madero, President; Domingo Valdez Llano, Vice-President; Madero's brother in law, Gabriel Escalante, First Vocal [partner of the failed company Escalante e Hijos, from Mérida]; Nestor Pino Suárez [the vice president's brother]." Among other partners, Scherer also mentioned José Vasconcelos, Andrés Troncoso, and José Mestre. The letter also mentioned that the shares would be distributed among the ten founders who claimed a right to them because of "having already secured contracts with the government of almost all public works planned and projected in the country."[90]

Madero's government would be taken down shortly after, so this construction company never formed; nor was this coalition between businessmen and the government created, which would have used the CBPM as its main bank. While this may be the case, this correspondence says a lot about how government project planning was performed at the time. This continued during the tenure of Madero, the democratic president who, in theory, looked to replace the methods of the Díaz administration to create a different government. This evidence confirms that Madero had only been excluded from the economic network protected by Díaz and that he would look to generate his own network once in power that would operate similarly to his predecessor's at least in economic terms.

The Company's Network with Politicians in Subsequent Revolutionary Governments

In April 1924, Camilo Jean was elected to the CBPM board of directors.[91] By that time, Banamex had expanded its participation in the CBPM because the latter had faced funding problems. In 1921, the CBPM had declared a suspension of payments as a consequence of three situations: the poor economic conditions among La Laguna cotton producers, partly due to the fall in the international price of cotton; a temporary interruption of commercial activities between the port of Veracruz and the commercial corridor of Puebla and Mexico City because of the poor condition of the railroads after the revolution; and the declaration of bankruptcy by a financial institution in Guadalajara that was a debtor to the CBPM.[92] With this suspension, the French banking company nearly collapsed. It was able to continue operations, in part because of capital injections from Banamex, although it would not recover its position in the market in the rest of the 1920s. In March 1930, after months of negotiations, Banamex acquired the CBPM for approximately 800,000 pesos, a price that reflects the depreciation this company experienced in the previous decade.[93] The last payment was made in September 1956.[94]

The history of CBPM insider lending and its links with the government continued after Banamex acquired the CBPM in 1930. Banamex offered continuous loans to the bank's directors over several years, according to information obtained from the Archivo Histórico de Banamex. Banamex's story is well documented, and the fact that it kept close relationships with members of the revolutionary governments until its nationalization in 1982 was not new—it had acted similarly ever since the Porfirian era.

During the Porfiriato, Banamex enjoyed special privileges. For example, its bills were the only ones accepted by the government for tax payments, and the bank was virtually exempted from all preexisting or new taxes on equities, notes, and dividends. However, with the founding in 1925 of the Banco de México (Banxico), Mexico's central bank, private banks could no longer issue banknotes.[95] This compromised the powerful position Banamex had held since its inception, although it remained the largest private bank in Mexico for many years.

Agustín Legorreta was a key figure in the reconstruction of Banamex following the revolution. He entered the bank in 1902, became its president in 1920, and built a strong relationship with the postrevolutionary governments. Members of the Legorreta family controlled the bank until 1982. During Mexico's ISI period of the mid-1930s to mid-1970s, Banamex funded many projects in conjunction with foreign corporations and Nacional Financiera, a government development bank. One example of these joint ventures was Celanese Mexicana, founded in 1944, which Banamex strongly supported.[96] It was partly through their relationship with the owners of Banamex (particularly Agustín and Luis Legorreta) and their participation in joint projects that some members of the Jean family maintained a leading position in Mexican business in the following decades. This is studied in chapter 4.

In this chapter, we analyzed how the Jeans, a French business family, became successful in Mexico after their immigration to the country in the late nineteenth century. We have traced how they succeeded in a later period than that considered by the classic historiography of the Barcelonnettes in Mexico, which arose as a result of the study of success stories of their compatriots who came from the same region of France before. In addition, we have seen how the Jeans built their social networks but remained economically independent from their peers, which allowed them more flexibility when dealing with events such as the Mexican Revolution and its institutional consequences, and diversified their activities into sectors where Barcelonnettes typically did not invest, like housing construction. This family was also astute in developing close relationships with distinguished non-French partners of key banking institutions, like the Legorretas, and profited by marriage to the most important media family in Latin America, the Azcárragas. These factors allowed a branch of this family to remain part of the Mexican economic elite until the present day, as we will study in the following chapter.

We also saw the participation of members of the Jean family in an important banking company that flourished in the revolutionary period: the CBPM. We showed how this company was used by its shareholders to fund their own companies in keeping with the common practice of insider lending, which continued in Mexico well into the twentieth century through a concentrated banking structure that was reflected in the concentrated structure of the industries it funded. The CBPM partners had links with Porfirian politicians, and later with the Madero government, through the funding of various projects (crony capitalism). This close relationship with the government continued after Banamex acquired the CBPM in the 1930s, when members of the Jean family were invited to join Banamex's board of directors. Thus, it is also through the direct and indirect connections the Jean family had with government officials in the banking, housing, and media sectors that this family has maintained a prominent position within the Mexican business structure until today.

The next chapter analyzes the effect of the Mexican labor movement on textile mills and of the new labor regulations on the modernization of the Mexican textile industry. In addition, I study the growth of competition with new economic groups after the 1920s, the introduction of synthetic textiles to

Mexico by the mid-twentieth century, and the consequences all these changes had for the textile mills and other businesses owned by the Jeans. Finally, the next chapter delves into the continued presence of members of the Jean family and other Barcelonnette families within the Mexican elite throughout the twentieth century.

CHAPTER FOUR

Labor, the Decline of the Textile Business, and the Future of Foreign Immigrants in Mexico

Revolutionary corporatism benefited the Jeans' textile factories by limiting radical labor demands and allowing some flexibility, for example, in stopping production at times when the external conditions forced mill owners to take such measures in violation of labor contracts. Although federal labor arbitration powers might have adversely affected labor discipline and thus productivity, not only were radical demands limited by revolutionary corporatism but owners got tariff protection in return for accepting federal mediation in labor conflicts.

However, such changes within the system did not promote the modernization of existing mills. By the 1950s, the traditional cotton and wool mills, including those in which the Jeans had participated, had been undermined by the entry of new, smaller, more modern and competitive firms (owned by other networks of ethnic entrepreneurs) and the introduction of synthetic fibers. Ironically, the state helped the Jeans wriggle out of their last labor obligations when they got rid of their inoperative mills.

This chapter covers the rise of organized labor within the textile sector (which began to appear after 1912) and the effect of labor militancy on the Jean family's mills. It also covers the emergence of new labor regulation as a consequence of the Mexican Revolution and its effects on the modernization of textile mills. In addition, it shows the growth of competition with other entrepreneurs and products, which all traditional textile producers faced by the mid-twentieth century. Finally, the chapter covers the Barcelonnette group's persistence within the Mexican economic elite. It delves into the direct, indirect, and more long-term causes that led to the decline of the Barcelonnettes' textile business in Mexico, as well as the survival strategies employed by members of the Jean family and other members of the Barcelonnette community in Mexico.

After many years of strong performance, the majority of the Barcelonnettes eventually either shut down or sold their textile mills, which had been one of their most important businesses. The last mill the Jean family operated was La Magdalena, which closed in 1973. It is difficult to attribute the decline of the textile mills to a single cause. Added to the causes mentioned above, in some cases the generations that followed the companies' founders were unable to manage the businesses properly, and families discouraged members of the third generation from entering the textile business.

Other activities made up for the losses in the textile business. For example, the Jean family began to construct housing estates, which differentiated them from other Barcelonnettes. In addition to the social network the Jean family had, one of the most important benefits of their experience in the banking sector was the relationship they established with some of the owners of Banamex. These and other connections through social clubs were of great importance to the economic future of members of the Jean family.

THE EFFECT OF THE MILITANT LABOR MOVEMENT ON TEXTILE MILLS

In the late Porfiriato, the working class had failed to create strong, durable unions and had failed to have their demands fulfilled. This changed during the revolution as a result of strikes and labor unrest. Throughout the tumultuous years that followed, new labor organizations pushed for improvement of labor conditions. While this had many positive outcomes, the new labor dynamics established between workers, owners, and governments after the 1920s also hindered the modernization of mills in the textile sector. Despite this, the direct impact of the radical labor movement on the production output of Jean mills was not significant in the first half of the twentieth century. Here I highlight key points in the transformation of labor relations in the textile industry, beginning in 1912. I also examine the effects that labor militancy had on the Jeans' factories.

Life in factories was hard for most Mexican workers. Though some bosses may have displayed humane qualities, workers usually faced low wages and long working days before labor conditions and rights were formally regulated. In addition, factories offered little job security. This situation began to change when workers started drawing together around common values to improve their labor conditions. They created various types of mutual aid societies where workers made financial contributions to support their own well-being.[1] In addition, they created movements to appeal for workers' rights. Their struggle would continue even after the creation of syndicates.

It is difficult to measure to what extent anarchist ideologies influenced specific mills in Mexico. John Hart believed the anarchists to be the most influential group in the Mexican labor movement in 1880, with more than fifty thousand affiliates in the Congreso General Obrero de la República Mexicana.[2] According to Hart, before 1870, when workers were generally organized in mutual aid societies, these organizations could do little to modify the owners' control over labor contracts and wage policies. Hart also mentions that the bad working conditions in the mills, the long workdays (which fluctuated between twelve to eighteen hours), and the low salaries were ideal conditions for the propagation of anarchist and anarcho-syndicalist ideas.[3] However, Hart's view seems exaggerated. John Lear argues that "although mutual aid societies sometimes sheltered anarchists and socialists who advocated struggle against employers and the state, the more dominant mutualist idiom, and the one strongly encouraged by officials and employers, spoke not only of unity among workers but also of unity between workers and their bosses."[4]

Díaz's role in controlling labor radicalism was also important. He used methods of repression and marginalization, such as imprisonment and military conscription, to confront radical workers. Once the threats from labor declined in the 1880s, in part as a result of the growing Mexican economy, government support for moderate mutual aid societies weakened.

When labor unrest began to emerge again, beginning in 1905, there was a new shift in labor policy: Díaz began to accommodate a minimal level of workers' grievances.[5] For instance, after the textile uprising of Río Blanco in 1907, Díaz made efforts to initiate reform in factory regulations in the Orizaba region. Nevertheless, repression continued. He repressed workers who supported Madero, who at that time was the leader of the opposition party: the Partido Antireeleccionista.[6] Díaz probably had a genuine desire to make some changes to labor conditions after 1905, realizing that the emerging labor unrest that year could cause political instability in the regime. But he was not willing to confront employers, as they formed the financial backbone of the economy, and his government lacked a consistent labor policy and legal mandate to deal with workers' demands.[7]

In 1910, Madero's electoral campaign received strong support from urban workers. Most of these workers identified with Madero's liberalism, rather than with revolutionary ideologies such as anarchism or radical programs such as those of the Flores Magón brothers. However, there were some textile mills in the center of the country that may have had a stronger radical influence. This was the case of some of the mills owned by the Jean family. For example, La Magdalena was "a site of documented anarchist-led workers' militancy between 1876–1882 and 1911–1931 and continued strikes in the 1880's–1890's."[8] Ten of the eleven strikes that broke out in cotton textile factories in the Federal District between 1906 and 1911 took place in the La Magdalena, La Hormiga, and San Antonio Abad mills.[9] Another mill owned by the Jeans was Santa Teresa, which had much harsher working conditions during the Porfiriato than other mills according to Katz.[10] So it is not a coincidence that some of these mills were specific targets for the expansion of radical organization after 1910.

At the end of 1909, textile workers did not have the protection of labor contracts, adequate labor laws, or influential national unions.[11] The Porfirian governor of the Federal District, Guillermo Landa y Escandón, made efforts to strengthen the Mutualist and Moralizing Society of Workers of the Federal District in late 1909. This society would include representatives of workers, industrialists, and the government to solve labor conflicts in the capital city and its surroundings. However, the society was only inaugurated in April 1911, less than two months before Díaz fell, so it could do little to achieve its objectives.[12]

The workers' situation changed during the revolution. In December 1911, less than two months after Madero took office, a major textile strike began in Puebla. Workers from many factories rose up, soon followed by workers from textile mills in Tlaxcala and Mexico City, including La Magdalena and Santa Teresa. The two most common demands were for reduced working hours and improved wages.[13] This strike would define the labor policy that Madero's administration followed. In January 1912, the government convened a meeting of textile owners, in which the owners agreed to a 10 percent increase in wages and a shortening of the workday to ten hours.

After six months, a convention of the textile industry took place—the first of its kind. It brought together representatives from labor and industry, along with government representatives. La Magdalena sent two representatives, Luis Veyan and Tomás Reyes Retana.[14] The result of this gathering was the *Reglamento para las Fábricas de Hilados y Tejidos en la República*, a regulation for the textile mills, which the Ministry of Development published that same month. The industrialists also approved the Tarifa de Hilados y Tejidos, a new wage scale that guaranteed a minimum wage of one peso per day to textile workers.[15] This was an important step toward institutionalizing government participation in the incipient labor relations system. Until then, contract negotiations had been a mostly private affair.[16]

After the convention, the workers began to feel that they were strong enough to limit the owners' authority. Furthermore, they understood that it was difficult for the government to repress them and that they could win battles against the owners. Bortz shows how, in various mills, the workers began to be ruled "without any more law than their own caprice."[17] This shows how labor was emerging as a political force resulting from irreversible gains that workers made in the revolution. The government also started playing an active role in these changes through its new Labor Department, which supervised compliance with the new labor regulation in the mills. This practice continued after Madero's fall. For example, Miguel Casas, an inspector from the Labor Department, visited La Magdalena in December 1913 to check if it was observing the regulations and wages approved in the previous year.[18]

Although these changes were taking place, workers' ability to limit owners' control of the mills should not be exaggerated. The owners failed to pay workers according to the agreed wage scale on many occasions. For instance, José Pérez, a representative of the La Magdalena union, asked the Labor Department to send an inspector in March 1920 because "the wages in the weave department were far from being the ones agreed in the 1912 convention."[19] However, there had been advances for the workers that would never be reversed.

After the general strike of December 1911, radicals in Mexico City organized the Casa del Obrero Mundial. This was an anarcho-syndicalist association that gathered support from workers because the Madero administration had failed to give workers' organizations direct political participation or significant improvements in the workplace. However, it was not the anarcho-syndicalist ideology that moved workers to affiliate themselves with the Casa,[20] but their desire to "eliminate the worst abuses in industry[,] . . . asserting greater control over aspects of the work process, and assuring just wages and work conditions."[21]

The Casa soon began to acquire power within the labor movement in the Federal District. It attracted more followers than the official unions such as the Gran Liga Obrera de la República Mexicana created by the Madero administration, in central Mexico. After Madero's fall, his successor Victoriano Huerta closed the doors of the Casa.

When the Constitutionalists defeated Huerta, they found support against the revolutionary factions led by Villa and Zapata in the urban labor class represented by the Casa. Urban workers, mainly from Mexico City, organized six battalions in 1915 that became known as the red battalions, which fought against Villa and Zapata. Workers from La Magdalena and Santa Teresa participated in these battles as part of the third and fourth battalions.[22] In fact, in Mexico

City, unionized textile workers represented one of the Casa's most important components.

The battalions were ultimately disbanded after Carranza no longer required them to subdue the peasant guerrillas of the south and the insurgents of the north. Rising inflation, urban unemployment, and general instability led to labor discontent in major cities. In the second half of 1915 many strikes occurred in the capital involving different industries. On January 1916 amid strikes incited by the Casa Obrera Mundial in Mexico City, Carranza ordered the last of the Red Battalions to dissolve and the Constitutionalists violently crushed the strikes. This led to the fall of the Casa and represented a crucial moment for the Mexican labor movement, as the anarchists had been severely weakened in Mexico City.

The Casa went into decline after the repression of the Constitutionalists. However, by that time urban workers had gained sufficient collective power that they were able to force the faction that ultimately triumphed in the revolution to acknowledge their importance.[23] Despite the problems that led to the fall of the Casa, the workers' organizations grew and their influence continued to increase during the revolution. As Bortz notes, "as ruling class hegemony waned, workers became bolder, sometimes instigated or protected by revolutionary bands, wily politicians and new laws. . . . Meanwhile, clever revolutionary leaders saw the wisdom in creating new hegemonies in regions under their control."[24]

Cándido Aguilar, the governor of Veracruz, issued a decree in October 1914 that gave various benefits to the working class in his state. The reason behind this was probably the same one that drove Madero to convene the textile convention in 1912: to pacify and govern his state, which had important mill towns, including Orizaba. Additionally, the 1917 Constitution gathered together some of the demands that the workers had sought in the previous decade. Article 123 gave labor and capital the right to organize for the defense of their respective interests and allowed workers to bargain collectively and strike.

At this point, it was difficult to control the stronger labor movement that had emerged from the armed conflict. The textile workers continued to organize strikes in many places. For instance, the Santa Teresa mill had a three-day strike in 1920 to support a worker who had been dismissed without just cause.[25] However, one problem that arose from this stronger labor movement was that, as it strengthened, it hindered the modernization of the textile industry. Automatic looms had become commonplace in many industrialized countries, but the unions blocked their installation when certain mills attempted to set them up in the 1920s.[26] The owners of the Atoyac Textile Company in the central state of Puebla installed new automatic looms in 1923 but the unions blocked their operation. The worker who ran the looms was stabbed to death, and his successor soon started receiving death threats and promptly resigned. No one else dared to tend the looms, and they were abandoned until technicians modified them to become ordinary power looms.[27]

This militancy would continue for some years. After the death of the Casa, the CROM, founded in 1918, attracted some of its ex-members. Other ex-members founded the Confederación General del Trabajo (CGT) in 1921, which maintained the same anarcho-syndicalist ideology. The CGT was very militant in its first six years, but it was also a strongly persecuted labor organization.[28] This confederation attracted the unions of three of the Jean family's mills: La Magdalena, Santa Teresa, and the recently acquired Río Hondo.[29] La Magdalena and Río Hondo were two of the five most important cotton textile mills affiliated with the CGT.[30] This was also the case for Santa Teresa in the wool textile sector.

The CGT claimed to have eighty thousand affiliate members in 1928 and 1929, most of them in Mexico City.[31] Textile workers were once again one of the most important components of an anarcho-syndicalist organization. However, the government was clearly hostile to the CGT, and the industrialists, supported by the government, did not make any extra concessions to CGT affiliates. For example, mill owners in the Federal District closed their mills at various intervals in 1923 and 1924, arguing that raw materials were scarce. However, a report showed that some mills had enough material to operate for at least three more months. The CGT members declared that the plants should remain open or else the workers would take control of them, but the government, represented by Gen. Manuel Pérez Treviño, supported the owners. This led to various strikes in the mills.[32]

When Calles took office at the end of 1924, he was not sympathetic to independent labor organizations. With Luis Morones—the leader of the CROM and a new minister in the Industry, Commerce, and Labor Ministry—and one of his closest collaborators, he began to combat CGT unions. For example, although the CROM had a minority of affiliates in the Federal District textile mills, the government supported an attempt to invade the CGT headquarters in the San Ángel-Contreras area in 1925. This led to many violent revolts in the streets, strikes, lockouts, and government military-police intervention to support the CROM minority.[33]

By that time, the CROM was expanding its influence throughout the country by issuing laws and expanding its bureaucracy. Due to the difficult situation in which the CGT had been placed, some CGT affiliates began to see the CROM as an alternative. This helped to centralize control of the labor movement in government hands. Meyer argues that, in the absence of better information, by the mid-1920s "it may be agreed that the CROM had mustered 100,000 workers, artisans, office workers, small traders and, in theory, 50,000 agricultural laborers."[34]

The CGT would continue to battle for some time. In July 1925, the Junta de Conciliación y Arbitraje (Federal Arbitration Board [FAB]) accepted a claim made by the owners of three mills located in the San Ángel-Contreras region, one of which was La Magdalena. The owners asked for a readjustment in wages. The FAB supported the industrialists and this led to many conflicts. The national government blamed the CGT workers from La Magdalena because they prevented the entry of workers affiliated to the CROM to that mill and because they convened illegal meetings inside the factory.[35] In November of the same year, La Magdalena experienced intense fights between the workers of the CROM and the CGT after the owners hired members of the former.[36] In 1926, the owners of La Magdalena fired fifty CGT members, and the government sent federal troops to protect CROM workers and the plant.[37]

The CGT remained powerful in the Federal District until the end of the 1920s. However, there were two factors that substantially weakened it: the assassination of president-elect Álvaro Obregón, which weakened the CROM and made a better relationship between the CGT and the government possible, and the death of the most radical CGT leaders.

The Effect of Labor Militancy on the Jean Family's Mills

At this point, it is important to analyze the effects that labor militancy, which the Jean family confronted in their mills before the 1930s, had on these factories' production capacity. An obvious conclusion is that any mill owner would have preferred not to have workers affiliated to radical unions. It seems, however, that the presence of militant workers did not affect the level of production of the Jean family factories for a number of reasons.

First, the workers needed the jobs. They were, in general, poor people that came from rural areas looking for better opportunities and wages, so they could not stop working.

Second, there was a great deal of control over the workers in the mills; supervisors kept control over the workers and their activity by registering information about their performance on special cards. Since the supervisors were trustworthy employees with higher salaries, they were not easily bribed.

Third, although mill owners confronted a more dynamic and organized labor movement after the revolution, and gradually lost the control that they held over contractual negotiations, the federal government's rejection of radical ideologies and organizations benefited them. The government generally supported owners who confronted radical unions.

Fourth, although there were continuous strikes and lockouts, the market did not demand full-capacity production from the mills. For instance, industrialists from Puebla, Tlaxcala, and Mexico City sought permission from the federal government on more than one occasion in 1923 and 1924 to cut back on hours and wages in order to reduce their excess stock.[38] Haber argues that overproduction occurred on a fairly regular basis: "At least twice during the latter part of the Porfiriato, in 1901–2 and again in 1907–8. Throughout the years of the revolution (1910–17) and the 1920s, the problem was endemic."[39]

NEW LABOR REGULATIONS AND THE MODERNIZATION OF TEXTILE MILLS

The decline of the Jean family's factories was more the result of new labor relations that emerged after three textile conventions (in 1912, 1925–27, and 1937–39) than from the radical unions they had to confront. In addition, in the postwar period after 1945, Mexican cotton mills were challenged by a lack of modernization due to labor regulations and demands, combined with the emergence of new competitors in the textile sector and new types of fibers available in the market.

During the 1920s, the Jean family mills maintained their privileged position within the cotton textile industry. In 1929, La Magdalena alone was producing 2 percent of the total industry output. These were years in which the textile industry was facing a crisis, particularly as a consequence of the Great Depression. Between 1926 and 1932, the number of workers employed in the cotton textile industry decreased by around 25 percent, and revenues from cotton cloth sales dropped 30 percent.[40] However, these were not bad years for the Jean family—at least not compared to their competitors. As already shown, the business interests of this family expanded in terms of factories, properties, and other activities during that decade.

The presidents who came to power following the revolution could not impose their will on the strengthened labor movement that had emerged. Their general strategy was to build consensus around new labor institutions. However, the textile industry was faced with problems in the first half of the 1920s that seemed difficult to solve: workers wanted wage increases in a complicated economic environment, in which mills had been hit by reduced demand for their products. In fact, as mentioned above, many industrialists from Puebla, Tlaxcala, and Mexico City sought permission from the federal government to cut back on hours and wages in order to reduce their excess stock.

In an attempt to solve these problems, the Calles administration convoked a tripartite textile convention, which was similar to the 1912 convention. The event took place between 1925 and 1927, with participation from the labor representatives of 110 factories and the owners of 117 factories.[41] Camilo Jean attended as one of the five representatives of the industrialists.[42]

In general, the actions taken by the government during the convention aimed to extend federal authority on labor issues. The negotiations regarding wages divided industrialists, allowing the government to increase its role in the debate. The industrialists of Mexico City and the states of México and Veracruz supported the idea of establishing a minimum wage for all the industry. Meanwhile, the Puebla and Tlaxcala industrialists supported the idea of maintaining different wages for different regions, arguing that living expenses in their states were lower than those in the Federal District or Veracruz.

Since the Puebla and Tlaxcala industrialists were a majority, they won the debate and the minority had to accept increased costs in their regions.[43] Other issues resolved at the convention were the approval of bilateral commissions (*comisiones mixtas*) to solve conflicts between workers and industrialists, and the *cláusula de exclusion* (exclusionary clause), which gave union leaders the right to expel members for antiunion activities; they "closed shop," excluding nonunion members. These two aspects strengthened the labor bureaucracy and its alliance with the federal government.

The federal government emerged as the winner from this convention because neither the owners nor the workers were satisfied by the *contrato colectivo de trabajo* (collective contract) that had been agreed to there. Workers did not receive the wage increases they wanted, and they saw continued decreases in their real wages. Owners lost control of their mills with the establishment of comisiones mixtas. The federal government, meanwhile, became the "final arbiter of industrial relations."[44]

In addition, the new regulations generated more obstacles to industry modernization. In particular, "the wage list that was designed . . . fixed a maximum number of machines per worker and established specific wages-per-piece. Under these conditions, industrialists had no incentive to introduce better machinery because it would not enable them to reduce labor costs, since wages-per-piece had to remain invariable."[45] Additionally, in the late 1920s, the government imposed a legal restriction on the adoption of new technologies, including automatic looms. Consequently, it was necessary to increase the level of protection after the convention to keep the industry running. Ad valorem tariffs, in particular, were substantially increased. The ad valorem tariff for coarse unbleached and white cloth rose from 32.5 percent in 1926 to

186.3 percent in 1927. In the case of fine white and unbleached cloth, this tariff rose from 40.8 percent in 1926 to 215 percent in 1927.[46]

During the 1930s, the economic situation of the cotton textile industry changed for the better. Output grew more than 60 percent between 1932 and 1937, accompanied by an increase in the productivity of capital and labor.[47] Also, a new confederation of labor unions was founded in 1936, the CTM. Cárdenas saw organized labor as fundamental to the objectives of his administration and promoted the formation of this new umbrella labor organization.[48] This led to violent conflicts between the followers of the CROM and the CTM, especially in Puebla and Orizaba.

In 1937, in the middle of this conflict, the Labor Department summoned a textile convention to review the main agreements of the 1925–1927 convention. At this convention, as at the previous one, the owners were divided between the majority (mainly owners of mills in Puebla and Tlaxcala) and the minority (mainly owners of mills in Mexico City and the states of México and Veracruz), as they became known. The labor delegates were also divided between the CTM, the CGT, and two factions of the CROM. Some cotton textile industries still had CGT members. For instance, two of the Jean family factories (La Magdalena and Río Hondo, and in all likelihood Santa Teresa) were still cataloged as CGT mills.[49] However, the CGT had become much less radical. In fact, the CGT and the CTM were allied at the convention against the CROM and showed their support to the government as opposed to the owners. In December 1937, the CGT and the CTM jointly led a strike to force the owners not to "create difficulties for the government."[50]

The main issue of the convention was again wages. The divisions among owners and workers on this topic delayed the negotiations. The issue was finally transferred to President Cárdenas, who contributed to establish a new collective labor contract in April 1939, which stipulated an industry-wide minimum wage of 2.80 pesos. This was a low wage, closer to what industrialists had proposed.[51] The contract also approved a new industry-wide wage scale and maintained the workweek at forty-eight hours.

The main result of the 1937 convention was, perhaps, the establishment of a collective contract in itself. This strengthened the federal government's control over industry. In a way, both labor and owners benefited from the convention since they both obtained advantages from the new system. That is, the inflexibility of the wage schedule that had been agreed to at the 1925–1927 convention remained unchanged, maintaining the disincentive to undertake technological innovations. Thus, workers' desire to avoid technological change to keep their job was granted. So the government supported the workers and protected the industry with higher tariffs giving the owners a captive market.[52]

The problem was that the textile industry was confronting substantial backwardness by the early 1940s.

WWII was the last period in which the traditional cotton and wool mills that had been present since the mid-nineteenth century would have high rates of production. Cotton textile exports during the war represented 60 percent of total manufacturing exports. During that period, Mexican textile mills operated in three shifts of eight hours per day, and textile exports mainly satisfied US demand.[53] Additionally, textile products were also sent to other Allied countries; for instance, "the Jean family's factories, which [also] worked day and night, exported part of their output to France, via the Port of Veracruz."[54]

However, the United States resumed its textile production by the end of the conflict to meet the needs of its internal market. Mexico, which was confronting an overvalued exchange rate, suffered a rapid reduction in manufacturing exports. In real terms, cotton textile production decreased by around 11.5 percent between 1946 and 1947, with a small recovery after that year due to an increase in internal demand.[55]

Furthermore, the modernization of the mills never took place. After 1945, the industrialists made another attempt to modernize their mills by trying to change the legal restrictions. In that year, the "CIVSA's president explained at [a] . . . shareholders' meeting that it was urgent for Santa Rosa, as well as for the Mexican textile industry as a whole, to fully modernize its equipment in order to be able to produce intensely in 'conditions of efficient competition.' . . . It was a matter of life and death for the national industry."[56] However, their efforts failed, as "only new plants established after the war were exempt from restrictions imposed by the industry-wide labor contract."[57]

Workers basically continued obstructing any modernization efforts, even those that were taking place in new plants. Although they argued that they were not against modernization, their requests to the government did not show that. For example, the unions of four mills, owned by the Compañía Industrial de los Hermanos Alfonso y Casimiro Jean, joined together in 1942 in what they called the Pact of Solidarity and Mutual Aid to discuss the problems that workers confronted in different factories. The mills were La Magdalena, Santa Teresa, Río Hondo, and La Industria Nacional, and their unions were La Lucha, La Igualdad, Resurgimiento, and Acción Social, respectively.[58]

These unions collectively sent a letter to Pres. Adolfo Ruiz Cortines in 1953 in which they mentioned that, among other issues, "they were not against the modernization of the textile mills as long as the industrialists fulfilled the labor laws and the collective contracts."[59] The problem was that, besides the rigid wage list, the labor contract forced the industry to maintain the same number of workers in employment; "any worker who left the mill for any reason had to be replaced. Moreover, because it established a promotion system based on seniority, it prevented firms from choosing and promoting personnel on the basis of aptitude and effort."[60] The union also "asked for the standardization of the labor system in modern mills so that non-modern mills could subsist."[61] In other words, they were against the exemptions in the labor contract that modern mills enjoyed because this would generate a further technology gap between mills.

The problems for the Jean family worsened during the 1950s, and their relations with the unions also became more difficult. In November 1953, La Lucha sent another letter to the president complaining that the owners planned to close La Magdalena for an indefinite period without any compensation for the workers, to reduce the workday by half, and to maintain vacancies. They asked that the president reject a request made by the owners to the Junta de Conciliación y Arbitraje in which the industrialists argued that "the economic situation was bad and that they needed to take these measures." According to the union, "there had been many dismissals without fair cause and without compensation." They also claimed that "the owners exaggerated the bad textile industry situation in order to make all these changes so they could modernize the mills."[62]

La Magdalena closed in March 1954. According to some reports, an artificial conflict led to the shutdown. In those reports, two unions from Puebla asked the president for the "fast and fair solution of the artificial conflict that led to the close of the cotton mill La Magdalena."[63] The mill was reopened in May 1954, at which point La Lucha union sent a very friendly letter to the president, thanking him for the reopening of the mill. They offered their most ample support to "the government that he honorably presided." They also called him a patriot.[64] This represented a notable change in the labor-state relations for this originally anarcho-syndicalist union.

In April 1955, a strike began at the Santa Teresa mill due to a reduced workday and the condition imposed by the owners that vacancies would not be filled. The union that represented the workers asked the president to either expropriate the mill or reopen it and require the owners to follow the collective contract. The owners had already requested recourse and once more had cited the bad economic situation before the Junta de Conciliación y Arbitraje.[65] The president intervened to reopen the mill, supporting the workers' requests again.

It seems that all the measures taken by the owners, such as temporarily closing the mills without compensation, reducing the workday, or maintaining vacancies, were efforts to slim the workforce, obliging employees to look for other work in order to force the modernization of the mills and to allow them to become competitive again. The workers recognized this situation, as they mentioned it in their letters to the president. However, the modernization of the mills would not occur. The labor unions were strong and their close relationships with the government were strengthened even more during the Adolfo López Mateos administration (1958–64).[66]

THE GROWTH OF COMPETITION WITH NEW ECONOMIC GROUPS AND THE INTRODUCTION OF SYNTHETIC FIBERS

After World War II, the textile business in Mexico was impacted by the introduction of synthetic fibers and the participation of different entrepreneurs in the sector—Eastern European Jews and Lebanese and Syrian immigrants among them. Between 1956 and 1965, the production of synthetic fibers in Mexico increased by 116.5 percent. These entrepreneurs were strengthened due to their economic activities in wartime, and they began to present serious competition to the Porfirian entrepreneurs until the shutdown of most of the traditional textile mills in the 1960s.[67] In some branches of the textile industry, the entry of new firms was widespread. Literally hundreds of enterprises sprang up during this period. In addition to being new, these firms had two other major attributes. The first was their size. Almost none of them had capital in excess of 100,000 pesos; in fact, most started with less than 10,000 pesos. They survived because there were no significant economies of scale in the products they manufactured.

A second attribute was that their owners were, for the most part, foreigners like the Porfirian giants. These entrepreneurs were predominantly Eastern European Jews and Lebanese and Syrian immigrants who had come to Mexico in the 1920s fleeing religious persecution.[68] Many of the Syrian and Lebanese immigrants were Jews and Maronite Christians, and they had set themselves up as petty traders in the cloth business.[69] For these entrepreneurs, Mexico became an alternative destination when the United States closed its doors to them after immigration restrictions following WWI.[70]

Many started out selling socks, underwear, or similar products door to door. By the 1930s, they had amassed sufficient capital to enable them to become the owners of small mills. By 1938, the tax register for the textile industry was dominated with names of owners like Eli Dwedk, Izzat Nacif, Amade Zidam, Leon Zakowsky, Jorge David Assef, Jacobo Farji, and Alejandro Kleyff.

WWII marked the beginning of fierce competition within the textile industry; the era of synthetic fibers had begun. Polyester, *artisela*, and rayon were some of the new materials that consumers were looking for in the market. Some of the small entrepreneurs who had come to Mexico in the 1920s capitalized on this opportunity and began to focus on producing synthetic fabrics. This was combined with the fact that 95 percent of the looms and 85 percent of the spindles in Mexico in the early 1950s had been built before 1925,[71] and it was too late to modernize the preexisting mills. There had been complaints about the old machinery in use dating back to the 1940s, but this technology was obsolete by the end of the 1950s and consumers were not demanding cotton textiles in the same quantity as before.

In 1942, some small mills in Mexico began to produce rayon yarn textiles in small quantities. Secondhand equipment for the production of rayon yarn was purchased in the United States by a Mexican firm and installed at a plant near Mexico City. Rayon yarn was supplied to weaving mills at a rate of approximately 1.5 million pounds per year. The quality of the yarn was low and the costs of production were high, but the weaving mills had no trouble disposing of its output during the war years. Toward the end of the war, the Celanese Corporation of America bought and reorganized this only firm in Mexico producing rayon yarn under the name Artisela Mexicana. New equipment was added, plant capacity was expanded, and steps were taken to improve the quality of the product.[72]

Beginning in 1944, Celanese Mexicana S.A. began to open factories in different regions, some new to industry. Due to their need for a great deal of water, the factories were mostly located in rural areas, which helped establish a new pattern of industrialization. The factory that Celanese Mexicana installed in Ocotlan, Jalisco, in 1946 represented one of the most significant investments in industry of the decade. The one opened in Zacapu, Michoacán, in 1946 was the most important enterprise in the state of Michoacán for decades.[73]

The large factories producing synthetic fiber both supplied it to a multitude of small and medium enterprises and imposed dynamism on others. They also managed to make blends and converted their traditional competitors—cotton producers—into buyers. The synthesis seems to have been fruitful; the "natural" innate goodness of cotton benefited from the "practical" qualities of synthetic fibers and vice versa.[74]

Between 1956 and 1965, the production of synthetic fibers grew from 25,586 to 55,392 tons, an increase of 116.5 percent. The volume of cotton products was much higher in 1956, at 153,810 tons. However, its growth rate was much smaller in the same period. Production had only increased by 7 percent from the mid-1950s to the end of the 1960s, particularly affected by an agricultural crisis in the second half of the 1960s.[75] Wool production decreased between 1954 and 1969, and its volume was half that of artificial fibers in 1956.[76]

La Magdalena, the last mill in the hands of the Jean family, shut down in 1973 after six years of strikes and one year before the production of artificial fibers surpassed the production of cotton textiles. Santa Teresa had closed its doors in 1965.[77] Río Hondo had also shut down in the late 1950s, and La Compañía Industrial de Toluca and the two mills located in Atlixco (El Carmen and La Carolina) were sold. The Jeans department store, La Francia Marítima, and its remnants, was sold to the Saba family in 1981.[78] This was a Jewish family of Syrian origin that had come to Mexico earlier in that century.

By the late 1970s, the Jean family textile business had ended. In early 1973, the Supreme Court ruled in favor of the workers of La Magdalena after a six-year strike that broke out due to violations of the collective contract. The company had to pay 47 million pesos to compensate the workers. However, this payment was not made, and the company's properties were seized and sold off cheaply. This situation was a relief for the owners, rather than a problem; they got rid of an old and uncompetitive mill without having to compensate their workers directly.

THE PERSISTENCE OF THE BARCELONNETTES WITHIN THE MEXICAN ELITE

An important number of Barcelonnettes were unable to overcome obstacles following the Mexican Revolution. Despite early economic successes, the revolution, which coincided with WWI, and the economic crisis of 1929 forced many of their companies into bankruptcy. Such was the experience of Joseph Ollivier, a central entrepreneur in the Barcelonnette network. In contrast, the Jean family participated in various economic sectors in addition to textile mills, such as banking, housing, and electricity, allowing them to maintain their wealth and businesses—which is also the case of the Ebrard and Michel families, for example—for a longer period, and despite the eventual division of the family.

Following changes in regulatory, labor, and market forces, the Jean family never truly recovered the economic power they had enjoyed as a whole in the first half of the twentieth century. However, there were other factors that allowed members of this family to remain among the top business elite, particularly through social relationships. For Pablo Jean, his brother Casimiro, and other members of this branch of the family—which descended from Adrián Jean, the first Jean in Mexico—who also maintained close relationships with other prominent families,[79] these social networks and family ties provided much-needed support in the face of adverse conditions.[80]

For the Jeans, social networks cushioned their growing failures in the cotton and wool textile sectors and allowed diversification of activities. Labor in Mexico had grown considerably since the revolution, especially during the golden age of the PRI as political stability was maintained, and changing labor policies was difficult even for the PRI governments as workers gained status. Despite this, the Jeans' connections, including government officials, grew through Banamex, Televisa, their companies in the housing sector, and also Celanese, even as their traditional textile business weakened. This was due to connections with families such as the Legorretas, Azcárragas and Rivera Torres.

In the sectors where most of these companies grew, privileges for entrepreneurs and linked politicians prevailed, keeping formal institutions weak. In the previous chapter, we explained, for example, the power of manipulation of public information by Televisa to support government interests in exchange for prerogatives since its founding in the 1950s. A recent study even suggested that the relationship between Televisa and the three Mexican federal governments in the period from 2000 to 2018 was close to what has been called presidential capture because Televisa's influence over executive power was clear and consistent.[81] In fact, Peña Nieto began his presidential term in 2012 with a huge debt to settle with Televisa, given the support the television company gave in building the presidential couple's image. "This allowed Azcárraga Jean to emerge from a long debate about the Telecommunications Law, much less prejudiced than Carlos Slim, and with the green light to monopolize cable TV and to continue benefiting from large purchases of official advertising." In each recent presidential period where Televisa has lost ground, "it has not been the president but other regulatory powers or the Supreme Court who have given the ruling."[82] The impressive growth of media social networks and paid sites that offer a range of content such as movies, TV shows, documentaries, videos, and so on has also affected its weight in the media.

In addition, as mentioned in chapter 3, Banamex continued to have crucial importance for the development of its shareholders' projects, since insider lending continued at this bank until at least 1982 when it was nationalized. Banamex also strongly supported the creation of Celanese.[83] As explained in chapter 2, the private national capital that participated in this large venture came from the old guard. Moreover, crony capitalism in the housing sector and its consequent effect on the formal institutional weakness there can clearly be seen from the 1930s in the urban planning of Mexican cities.

The construction of housing in Mexico City depends on the available areas and, above all, connections between developers and government officials, with little regard for whether it is carried out in areas already saturated with housing development or with inadequate roads to access them.[84] In these cases, the joint interests of politicians and business leaders have more weight than the application of construction laws and regulations and adequate urban planning. Most of the municipalities in Mexico City have this problem today, which is replicated in most cities in Mexico. The Jean family's partners in the housing sector, the Rivera Torres family, used their contacts with politicians to fraudulently obtain more land in the south of Mexico City in the second half of the twentieth century, where they planned to build more housing. The southwest of Mexico City has some of the most serious problems with roads and housing saturation.

Next, we will study some specific cases of failure and survival among the Barcelonnettes.

The Case of Joseph Ollivier

The case of Joseph Ollivier is very different from that of the Jean family. There were obstacles he could not overcome, despite being one of the greatest entrepreneurs of the time and the most central entrepreneur in the Barcelonnette social network in Mexico. Joseph Ollivier had been extremely prosperous in the textile industry and in banking, but in the early twentieth century, when he decided to enter the sugar industry, he was less successful. In early 1900, the environmental conditions of the Pánuco were not suitable for optimum production and Ollivier invested substantial capital in an attempt to make the business prosper. This began to affect J. Ollivier y Compañía's cashbox, and it also affected the BLM, of which he was a major shareholder; the same happened with the Banco Suizo Francés, of which he was a representative. By 1910, Azucarera Pánuco had accumulated a debt of 1.5 million pesos, compared to 1.7 million in equity.[85] Joseph Ollivier died on April 5, 1910, but the business continued to run.

As the revolution approached in Mexico in the 1910s, the favorable political conditions that had allowed some of the Barcelonnettes to develop for thirty years now worked against them. According to Patrice Gouy, an Ubaye valley native wrote to his family in 1913: "If it were not for the revolution, maybe I would have returned to France [rich], but what can we do, the savings that many of my comrades and I had, were invested in agricultural businesses and others, and that is not worth anything anymore. We must start all over again."[86] At the same time, the declaration of war between France and Germany in August 1914 increased confusion and destabilized the Barcelonnette colony. All young French people were eager to defend their country. Thirty-nine employees of La Ciudad de Londres went to France to make themselves available to the military authorities; five of them belonged to the Ollivier family or those of its partner-managers.

Although the situation calmed down after the revolution, the economic situation of many Barcelonnettes was never the same again. Following the revolution and WWI, the world economic crisis of 1929 represented a death blow for Ollivier y Compañía Sucesores, which declared bankruptcy in 1932, unable to pay its debts. Subsequently, the parent company in Paris also went bankrupt.[87] Many other Barcelonnette companies suffered and could not survive this era of upheaval.

The Case of the Jean Family

The labor movement became a strong impediment to technological changes in the textile mills from the 1920s. Partly due to this situation, the next generations of the Jean family were discouraged from entering the business.[88] As we have seen, the Jean family entered into many areas of the economy other than the textile sector during the first decades of the twentieth century—banking, housing, and electricity generation being the most significant examples.

The Jeans were not among the most central Barcelonnette bankers in Mexico; their experience in this sector was similar to that of other average French investors. They obtained credit to finance their own textile production, and their bank provided loans to partners, friends, relatives, and other companies with French participation, as well as to others. These efforts helped them to strengthen an important social network and to overcome the weaknesses of the Mexican institutional framework of credit transfer. In addition, they built relationships with revolutionary politicians—different from those of the Porfiriato—through banking, something that did not occur with other of their countrymen. However, the banking business ceased to be a profitable experience for the owners of the CBPM at some point during the 1920s, and it was sold to Banamex in 1930. It was partly through their relationship with the owners of Banamex, particularly Agustín Legorreta and Luis Legorreta, that some members of the Jean family maintained a leading position in Mexican business.

The fate of José Jean's family is very interesting because it is the polar opposite of that of Adrián Jean's family, who established relationships with prominent families from the Mexican elite like the Azcárragas and the Legorretas. José Jean, as we have seen before, was the fourth and last member of the first generation of the family to come to Mexico. He was also the first to pass away, from a heart problem derived from his participation in WWI, according to his family. José had two sons: Roberto and Huguette. Huguette died young, and Roberto worked directly with his cousins (Camilo's sons), the Jean y García brothers: Camilo Alfonso, Marcelo Casimiro, and Carlos Luis.

However, the participation of José's family in the family business was notoriously weakened. Rather than support José's widow, his relatives began to gradually limit her family's shareholding in the companies. Roberto Jean eventually began to work in other activities completely separate from the family businesses when the textile business was weakened. For many years until he died, he was the general manager of the Club Deportivo Chapultepec. Roberto Jean also broke away from the French colony; for example, his children did not learn French. Part of this was caused by resentment toward his family and the negative experience of being educated at a boarding school in France in his youth.

Camilo's progeny ended up being more important to the core family business because of the early death of Adrián Jean in 1936. However, Adrián's widow (Zoé David) and his sons (Casimiro and Pablo) did keep an important part of the company shares, unlike José's widow. This was because Adrián had been the initial pillar of the Jean family's business in Mexico. According to Roberto Jean, Camilo's sons could not adequately handle the textile business—particularly Marcelo Casimiro and Carlos Luis were spoiled daddy's boys. The other Casimiro, Adrián's son, also played an important role in the textile business, while Pablo, his brother, focused on nonfamily businesses: Banamex and Celanese.[89]

Pablo had participated in textile companies and in the real estate business. He had also focused on the trade and administrative activities of La Francia Marítima.[90] Eventually he became closer to the Legorretas, a relationship that his family had strengthened in social clubs, particularly in the Club Hípico Francés, an equestrian club founded by members of the Barcelonnette colony. This relationship and his own abilities allowed him to become an important partner of Banamex and Celanese Mexicana.[91] He became a proprietary member of the Banamex board of directors in 1957 and held this post until 1979, when he was appointed an honorary member of the board of directors until the nationalization of the banks in 1982.[92]

After its establishment in 1944, Celanese Mexicana soon became one of the leaders in Mexican synthetic textile production. Constant funding provided by Banamex supported the growth of this company. In fact, it was classified as the fourteenth-most-important company in the country between 1944 and 1980, including private and public capital and financial institutions, due to its economic influence.[93] In 1959, Pablo Jean was appointed general director—a role that he filled for the next two decades.[94] Pablo also became president of the Club Hípico Francés. This club is where Emilio Azcárraga Milmo, president of Televisa, met Pablo Jean's daughter Nadine.[95] Their son, Emilio Azcárraga Jean, who replaced his father at his death in 1997, is currently the wealthiest member of the Jean family in Mexico. However, he is not close to other members of the family.

At some point, the Jean family became divided.[96] From the first generation,

José had arrived late and was the first to die in the late 1920s. Adrián died in 1936. When the production of cotton and wool textiles transitioned into passive income for the Jean family, the other two brothers, Camilo and Alfonso, became more involved in the operation of the construction business in Mexico City. Adrián's branch became more involved in the construction business in the state of Mexico, in the commercial activities of La Francia Marítima and in the operation of new commercial businesses, in conjunction with other members of their new closest social network, which included the Legorreta family. For example, Parmex, created in the 1960s, was an importer of wines and liquors. Three of Adrián's sons founded the company—Pablo, Casimiro, and Emilio—in conjunction with the Legorretas. Claude, Adrián's oldest grandson, also worked there. This company supplied all the wine and liquor to Banamex, among others.[97] After Parmex, Emilio continued with the liquor business and founded a new company called Cittec.[98]

Members of the Jean family who were more engaged with the textile mills clung to them and sold them late, which weakened them economically. Other Barcelonnettes sold their factories at a better time, keeping only their stores, as was the case with the owners of the department store Liverpool. The textile factories frequently struggled in the hands of new buyers such as Gerardo Rodríguez, who purchased the Río Hondo factory in the 1960s, following which "it broke down in his hands."[99] Gerardo Rodríguez was a nephew of Alberto J. Pani, an important public servant of the federal government in the 1920s and 1930s, a member of the Club Hípico Francés, and later a key leader in the hotel industry. Relations with politicians of the time through the Club Hípico Francés gave members of the Jean family an opportunity to rid themselves of old factories, in spite of their initial stubbornness in continuing to operate them.

In the late 1930s and throughout the 1940s, companies belonging to the Jean family bought and sold parcels of land in different parts of Mexico, such as Oaxaca, Michoacán, Puebla, and the state of México.[100] This may have been the result of speculation, but there is also evidence that they were seeking to expand the construction business begun in Mexico City elsewhere in the republic. The Jean family also expanded its properties in the country as a result of the liabilities that some of its clients had with the CBPM and La Francia Marítima. These clients left properties as collateral in exchange for credit and goods.[101] This guarantee was exercised in some cases, which increased the assets of the Jean family's companies. Some of these properties were sold and some were used for the construction business.[102]

As with other Barcelonnette companies, the commercial business La Francia Marítima could not maintain the vertical integration that characterized the

Porfirian period and the first decades after the revolution; that is, the textile mills associated with this store no longer supplied products to be sold there. Some textile products began to be obtained from factories owned by Jews or Arabs. In a later period, some clothes, fine lace, and cloth were imported from France, using another company founded by the Jean family called Astor. Ultimately, as mentioned above, La Francia Marítima was sold in 1981.

Many notable intellectuals, such as Daniel Bell, Thorstein Veblen, and Pierre Bourdieu, have speculated on the relationship between economic and cultural capital. According to Bourdieu, cultural capital refers to the cultural knowledge that serves as a currency that helps us navigate culture and alters our experiences and the opportunities available to us. Cultural capital includes material objects and formal and informal education. Bourdieu's analysis also focuses on the symbolic elements that embody cultural capital, such as tastes, manners, skills, and credentials.[103] There is also some fine historical and ethnographic work on the evolution of Latin American elite families over generations (e.g., by Stuart Voss and Larissa Adler Lomnitz, among others) that presents evidence on how the construction of wealth in these families has affected cultural capital in Latin America.

Related to this, the study of social mobility has generated a boom among intellectuals and institutions in recent years. Social mobility refers, in general terms, to the ascending or descending movements made by individuals, families, or social groups within a given socioeconomic system. Even though cultural capital is not necessarily about money, it could be exchanged for money. So, an ascendant variation in terms of social mobility will allow an individual to access new opportunities to increase cultural capital, which will be reflected in most of their decisions and activities in different arenas in the future. In Mexico, the Centro de Estudios Espinosa Yglesias is the main think tank that specializes in the study of this topic. Next, I use the prosopography that I constructed of the current generation of Jeans to address larger questions raised by scholars and institutions like these.

The Current Generations

Various Barcelonnettes families arrived in Mexico without economic capital. When they eventually built this capital, especially from the last third of the nineteenth century, it put them in a predatory position within leisure, according to Veblen. A large proportion of Barcelonnette descendants could access new alternatives to cultural capital; that is, diverse activities and professions of another nature, not necessarily related to the effective creation of wealth through productive work. In that sense, Veblen qualifies leisure as a predatory aspect since it ultimately dissociates itself from the generation of new wealth.

This, in turn, creates class distinctions of manners and diverse tastes that give capitalism its cultural legitimacy.[104]

Bell delves into these ideas, studying the cultural contradictions of capitalism, and mentions that the prevailing capitalist philosophy supports the idea that capitalism "serves as the basis for freedom, the elevation of the standard of living and the overcoming of misery." Bell relates this aspect to the fact that modern culture, which has a clear individualistic character, is defined by the extraordinary freedom to achieve self-realization. This freedom provides ample space to perform a wide range of activities once economic liberty has been obtained.[105] That is partly why we can observe a diverse range within the activities and professions carried out by the new generations of the Jean family.

Larissa Adler Lomnitz and Marisol Pérez Lizaur, who have studied the activities and professions of descendants of elite Mexican business families, mention that these are related to the same family business or to professions associated with business or to professions with their own prestige. "Being employed by a company is considered a step towards a business career, but lifelong employees are despised by conformists. The independent professions are estimated if they have their own prestige (doctors) or are useful to build a company (architects, engineers, chemists). Political posts [which is not the same as having relations with politicians] or employment in public administrations are rejected as inadequate for the Gómez,"[106] which is the family that Adler Lomnitz and Pérez Lizaur studied. Balmori, Voss, and Wortman, analyzing this topic in families of the Argentinean economic elite, expanded the list of useful professions to business activities, mentioning qualifications in law.[107] Adler Lomnitz and Pérez Lizaur affirm that the Gómez family in Mexico did not value cultural activities, "such as reading, attending a concert or visiting a museum, which are activities appreciated by other bourgeois cultures, [but] perceived by the Gomez as a waste of time."[108]

These aspects force us to differentiate between families of the Mexican economic elite because the values that guide them (defining value as what is chosen instead of other alternatives at a moment in time) cannot be generalized. That is, it cannot be generalized that access to economic capital is necessarily reflected in similar cultural capital preferences among families that have had access to wealth.

In addition, Bourdieu states that economic capital can be used to obtain cultural capital, but this is not a rule, and, in this regard, distinctions exist even between members of a family. Bourdieu describes the sophisticated manners and tastes of the ancient nobility, who valued art and literature, and contrasts them with the more materialistic tastes and badges of the new rich, who often prove their status with luxurious styles of life, large houses, and cars.[109] This leads us once again to conclude that the aspects that have weight in each elite family's cultural capital decisions are variable, depending on their origins and their values.

When the Jeans arrived in Mexico, French culture was the most appreciated in the world. This gave them immediate social ascent and many opportunities, thanks also to racial aspects and the Mexican culture discussed above. In addition, the region from which the Barcelonnettes came (southeast France) was also influential in determining their cultural position from their arrival in Mexico. In Barcelonnette, many of them had been engaged in activities such as teaching and the priesthood, which they mixed with itinerant commerce and sheepherding; as mentioned before, the Barcelonnettes stopped supplying their excess priests and teachers to the surrounding regions of France when Mexico began to offer better alternatives. Thus, they also arrived in Mexico with a higher cultural level than other groups that became wealthy in this country in the same period. The economic capital they earned over the years was used to increase this cultural capital.

Although not all the Jeans persisted within the economic elite over the years, all remained within the middle class.[110] They had access to private education and shared spaces with members of Mexico's elite, which allowed them to maintain their values: art, culture, travel, academic preparation, and luxuries, among others. Adler Lomnitz and Pérez Lizaur describe this as "the taste for the good life: good schools, beautiful cars, swimming pools, trips, and friendships with the offspring of important people. . . . [That is,] they are taught the values inherent to their social class."[111] In other words, the ascendant social mobility that they once experienced in Mexico has never ceased to give most members of the family access to cultural and social spaces that have allowed them to perform multiple activities and practice diverse professions in different sectors of the economy; some of them, in line with Veblen's ideas, not necessarily related to the effective creation of wealth through productive work.

Many members of new generations of the Jean family have lost the link with French institutions, partly because they have assimilated into Mexican culture over the years. Many have married Mexicans and live in Mexico City, Puebla, and the state of México—still the states in which the Jean family's business developed. They have attended private schools, such as Oxford School in Mexico City, Centro Escolar Cedros, and the Instituto Cumbres, and they have studied at a wide variety of private universities in Mexico, like the Universidad Anahuac, the Universidad Panamericana, and the Instituto Tecnológico Autónomo de México (ITAM).

Current members of the Jean family perform a variety of activities, mainly in the private sector, in areas such as municipal and cleaning services, the media, and the artistic, commercial, and education sectors. Pamela Jean, a member of the fourth generation of the Jeans in Mexico, is a professor in communication studies at the Universidad Anáhuac and works for several media enterprises, like Cadena 3 and Efekto TV. She also founded a company that focuses on effective communication, Lenguaje Persuasivo,[112] and is in a rock band called Leftovers. Christian Jean, also a member of the fourth generation, has a fairly popular rock band named Reyno, formed in 2012, which had released three studio albums and one live album at the time of writing.[113] Guillermina Jean is the director of retail sales for MEPSA, a provider of kitchenware and glassware for hotels, resorts, restaurants, universities, cruise ships, industrial kitchens, dining rooms, and executive culinary schools.[114] Thierry Jean is one of around forty members of the board of directors of Club France today. His family manages a business, Optical Securities de México, which focuses on brand protection technologies and systems and document security technologies. Regina Jean established herself in Puebla and has become a promising modern art painter.[115]

Other Barcelonnettes

The Ebrards and Michels are two other families from the Barcelonnette valley, some of whose members remain prominent within the Mexican political and economic elite in the present day. El Puerto de Liverpool and the corporation J. B. Ebrard and Co. were established in 1847 by Jean Baptiste Ebrard. Following the pattern of his countrymen, he developed relationships with other large company employers. He (J. B. Ebrard and Co.) and Manuel Ibáñez of Spain, for example, founded the BMM with other Barcelonnettes in 1882. This was followed by the foundation of Robert Tron and Co., again by Ebrard and other Barcelonnettes. By 1889, three of these companies (J. Ollivier and Co., J. B. Ebrard and Co., and J. Tron and Co.) partnered to found yet another: the CIDOSA. They remained partners until 1930.

J. B. Ebrard and Co., which later became J. B. Ebrard y Compañía Sucesores, also participated as a shareholder in Banco Central Mexicano and Compañía Bancaria de Paris y México, as well as in manufacturing companies, including the Compañía Explotadora de las Fuerzas Hidroeléctricas de San Ildefonso S.A., the Fábrica de Papel de San Rafael y Anexas S.A., and the San Ildefonso Fábrica de Tejidos de Lana S.A.[116]

The name Ebrard remains familiar to Mexicans, since Marcelo Ebrard Casaubon was the mayor of Mexico City from 2006 to 2012 and was appointed secretary of foreign relations (the equivalent to secretary of state in the United States) in the cabinet of the leftist federal government headed by Andrés

Manuel López Obrador in 2018. He is currently the closest man to the president. Having studied international relations at El Colegio de México from 1977 to 1981, he soon became involved in Mexican politics. Positions he has since held include federal deputy, undersecretary of foreign relations, and secretary of public security in the Mexico City government, with the support of various political parties, including the PRI, the Partido Verde Ecologista de México (PVEM), and the Partido de la Revolución Democrática (PRD).

The only business group of Barcelonnette origin continuing to trade successfully under the same name since the Porfiriato is led by the Michel family. Alphonse Michel partnered in J. B. Ebrard and Co. in the late nineteenth century in the running of El Puerto de Liverpool and holds shares in several Liverpool-associated banks and industries.[117] Max Michel Suberville, who died in 2016, was the thirteenth-richest billionaire in Mexico that year, according to *Forbes* magazine. He played a great role in convenience store chains and Coca-Cola's bottler, Fomento Economico Mexicano (FEMSA). A major shareholder in Liverpool, he also served as an honorary company chairman.[118]

There are now more Mexican residents of Barcelonnette origin than there are Barcelonnettes in the Ubaye valley. A great number adjusted to Mexican culture as they married Mexicans. Institutions begun by their ancestors are still central to many, as they still operate Club France, the Panteón Francés cemetery, and the Liceo Franco Mexicano. Henri Bremond—president of the Liverpool council estate, a shareholder in Banamex and Aeromexico, and chairman of the Patronato de la Asociación Franco Mexicana y Belga—has said that the presence of the Barcelonnettes in the Asociación Franco Mexicana y Belga, in particular, remains very noticeable even today.[119] In fact, the Panteón Francés provides an important source of income for some, one that continues to grow thanks to the cemetery's association with Mexican elites.

When asked how he successfully maintained the only major Barcelonnette-controlled department store, Bremond explained that they had kept abreast of labor issues and subdued anarcho-syndicalist presence. He noted they have no union and that their workers are skilled. "The department of human resources does an excellent job maintaining a positive work environment and is selective in its hiring," he said. The expansion of their retail business to provide customer credit, real estate, and even insurance clearly owes itself to those sound practices.

Finally, Bremond mentioned another key factor for survival: "We have always gotten along with the government. I visit Peña Nieto often, but this is historic; we hardly would have survived without it."[120] Minouche Suberville, former president of Raíces Francesas en Mexico, said as much in a July 2012 interview: "Whoever tells you that the Barcelonnettes did not have close links with the government is lying. During the Porfiriato, politicians were directly linked to the banks controlled by Barcelonnettes, and in other economic sectors controlled by the French, even though the politicians did not appear on the councils and did not sign, many of them were closely linked to the businesses." "The Tron family, of Barcelonnette origin, who grew wealthy in Mexico, granted use of their tomb when Porfirio Díaz died in France, where he was temporarily interred before being moved to Montparnasse Cemetery," she said.[121]

In this chapter, we have studied aspects that led to the decline in economic power of different members of the Barcelonnette group in Mexico. We explained the elements that allowed some Barcelonnette families to remain within the economic elite. We have seen that labor militancy and the emergence of a new labor regulation as a result of the Mexican Revolution had serious consequences for the modernization of traditional cotton and wool textile mills in the whole country. In addition, the growth of competition with synthetic textiles and their producers toward the mid-twentieth century displaced traditional producers, who sought alternative forms of subsistence such as housing construction, in some cases with great success. Another key aspect of the subsistence of a large percentage of this French group was their connection, even through marriages, with other powerful families of the Mexican economic elite.

In chapter 5, we continue to examine the progress of relationships between business leaders and politicians and the appearance of new groups of cronies during the twentieth century. I show how old business practices persist in Mexico and how these hinder the creation of a strong institutional environment supported by the rule of law. I argue that crony capitalism is one of the most difficult forms of corruption to control in modern-day Mexico, despite regulatory advances.

CHAPTER FIVE

Reflections on Corruption in Mexico

With the passage of time, the French business network created by the Barcelonnettes throughout the Porfiriato and the first third of the twentieth century vanished. Descendants of the first Barcelonnettes began to fuse with the rest of Mexican society, and those who persisted among the business elite after the Mexican Revolution gradually lost the characteristics that had distinguished them during the Porfiriato. Their absorption of local culture made them ever more Mexican; for example, speaking Spanish instead of French, sending their children to schools and social clubs outside of the French community, and marrying Mexicans. Also, important operating mechanisms of their social business networks disappeared. Migration from Barcelonnette to Mexico had almost stopped by the beginning of the twentieth century, so Barcelonnette entrepreneurs in Mexico could not continue to hire French employees exclusively. Supply chain dynamics and the growth of enterprise through Barcelonnette partnership could not be maintained.

However, the decline of the classic business dynamics that these ethnic entrepreneurs employed did not weaken crony capitalism in Mexico, for reasons that will be discussed in this chapter. Crony capitalism and insider lending played a key role in the stabilization and growth of economies that were adopting the paradigm of global capitalism.[1] In fact, countries that readily embraced capitalism in the late nineteenth century, such as Mexico, faced a variety of institutional weaknesses (which some neo-institutionalist authors have exaggerated), including regulatory and legal omissions. However, having previously solved institutional weaknesses, crony capitalism deeply limited the construction and evolution of formal institutions, including that of a robust legal system, keeping them weak and sequestered to the benefit of a few individuals in the medium to long term (to the present day).[2]

In this chapter, I examine the extent of crony capitalism and the ways in which it has permeated Mexican business culture throughout the twentieth century to the present day. I discuss the strategies that recent Mexican governments have employed to favor friends in various economic sectors. In particular, I show how the privatization of public companies implemented by president Carlos Salinas (1988–94) created a new group of wealthy Mexican businessmen. These included Carlos Slim who, ironically, also comes from a current of migration of ethnic entrepreneurs in Mexico, this time from the Middle East. The new group of entrepreneurs strengthened by Salinas was different from the traditional entrepreneurs and business families, some of whom had maintained control of the economy in Mexico since the Porfiriato. However, not all entrepreneurs of the Porfiriato were necessarily weakened in this new period. Some survived, as is the case of some members of the Jean family.

This chapter demonstrates how old business practices permeate contemporary business in Mexico and how these practices continue to hinder the creation of a strong institutional environment supported by the rule of law. I examine why this system has survived for so long. This chapter covers a selection of issues that still remain relevant and that are directly related to the most important concepts addressed by this book, including crony capitalism, networks, and corruption.

NEW GROUPS OF CRONIES IN MEXICO

An important number of entrepreneurs maintained their position within the Mexican power elite from the Porfiriato through to the late twentieth century as a result of crony capitalism. Between the 1940s and 1960s, when the traditional Porfirian economic elite continued to participate actively, the Mexican economy showed stable growth within an ISI model that required strong state involvement. However, the Mexican economy began to deteriorate from the 1970s and a change in economic paradigm was adopted during the 1980s, in great part due to pressure from developed countries (particularly the United States and the United Kingdom). This led to the liberalization of the economy, which included the privatization of most state-owned companies, and a restructuring of the economic elite as new business entrepreneurs were granted access to opportunities. Despite the emergence of greater economic competition, the neoliberal reform mainly led to a change in business leaders without changing the way of doing business in Mexico, ultimately supporting a new generation of cronies.

Despite the emergence of other business groups and the consequences of the Mexican Revolution, a large number of entrepreneurs were able to maintain their positions within the power elite in Mexico since the late nineteenth century. In addition, the business models for privileged individuals did not change much during the golden age of the PRI in Mexico (1940–70) compared to the golden era of Porfirio Díaz, except that new players played fundamental roles in the new coalitions of power within the new government corporatist model. In particular, these were organized industrial workers and peasants.

Table 5.1 shows some of the most influential Porfirian companies in Mexico between 1920 and 1980.

After the Mexican Revolution, beginning with the administration of Lázaro Cárdenas (1934–40), Mexico experienced a period of relative economic stability that it had not had for many years. This was an important factor in the growth and development of the economy, to the extent that the period between 1940 and the end of the sixties is identified as the "Mexican miracle."

This situation of price stability and economic growth of 5 percent on average in real terms was not unique to Mexico; the world generally benefited from significant economic stability during this period. In Mexico, beginning with the administration of Ávila Camacho (1940–46), the foundation was laid for the state to strategically adopt ISI. Although Mexico saw its industry grow in the Díaz period, a process that was strongly resumed in the 1930s and during WWII, ideological considerations began to emerge in the world that strengthened the idea that developing countries should minimize their imports, often manufactured, in favor of substitutes produced locally, promoting domestic growth. Mexico adopted this model, like most countries in Latin America, due in part to the influence of the Economic Commission for Latin America and the Caribbean (ECLAC) and the ideas of Prebisch and Singer regarding industrialization.[3] Import substitution resulted in extensive state involvement in the economy, which had the following characteristics:

An essentially closed economy with a high level of protectionism through special taxes and duties

Building measures for industrial growth through tax incentives

The growth of the finance industry, mainly through Nacional Financiera (a public development bank)

Central bank actions regarding monetary policy to balance the economy

Expansion of state enterprises

Table 5.1. Most influential Porfirian companies and banks, 1920–1980

Company	Owner	Sector
Banca Serfín, founded in 1977 and included the Serfín chain, Banco de Londres y México (1864), and Financiera Aceptaciones, S.A.	Private	Banking
Banco Nacional de México, S.A., founded in 1884, managed by the Legorreta family	Private	Banking
Cervecería Moctezuma, founded in 1894 in Orizaba, Veracruz, managed by the Suberbie brothers, then by Alberto Bailleres	Private	Manufacturing
Compañía de las Fábricas de Papel San Rafael y Anexas, S.A., founded in 1894 and managed by San Rafael Group and Banamex	Private	Manufacturing
Compañía Fundidora de Fierro y Acero de Monterrey, S.A., founded in 1900 by a group of Mexicans and Americans that included Antonio Basagoiti, Leon Signoret, and Vicente Ferrara	Private	Manufacturing
Compañía Telefónica Mexicana (TELMEX in 1947 after a merger), founded in 1882	Private-public-private again in 1991	Communications
El Puerto de Liverpool, founded in 1847 and owned partly by the Suberville family	Private	Retail
Ferrocarriles Nacionales de México, founded in 1908 through a partial nationalization of privately owned railroad lines and taken over by the government in 1937	Public	Transportation

Source: Based in part on data from Camp, *Los empresarios mexicanos*, 199–212.

Economic strategies were developed as general statements of national economic policy during this period and adapted to each president's administration. National economic policy would transform its political discourse according to the situation. This flexibility was shared by public administration, as the impetus for industrialization required governmental bodies to resolve the increasing complexity of a growing capitalist system to ensure the stability necessary for development.[4]

After the "Mexican miracle," some economic variables began to deteriorate during the 1970s, including price stability and the exchange rate, and deficits in public finances accompanied these changes, as well as external indebtedness.[5]

The heads of developed countries, led by Reagan and Thatcher, pressured the "developing" regions to change the economic model and approach to liberal paradigms that were resurgent in the world. They were able to exert this pressure partly because Latin American countries, starting with Mexico, could not continue to pay their huge foreign debts, ultimately declaring a moratorium in 1982. This situation allowed for international support from the IMF and the World Bank as countries initiated a series of economic adjustments: liberalizing the economy, reducing the state's role in it, encouraging the payment of foreign debt, and implementing fiscal deficit reductions and programs to control inflation.

The adjustment plan, termed the Immediate Economic Restructuring Program (PIRE) by Pres. Miguel de la Madrid (1982–88), played an important role in the privatization of parastatal organizations. By September 1985, 205 different entities had settled, transferred, sold, or merged, and 261 were in the process of doing so, leaving around 700 of the 1,155 that had existed in 1982. De la Madrid's successor, Salinas (1988–94), accelerated the process of liberalizing the economy; in fact, the privatization of the largest firms did not take place until Salinas came to power. He privatized banks (which López Portillo nationalized in 1982) as well as other public companies such as state-owned airlines, steel plants, and the state telephone monopoly. The revenue generated from the sales of these companies helped reduce the country's public debt until it was able to generate a fiscal surplus in 1992.[6]

The trade liberalization measures and sale of public enterprises, particularly in banking, weakened the position of the traditional economic elite that originated in the Porfiriato, who still held considerable economic power in the early 1980s (table 5.2).[7] These measures had more impact on the restructuring of the economic elite than any other event in the twentieth century, including the 1910 revolution.[8]

The restructuring of business groups that followed bank nationalization did not strongly threaten the status of industrial groups financially supported by the banks. However, entrepreneurs whose primary source of revenue was the banking system disappeared from the pinnacle of business.[9] Examples of this include Manuel Espinosa Yglesias, Pablo Deutz, José María Basagoiti, and Agustín Legorreta.

Privatization, deregulation, and new rules to attract foreign direct investment were initially beneficial, as they gave access to a variety of entrepreneurs who had no access to the big leagues during the 1970s and 1980s. These measures seemed to move the Mexican economy toward an economic model of perfect competition, away from one that facilitated monopolies. For example, the relative power of Grupo Alfa, a company that emerged in the steel sector in northern Mexico, dropped dramatically, allowing new Mexican and foreign

Table 5.2. Main economic industry groups before the bank expropriation of 1982

Industrial group	Family	Stock participation (%)
Cifra	Arango Arias	46
Hulero Euzkadi	Arocena-Urraza	34
Banca Cremi y Casa de Bolsa Cremi	Bailleres	99
Cervecería Moctezuma	Bailleres	40
El Palacio de Hierro	Bailleres	58
Industrias Peñoles	Bailleres	71
Mexicana de Aviación	Ballesteros	36
Moresa	Basagoti	28
Tabacalera Mexicana (Cigatam)	Basagoti	26
VISA	Garza Lagüera	72
Alfa	Garza Sada	78
Grupo Continental	Grossman y Grossman	60
Sociedad Industrial Hermes	Hank González	70
Consorcio Aristos	Kalchky Kaplan	63
París-Londres	Lebrun Cuzin y Charpenel	67
Loreto y Peña Pobre	Lenz	40
Industrias Syncro	Levin Podvilevich	56
Grupo Industrial Saltillo	López del Bosque	87
Holding Fiasa	Rodríguez Ruíz	63
Vitro y Cydsa	Sada González	53
Desc	Senderos Irigoyen	56
Grupo Industrial Bimbo	Servitje Sendra	80
Grupo Celulosa de Chihuahua	Vallina	52
Ponderosa Industrial	Vallina	89

Source: Morera Camacho, *El capital financiero*.

investors to participate in the sector. Before that, the Garza Sada family, the major shareholders of Alfa, was the only Mexican family that appeared on the list of billionaires in *Forbes* magazine.

Unfortunately, in the end, neoliberal reforms only passed the baton among the leading business owners in Mexico without changing any fundamental characteristics of the way of doing business. Despite the economic changes that emerged in the twentieth century, the economic groups have kept similar practices in their operations inherited from the Porfiriato. They can be identified by the following characteristics:

> Ownership and operation are in the hands of a small number of major shareholders.
>
> The links between the companies that form a network are long term. While legally independent, companies share ownership through informal mechanisms such as family or social relationships and the overlap of members of the boards of directors (interlocking directorates).
>
> Their network architecture leads companies to be integrated vertically or with a certain level of diversification (related, nonrelated, or geographic).
>
> For funding, companies are supported mainly by retained earnings that are distributed through their domestic capital markets or by the investment of securities in international financial markets and credit extended by the financial wing of their holdings (banks, brokerage firms, and insurance companies).
>
> There is some overlap between the majority shareholders, the boards of directors, and senior executives of various companies.[10]

These features, which still persist, cast doubt that Mexico has experienced a managerial revolution like the one that took place in the United States during the establishment of the railroad. In the latter case, the size of the companies and the multiple geographically dispersed units whose operations had to be coordinated meant that job functions became well defined and organizational charts were created to show chains of command and lines of communication.[11] In that way, skill management (by salaried managers) became fundamental to implement this managerial revolution.

In 1994, *Forbes* magazine showed fourteen Mexican billionaires on the list of the world's richest men. This was because there had been an exponential increase in the number of rich individuals from the country at the end of the Salinas administration, which was possibly only achieved as a result of monopoly profits. From that list, Carlos Slim, Roberto González, and Ricardo

Salinas Pliego stand out in particular. González developed the market for dry corn flour for tortillas, one of the most consumed foods in Mexico. He also acquired Banorte, one of the banks privatized by Salinas. During the process of privatization of state monopolies, Slim took control of Teléfonos de México, the only company providing telephone services in the country. Salinas Pliego became the top Mexican retailer of household appliances and also bought TV Azteca, the only other broadcaster in Mexico besides Televisa, from the government. In the late 1980s, none of these entrepreneurs were among the richest in Mexico. This does not mean that they had no links with members of the old economic elite, but their historical roots in business did not come from the traditional economic elite.

In the same way that Porfirian entrepreneurs shared the productive apparatus of the country with other economic groups that emerged later during the golden age of the PRI, the following have managed to survive to the present day: Arango (Aurrera-Walmart), Baillères (Grupo BAL), Azcárraga (Televisa), Michel Suberville (Liverpool)—the latter two with Barcelonnette blood. There are also a large number of foreign investors who have entered key sectors of the Mexican economy more recently. After an initial round of privatization of eighteen banking institutions that began in 1991, another round of mergers with foreign banks took place starting in the early 2000s, with Banamex-Citibank, BBVA-Bancomer, and Santander-Serfin among the most notable.

The growth of Mexican billionaires would be worth celebrating if the income growth of the general population had increased proportionately. However, Mexico is in the top 25 percent of the countries with the greatest economic inequality in the world. The Global Wealth Report for 2014 indicates that 64.4 percent of all income in Mexico was held by the top 10 percent of the population (table 5.3).[12] In addition, there is another problem with this newly created billionaire class in Mexico: most wealth creation has not come as a result of innovation. That is, entrepreneurs operating in Mexico are not creators of new ideas that become attractive products, whereby consumer preferences determine the rise of entrepreneurs in wealth. Their wealth is generated by the Mexican political-business system, which is based on cronyism and new forms of corruption, as we will see in the next section.

The Legorreta family is an example of an entrepreneurial family that played a key role in the elite during the ISI period but was excluded from the reprivatization that followed the process of bank nationalization. As we have seen, the Legorreta family played a key part in the Jean family's survival within the sphere of power in Mexico. Legorreta stood at the helm of Banamex until 1982, when it was expropriated. It was reprivatized in 1991, and, with the group led by Legorreta not allowed to buy back the bank, it was acquired by

Table 5.3. Richest Mexicans in the world, 2015

Rank	Name	Net worth (billions of US dollars)	Age	Source of wealth
#2	Carlos Slim Helu	77.1	75	Telecom
#77	German Larrea Mota Velasco	13.9	62	Mining
#121	Alberto Bailleres Gonzalez	10.4	84	Mining
#168	Ricardo Salinas Pliego	8	60	Retail, media
#201	Eva Gonda de Rivera	6.7	—	Beverages
#265	Maria Asuncion Aramburuzabala	5.6	52	Beer, investments
#381	Jeronimo Arango	4.3	89	Retail
#462	Antonio del Valle Ruiz	3.7	77	Chemicals
#577	Emilio Azcarraga Jean	3.1	47	Media
#782	Carlos Hank Rhon*	2.4	67	Banking
#894	Jose and Francisco Jose Calderon Rojas	2.1	61	Beverages
#1,054	Roberto Hernandez Ramirez	1.8	73	Banking
#1,312	Max Michel Suberville (perished in 2016)	1.45	83	Beverages
#1,324	Alfredo Harp Helu	1.4	71	Banking
#1,500	Rufino Gil Gonzalez	1.25	67	Steel
#1,533	David Penaloza Alanis	1.2	41	Toll roads

Source: Data from "World's Billionaires." *Forbes*, accessed on December 2, 2015, http://www.forbes.com/billionaires/list/#version:static_country:Mexico

*Roberto González died in 2012, but his interests are represented in this list by Carlos Hank Rhon, his son-in-law. Carlos Hank González, Roberto González's grandson, took over control of Banorte.

shareholders of the financial group Acciones y Valores de México (ACCIVAL), which had been founded twenty years before. Among the shareholders were Alfredo Harp Helú, a CPA who started in the business sector in 1970, and Roberto Hernández Ramírez, a business manager and former director of the ACCIVAL for several years. Both names can be found in table 5.3, which lists current billionaires. In 2001, Banamex was sold to Citigroup.

Agustín Legorreta was allowed to participate in the reprivatization of banks but to a very marginal extent and with a bank that had far less importance and economic clout than the one he had possessed before nationalization.

Legorreta became the head of the new financial group Multibanco Comermex, and claimed in February 1992 that this bank's disincorporation process had been transparent and a good deal for the government.[13] Eleven years later, the "good deal" ended up almost entirely in the hands of Scotiabank.

The privatization that occurred in some countries, like Mexico, was equivalent to the process of deregulation that took place in countries including the United States, especially between 1970 and 2000. It was done on the grounds that simpler and fewer regulations would lead to a raised level of competitiveness and therefore higher productivity, lower prices, and more efficiency overall. This consequently led to corruption, crony capitalism, and changes to the economic status of particular groups that were similar to the effects that privatization had in Mexico and Russia. Enron in the United States provides a clear example of this. According to James Kenneth Galbraith, the key question that the promoters of privatization and deregulation neglected to ask regards the effects of the process of moving from public to private or regulated to deregulated. Failure to consider the potential effects of these processes caused so much chaos in privatization in Mexico, as was the case with the deregulation of power generation and natural gas in the United States.[14]

CORRUPTION AND THE MYTH OF TRANSPARENCY AND ACCOUNTABILITY IN MEXICAN PUBLIC INSTITUTIONS: A NEW FORM OF CRONY CAPITALISM FOLLOWING THE LAWS

Corruption is a problem in most of the world, but Mexico is among the worst countries for corruption.[15] It has remained a constant despite changes in governments and governing parties, and academic circles have not addressed this problem with sufficient depth. One of the most pervasive forms of corruption is present in the acquisition of goods, services, and public works by government institutions from private entities through collusion, leading to one of the biggest areas of crony capitalism in Mexico today. Challenges remain in the implementation of transparency laws despite the creation of the National Anti-Corruption System in 2015, and many analysts consider these efforts to be mere simulations.[16] The persistence of corruption and the inability to curb it through adequate implementation of regulations has led to negative effects on labor markets and social mobility.

The NGO Transparency International (TI) was created in 1993. Since 1995, it has published an annual report on the state of corruption in the world, with the aim of putting the issue on the international agenda and finding ways to fight it. Figure 5.1 shows this index of the perception of corruption in 2014.[17]

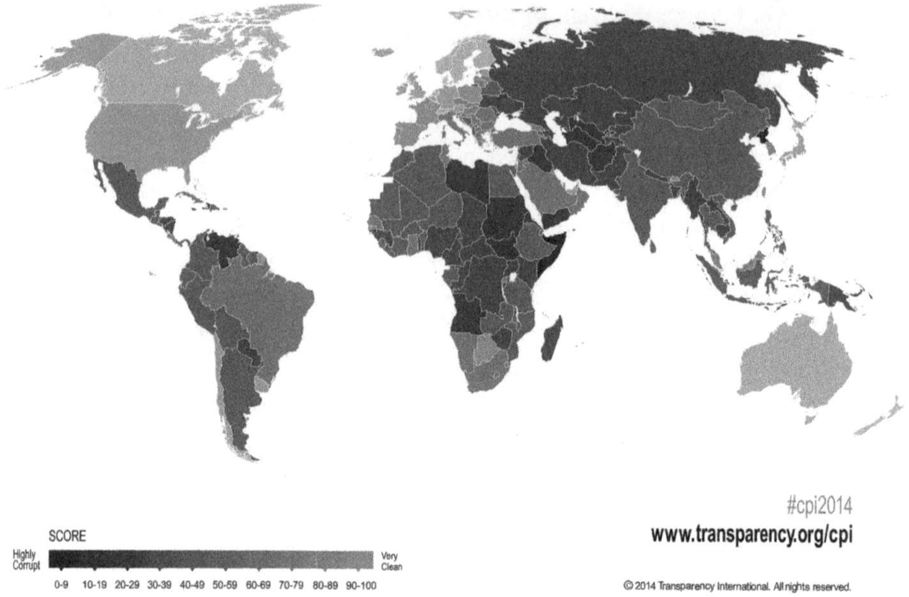

Figure 5.1. Index of the perception of corruption, 2014. (Transparency International, "Corruption Perceptions Index 2014: Results")

Corruption has permeated spaces one might think are less prone to it, such as the Vatican today. However, corruption in the Vatican, as well as the excesses of some of its leaders, has been a persistent problem throughout the centuries. The current pope, Francis, has acknowledged that corruption continues to eat through the Vatican.[18]

Figure 5.1 shows that approximately two-thirds of the countries in the world have serious corruption problems. The following countries are the twenty most-corrupt places in Latin America, according to the 2014 report: Venezuela, Haiti, Paraguay, Nicaragua, Honduras, Guyana, Guatemala, the Dominican Republic, Ecuador, Argentina, Mexico, Bolivia, Suriname, Panama, Colombia, Trinidad and Tobago, Peru, Jamaica, El Salvador, and Brazil. Mexico ranked seventy-second out of 175 countries and territories included in the TI index for corruption in 2014. It is readily apparent that corruption and impunity are currently the biggest problems facing Mexico, and this has not changed—some might say it has even increased—in spite of the change of ruling political parties in government.

One aspect of corruption in Mexico that has not been addressed in the depth required within academic circles, and one where there is currently a strong drain on public resources, comes from the "theater" of purchases, service provision, and recruitment for public works by Mexican public institutions. Supposedly they are subject to a comprehensive system of controls to prevent corruption, including regulations for transparency and accountability.[19] However, public servants (generally high-ranked) at an institution collude with administrative employees, usually including the head of the administrative office for that institution ("Oficial Mayor") who is responsible for acquisitions of goods, services, and public works and with their business contacts. Together, they have discovered how to get around the entire anticorruption legal structure, doing business among themselves with public resources. This type of corruption, according to the classification presented in table 5.4, is collusive and falls under the classification of political corruption. That is, these are acts by senior public servants with connections to companies. However, since corruption is a phenomenon that operates in networks and the diverted public resources from corrupt actions in these cases also reach bureaucrats (lower-ranked public employees), this type of collusive corruption also falls under the classification of bureaucratic corruption.

This is where the biggest area of crony capitalism exists in Mexico today. In that sense, current crony capitalism can be defined as a form of collusive corruption between businesspeople and politicians that occurs in networks

Table 5.4. Types of corruption

	Bureaucratic corruption	Political corruption
Extortive corruption: the public servant extorts the citizen by doing his job conditionally in exchange for gifts or money	Provision of services (health, education, licenses, police)	Licenses, property, expropriation, court rulings
Collusive corruption: implies the collusion between different elements of the private and public sectors at different levels; public servants divert or misuse the public budget	Arrangements to avoid or deviate from standards (taxes, quality control, permits), public procurement	"Close links" between companies and politicians (with the capacity to manipulate regulations, including public services and works'), high-level recruitment, tax exceptions

Source: Based on Organisation for Economic Co-operation and Development (OECD), *Consequences of Corruption.*

and reaches the political and bureaucratic levels of public administration. Privatization processes, such as those highlighted in the previous section, do not occur every day and thereby particularly favor the friends of politicians.[20] However, there are other constant opportunities to favor those friends; for example, public tenders for goods, services, and public works of all kinds. These friends, in return, transfer a percentage of the earnings from the business into the politicians' bank accounts (or the accounts of people that function as their "strawmen"), among other mechanisms to compensate them. The problem with this kind of corruption is that it is almost impossible to trace if carried out meticulously.

The Procurement Process (the Main Mechanism of Contemporary Crony Capitalism in Mexico)

We will focus on the Law of Acquisitions, Leases, and Public Sector Services (LAASSP) to understand the model of corruption (crony capitalism) related to this law. Through the LAASSP, all purchases of goods and services by the government are regulated. This law applies to all levels of government when local government acquisitions involve federal funds. This means that states and municipalities have their own norms with regard to acquiring goods or hiring services when using local resources—an issue outside the scope of this chapter. The application of the Law of Public Works and Related Services is also beyond the scope of this chapter. However, in both cases, the consequences are very similar to those that we will study next.

There are three basic procedures for the acquisition of goods and services: public tender, inviting at least three suppliers, and direct award. According to Article 42 of the LAASSP, public institutions may avoid a public tender procedure when acquiring goods and services (either inviting at least three suppliers or awarding directly) when the amount of each transaction does not exceed the maximum amounts established for that purpose in the federation's Expenditure Budget.

The maximum monetary sum for each purchase that comes as a direct award or an invitation to three suppliers is determined on the basis of the authorized budget of each public institution.[21] In general, the annual sum of operations conducted through direct awards and invitations to three may not exceed 30 percent of the assigned acquisitions budget at each public institution. However, autonomous public institution (such as universities, the National Human Rights Commission, the National Electoral Institute, etc.) are permitted by law to decide the amounts and limits for themselves. Public tenders may be national or international (based on international trade agreements Mexico has signed). Each public institution has a specific area in charge of internal acquisition policies and an internal acquisitions committee, which has to follow the restrictions the law imposes.

The exercise of public resources is subject not only to the laws of acquisitions and public works stated above but also to the whole system of transparency and accountability. However, public servants of every institution have found ways to manipulate the system and favor their entrepreneur friends. Direct awards and invitations to three have virtually no restriction on buying from whichever suppliers (entrepreneurs) the public servant wants. For example, with an invitation to three suppliers, a corrupt public servant will simply issue a formal invitation to three suppliers, who are themselves often in collusion, and select the bid of the prechosen supplier.

Once the acquisition is concluded, the supplier shares its profits with the public-servant abettor(s). This may take the form of cash or bank deposits in "strawmen" accounts (called "the tithe," representing at least 10 percent of the profit), a luxury holiday, or provision of a special personal service related to the business activity of the benefiting company. In the case of public tenders, payments may include luxury homes at a discount (as with the white house of Peña Nieto) or the financing of political campaigns.

The process is a little more complex with public tenders because there are often disagreements among suppliers who did not win the bid, but the strategy employed by public servants in charge of such tenders is to determine specific product features that only their friend (supplier) can offer. Public tenders come with numerous requirements, so institutions can easily disqualify unwanted participants.

Today there are public servants who make acquisitions with expert management, "complying" with the law, making it virtually impossible to detect corruption unless there is negligence on the part of the public servants or businesspeople involved in the process (for example, when their calls are tapped or when they are photographed in public places). Although there are other similar forms of corruption, such as the use of framework contracts, public tender manipulation is a very common and extensively used form of corruption that includes politicians and businesspeople. It is perhaps the most lucrative form of crony capitalism that exists today.

It is noteworthy that not all tenders, direct awards, or invitations to three are fixed. There are some that are handled more cleanly, which is part of the theater of transparency. This is clearly only one type of corruption, but it is a fundamentally problematic one because it is so difficult to control. Under current legislation, the ethics of the people involved are the only effective limit to this type of corruption.

Labor Markets and Social Mobility in Mexico as a Consequence of Crony Capitalism

Closed social networks with links to influential politicians still exist as a mechanism that limits competitive markets and social mobility. Here, we will focus on social mobility in the labor market. A significant percentage of the jobs in the world are obtained through contacts, regardless of whether the country is economically developed. For example, Granovetter found that about 50 percent of jobs in the US state of Massachusetts were obtained through contacts.[22] In Mexico, most young people are not hired through competitive search markets but by using networks. To find a job, networks, rather than knowledge, are what really count in this country. According to a survey published in 2005, 31.6 percent of young people in Mexico got their first job through being hired by a friend, 18.2 percent were initially hired by a relative, 18.9 percent were recommended by a family member, 9.7 percent were recommended by an acquaintance, and only 4 percent got their first job through an employment agency.[23] Given the high percentage of referrals involved, young people entering the labor market do not necessarily have proper training nor the level of preparation required.

This analysis can be applied to different social strata, since networks vary considerably by stratum without being totally mutually exclusive. Many of the better-paying jobs are landed by friends, acquaintances, and relatives of some well-positioned contact, without necessarily being well qualified, which limits the possibilities for other individuals who may be better qualified for the job. Rarely is it the case that the friend or relative of the well-positioned contact is the best qualified for a certain position.

If we analyze this topic further, individuals whose contacts are not related to those in high public and private positions will struggle to rise to high positions, or their efforts will have to be much greater for them to ascend, since most of the highly sought-after public and private positions are taken by members of the power elite and their contacts. Those who manage to rise through the ranks and who did not originally belong to a network owe their success to a combination of skills, ranging from loyalty to their superiors, negotiating skills, and outstanding aptitude for business and/or politics.

However, there are other factors permeating the social network that give access: marrying network members always helps, and racial homogeneity and social status play an important role, especially for the business elite. For example, there are individuals or groups who share similar features or cultural values to Mexico's economic elite and who find it easier to penetrate certain areas, even though they do not come from these areas. Several groups of foreigners who arrived in Mexico in a condition of poverty, like the Barcelonnettes, have been assimilated by power groups in that country, although they did not have a similar socioeconomic status in their original country. While the Barcelonnettes are no longer the richest group, they remain fully integrated into the Mexican elite and race was of fundamental importance in this case.

To exemplify some of these assertions, I end this section with a story. The case was recently released of one of Carlos Slim's employees: Adrián Ramírez. The latter stated that he had managed to climb to an important position in Slim's business structure by the mid-2000s after starting from scratch thanks to his ability in business and his loyalty. This is a case of exceptional social mobility. Ramírez began as a bricklayer in the city of Delicias, Chihuahua, and took over Slim's telephone company, making it one of the most important in Colombia. Comcel, the company headed by Ramírez in Colombia, had triple the customers of Telefónica (its closest competitor) by 2007.

However, Ramírez was never able to penetrate the social sphere of Slim and his closest associates. According to Ramírez, "aristocratic family-name managers end up creating bureaucracies to maintain power at the expense of companies."[24] Ramírez defined them as "yellow ducks," considering himself a "black duck" for his humble origin, darker skin, and being the product of public education. He also thought that the "black ducks" were more creative and innovative. "The 'yellow ducks' do not let the 'black ducks' pass and become restless when the 'black ducks' begin to do things better than them."[25] Ramírez ended up on bad terms with Slim and his network, and he lost his job by the end of that decade.[26]

This is an exceptional, though temporary, example of ascendant social mobility, which was the product of Ramírez's outstanding qualities and a little luck. However, even cases like this do not occur except on rare occasions, and it is even more exceptional to permeate the social network sphere of the elite; a division is always maintained.[27] This division, along with widespread public concern about corruption, is partly what handed victory to Andrés Manuel López Obrador (AMLO) in the 2018 presidential elections. However, it seems that AMLO has also generated his own network with entrepreneurs. But the benefits obtained as a result of these alliances are likely to be used to perpetuate his regime, rather than to enrich people individually.[28]

AMLO has directly awarded more than 70 percent of public contracts in the first months of his government.[29] Regardless of whether the profits from these contracts are shared between businesspeople and politicians—which is not likely to happen because of the anticorruption discourse that AMLO uses and possibly because of a genuine intention to control corruption—AMLO favors businesspeople close to him. This arbitrariness in the management of public contracts applied by AMLO does not contribute to the formal institutional strengthening of the country. Rather, it generates biases and loyalties that may perpetuate his political regime at the expense of democratic consolidation, and it excludes other entrepreneurs as capable as those favored but punished for not belonging to the president's network.

In this chapter, we have analyzed how some elements of the type of capitalism implemented in Mexico during the Porfiriato have remained to the present day, benefiting new groups of business leaders allied with different governments over time through so-called crony capitalism. We have also seen that the techniques used to carry out this type of corruption (collusive corruption) have become more sophisticated. For example, on many occasions strategies have been implemented without violating the processes demanded by the laws of acquisitions of goods, services, and public works to enable businesspeople and politicians to benefit from public resources. The deviation of these public resources has had clear consequences for the progress of other groups in Mexican society, affecting social mobility—a topic that has also been addressed in this section.

Conclusion

Since I started studying crony capitalism, my perception of it has changed. The origin of crony capitalism goes back to the origin of capitalism itself. In fact, in many countries, crony capitalism has been instrumental in consolidating the productive apparatus. The need for capital for investment, for example, was one of the main features that stimulated the formation of social networks between entrepreneurs and government officials. However, crony capitalism in Mexico, which was a mechanism that could overcome institutional weaknesses during the Porfiriato, has paradoxically become a factor that weakens the few institutions of influence.

By studying the economic success of the Jean family, as exemplars of entrepreneurial immigrants, we have analyzed the characteristics of crony capitalism in the early twentieth century in urban and central Mexico. The story of the Jean family fits the general entrepreneurial pattern of many other Barcelonnette families who immigrated to Mexico: they rose from lowly positions to prominence in the textile industry and then diversified into other businesses beyond. However, there were also important differences between the Jeans and other Barcelonnettes. For instance, the Jeans kept their textile business within the family and did not participate in the large textile companies created by other Barcelonnettes, such as the CIDOSA and the CIVSA. Despite avoiding large consortia, they maintained a very important position in the Mexican textile business. Additionally, the Jeans' diversification into different regions and into sectors such as construction and hydroelectric power were business actions not undertaken by many other Barcelonnettes.

After many years of good performance, the Jeans shut down or sold their textile mills, which represented their most important business. Their last mill, La Magdalena, closed in 1973. The many causes that drove these factories out of business included competition with other ethnic entrepreneurs, especially Arabs and Jews, who created businesses from the 1920s onward, and the introduction of synthetic fibers after WWII. In addition, the descendants of the Jeans' first generation were unable to manage the business properly. Finally, other factors such as organized labor within the textile sector, which strengthened after 1912, and economic policies implemented in Mexico that restricted foreign trade through tariffs affected the competition of traditional textile mills in the following years.

In banking, the Jean family's experience was similar to that of other Barcelonnette investors. They obtained credit to finance their own textile mills, and the CBPM provided credit to other associates and friends, including government officials, strengthening their specific social network. However, the Compañía Bancaria's financial problems led to its purchase by Banamex in 1930. In the end, their experience in the banking sector meant the Jeans consolidated a close relationship with some of the owners of Banamex, particularly the Legorreta family. This connection, as well as that developed with the Azcárraga family in the Club Hípico Francés, which the Jean family managed, proved to be very important for the Jeans' economic future.

For the Jeans, the decline in the textile sector was offset due to their social networks. These connections allowed them to explore new economic activities. In addition, despite the strengthening of organized labor in Mexico after the revolution, which weakened the core business of the Jean family, the Jeans' connections with government officials also grew—in banking through Banamex, in media through Televisa, and in housing through links with groups such as the Rivera Torres family. In all these sectors, the members of the Jean family who could participate maintained privileges greater than the rest of Mexican society and those entrepreneurs who did not have the same social connections but perhaps enjoyed the same capabilities.

In the last chapter of this book, we saw how crony capitalism evolved in Mexico throughout the twentieth century and how new cronies, some of them also ethnic entrepreneurs, in association with government officials, used laws to obtain lucrative public contracts, sharing profits among them. This type of collusive corruption is difficult to control because the most powerful members of elites in Mexico manage it or benefit from it.

A distinctive characteristic of crony capitalism today is that it hinders the cohesion and solidity of institutions. In Mexico, potentially robust institutions are often weakened in Congress, where laws are passed that support the interests of different individuals from the power elite. The day-to-day operation of formal institutions may also be compromised, with the breaking or bending of regulations, as dictated by the power elite. These are only two of the many mechanisms employed to avoid the proper use of formal institutions in a country where violating the law rarely has consequences, particularly for privileged individuals.

In present-day Mexico, the weakening of once-strong institutions can be exemplified by the recent restructuring of the Federal Electoral Institute as the National Electoral Institute, which has erased significant progress on electoral matters. Similarly, newly created institutions usually protect the interests of the powerful, such as the Anti-Corruption System, approved in April 2015, and the General System of Transparency and Access to Public Information, which actually limits the right of Mexicans to access information on the use of public resources and on human rights issues. The creation of these two institutions, in particular, was delegated in part to young politicians of dubious moral quality and who are linked with the PRI old guard.

The problem of crony capitalism in Mexico, and in other countries with common characteristics, is entrenched because the process of building and strengthening formal institutions (e.g., monopoly control) did not occur in the same way as it did in other countries throughout much of the late nineteenth and twentieth centuries. This condition has limited the evolution of formal process within big business in Mexico, where productive processes and relations are not dependent on specific agreements between members of the groups in power.

Throughout the twentieth century, more developed countries like the United States created certain types of formal institutions and laws that partially controlled some of the effects of crony capitalism, at least for some periods. However, Mexico has continued to use tailor-made contracts that ignore the reasons for the existence of the country's acquisitions and antitrust laws. Ignoring those laws has, for example, led to the creation of inefficient monopolies that result from assigning contracts to specific friends and not from innovation, as is the case for many monopolies that emerge in the developed world (although this is not to say that monopolies due to innovation do not need to be controlled).

Networks of economic groups are present in many developing countries, as well as in advanced economies. These business groups constitute a network of legally independent companies that maintain formal and informal links in the long-term and take coordinated actions. Evidence from Mexico shows that this pattern of networks is relatively strong and it has survived for over a century despite major political and economic crises and various technological, sociodemographic, and institutional changes.

When the development of capitalism in Mexico became stronger from the last third of the nineteenth century, the presence of discretionary institutions and the high production costs of economic activity led to the substitution of efficient market mechanisms. This is something that in Mexico remains the rule and not the exception as a result of the practices of these business groups. That is, to persist and protect their interests, these groups promote an environment in which the rule of law is limited. This environment is characterized by a legal framework that does not arise from consensus, a poor and biased system of administration of justice, and a set of beliefs and cultural patterns that gives way to corruption, opportunism, and narrow social confidence.

Nowadays, Mexico needs both good leaders who are ethical and prepared and a proper mechanism to guarantee accountability and block opportunity for corruption throughout all stages of public decision making.[1] However, it is impossible to guarantee that leaders will be ethical and that they will penetrate the highest levels of power. The existence of ethical leaders who penetrate the upper levels depends on several factors, including serendipity. That is why institutional mechanisms that function properly and independently of individuals are so important, though their construction is extremely complex and not always durable.

In addition, where society (including activists, journalists, and academics) speaks with a united voice, taking advantage of new communication technologies and proposing scrutiny in different areas of public administration, there is also an opportunity to remove trash from the system. This could exert pressure to properly centralize and regulate the new Anti-Corruption System through a series of recommendations, perhaps forcing the government to accept international supervision (if necessary) and to propose counterincentives to combat collusive corruption.

Notes

Introduction

1. Institutions are defined here as "humanly devised constraints that structure political, economic and social interactions." According to Douglass North, constraints are devised as formal rules (laws, constitutions, property rights) and informal restraints (customs, traditions, taboos, sanctions, codes of conduct), which usually contribute to safety and order within a society or market. North, "Institutions," 97–112.

2. See Paxman and Galindo, "Capitalismo de Cuates."

3. Rosenmüller and Ruderer, in the introduction to their book *"Dádivas, dones y dinero,"* mention that few academic studies of the nineteenth century (after independence) and the first half of the twentieth century put corruption at the center of their analysis. However, a large number of studies that come from the neo-institutionalist school speak of the concept of crony capitalism, which stands out in the late nineteenth and early twentieth centuries. For Mexico, this subject has been researched mainly by neo-institutionalists in the field of economics of corruption, such as Stephen Haber, and other authors, including Edward Beatty.

4. Haber, *Crony Capitalism*, 12.

5. Rosenmüller and Ruderer, *"Dádivas, dones y dinero."*

6. There are other studies of corruption in Mexico from the cultural perspective, or field of study. An influential one was edited by anthropologist Claudio Lomnitz-Adler and published in 2000 (Lomnitz-Adler, *Vicios públicos*). In the book, the authors discuss three specific issues that they consider key for understanding corruption. First, they observe the historical transformation of the discourses of corruption as indexes of political, economic, and cultural transformation of the country; second, they analyze the role of administrative and political corruption in the formation of social classes; and third, they study the relationship between corruption and forms of political representation. In *Vicios públicos*, the authors focus on showing that the study of corruption from these aspects offers a privileged perspective for the cultural study of national societies.

7. Not all studies on corruption in Latin American countries that have an economic

perspective would agree on this point. Some of them show a certain inflexibility in judging corruption, based on considerations of moral or economic progress. These views do not take into account changes in cultural perspectives on corruption over time. For example, see Quiroz, *Historia de la corrupción*. There are many other studies of corruption in Mexico, going back to the colonial period, such as Pietschmann, "Corrupción," and Rosenmüller, "El grave delito" and *Corruption and Justice*. However, these studies are more focused on corruption as it was understood (defined) in the colonial period, which was more concerned with judicial aspects (in Rosenmüller's words: "Corruption in Mexico's colonial period meant violating the proper finding of justice") and later evolved to include administrative aspects.

8. Morris, "La corrupción en México."

9. Blake and Morris, *Corruption and Democracy*.

10. Blake and Morris, *Corruption and Democracy*, 2.

11. Morris, *Political Corruption*.

12. Casar, *México*, 49. Unless otherwise noted, all English translations provided in the text are my own.

13. Morris, "La corrupción en México."

14. Ballinas, "Reseña de 'Corrupción y cambio.'"

15. Pardinas, "La corrupción en México."

16. Sandoval, *Corrupción y transparencia*. Another important recent work that addresses corruption from a multidisciplinary point of view is Campos, *MeTrOP*, a study by México Evalúa, Centro de Análisis de Políticas Públicas, A.C. It argues the importance of transparency in public works, which is necessary to combat corruption in different areas of the Mexican government. This issue had also been previously addressed in publications by the secretaría de la función púbica (e.g., Sandoval, *Corrupción y transparencia*). Finally, in addition to investigations carried out by activists, there are works that disclose the level and impact of corruption in Mexico in recent years. These include Kaiser Aranda, *El combate a la corrupción*, and Cortez, *Ensayo sobre victimización*.

17. https://www.transparency.org (accessed February 28, 2019); Merino Huerta, "Prólogo," 17.

18. Waldinger, Aldrich, and Ward, "Opportunities," 13–48.

19. Rath, *Immigrant Businesses*.

20. Rath, *Immigrant Businesses*, 2.

21. Kloosterman and Rath, *Immigrant Entrepreneurs*. These authors previously explored different case studies demonstrating various aspects of the economic environment that influence the immigrant entrepreneur. These studies provide some evidence of the concept of embeddedness, which refers to the degree to which economic activity is constrained by noneconomic institutions. Rath and Kloosterman, "Economic Context."

22. Flap, Kumcu, and Bulder, "Social Capital." There are other important books that are worth mentioning in this historiographical review, such as Waldinger, Aldrich, and Ward, "Opportunities," which explores the different cultural, political, and economic backgrounds of immigrants that could influence the development and transformation of communities.

23. DeHart, *Ethnic Entrepreneurs*, 1.

24. Echánove Trujillo, *Manual del extranjero*, 35.

25. Kenny et al., *Inmigrantes*, 30.

26. Riguzzi, "From Globalisation to Revolution," 358.

27. Riguzzi, "From Globalisation to Revolution," 366.

28. For a detailed evaluation of the political economy of the Porfiriato and aspects that still need further research, see Riguzzi, "From Globalisation to Revolution."

29. There are different debates on the level of crony capitalism that countries faced in the early stages of their capitalist model and also on the level and characteristics of crony capitalism they face nowadays. See Paxman and Galindo, "Capitalismo de Cuates."

Chapter One

1. Among the most significant works about the French in Mexico are "Los franceses" by Jean Meyer; *Los Barcelonnettes en México*, ed. Leticia Gamboa Ojeda; and *Franceses*, ed. Leticia Gamboa Ojeda, Guadalupe Rodríguez, and Estela Munguía. Javier Pérez Siller has also contributed important works, including "Los Franceses"; the chapter "De mitos y realidades" included in the Meyer book mentioned above; and as editor of the book *México Francia*. Jean-Louis D'Anglade is also important to mention for his monograph *Un gran patrón Barcelonnette* about the economic development and decline of a specific Barcelonnette entrepreneur in Mexico, Joseph Ollivier.

2. Meyer, "Los franceses," 5.

3. Grajales Porras and Illades Aguilar, "Sobre franceses," 30.

4. Pérez Siller, "Los Franceses," 340.

5. Sims, *Descolonización*.

6. Pérez Siller, "Los Franceses," 341.

7. The Pastry War was mainly the result of not signing a preferential trade agreement with France, although the excuse for intervention was a series of claims against the Mexican government by Frenchmen established in Mexico. A claim interposed by a French citizen who owned a pastry shop in the town of Tacubaya stands out. He declared that, in 1832, officers of then president Antonio López de Santa Anna had eaten in his bakery without paying the bill. This event gives the intervention its name. The French government demanded a hefty settlement for that claim and several more, which the Mexican government refused. A French walkout in the port of Tampico exacerbated tension between the two nations. As a result, between February and March 1838, ten French warships arrived in Veracruz.

8. Pérez Siller, "Los Franceses," 340–43.

9. Most of the Mexican registers of the French population do not maintain a record of descendants or partners; they primarily only take into account heads of family. Additionally, the rules regarding the control of foreigners in Mexico were not very rigid, so the registers may have left some individuals uncounted.

10. Galán Amaro, "Estrategias," 47.

11. Meyer, "Los franceses," 7.

12. Gaulot, *Sueño de un Imperio*, 24.

13. For an explanation of the arrival of Maximilian and his role as emperor of Mexico, see: Pani, *Para mexicanizar el Segundo Imperio*; Ratz, *Tras las huellas*; and Schmelzer, "Maximiliano de México."

14. Meyer, "Los franceses," 11.

15. Pérez Siller, "Los Franceses," 345–46.

16. Meyer, "Los franceses," 7.

17. Skerritt Gardener, *Colonos franceses*, 49.

18. A letter sent in 1900 by Joseph Proal to the notary François Proal describes to possible immigrants the conditions of life in the French colony, from the collection at Archivo Museo de San Rafael in December 2014.

19. Skerritt Gardener, *Colonos franceses*, 50.

20. Pérez Siller, "De mitos y realidades," 116–20.

21. Meyer, "Los franceses," 10.

22. Meyer, "Los franceses," 10.

23. Meyer, "Los franceses," 10.

24. Pérez Siller, "Los Franceses," 357.

25. Pérez Siller, "Los Franceses," 357–61.

26. Pérez Siller, "Los Franceses," 362.

27. Fernández Christlieb, quoted in D'Anglade, *Un gran patrón*, 63.

28. Arnaud, *Les Barcelonnettes*, 63.

29. See Fernández Christlieb, "La influencia francesa."

30. Hale, "José María Luis Mora," 205–6.

31. Hale, "José María Luis Mora," 205–6.

32. Although Díaz created a despotic liberal state in Mexico, he did so using Juárez's blueprints. Juárez and Lerdo de Tejada were not exactly uncompromising democrats. Juárez has been blamed for introducing machine politics, strengthening, for example, the figure of the *jefe político* and the *rurales*, two official bodies that were used in part to control (repress) the population and maintain order, often using violent means. In addition, the strategy of generating informal alliances (above the law) with regional strongmen to centralize national power, which was widely used by Díaz, arose from a strategy originally implemented by Juárez.

33. González Navarro, "Las ideas raciales." Charles Hale and William Beezley, among other authors, give a good account of the transformations that Mexico's liberalism underwent throughout the nineteenth century. See Hale, *Transformation*, and Beezley, "Kaleidoscopic Views."

34. Meyer, "Los franceses," 25.

35. D'Anglade, *Un gran patrón*, 84–85.

36. Meyer, "Los franceses," 28.

37. D'Anglade, *Un gran patrón*, 51.

38. Galán Amaro, "Estrategias," 73.

39. Gómez-Galvarriato Freer, "Los Barcelonnettes," 195–96.

40. D'Anglade, *Un gran patrón*, 110.

41. Topik, "When Mexico Had the Blues," 723.

42. Haber, *Industry and Underdevelopment*, 12.

43. Garner, *Porfirio Díaz,* 170–72.
44. Garner and Martínez Rodríguez, "Fomento," 91–92.
45. Sierra Moncayo, *Atlas histórico*, 264.
46. Gómez-Galvarriato Freer, "Los Barcelonnettes," 194.
47. D'Anglade, *Un gran patrón*, 133.
48. Meyer, "Los franceses," 30.
49. D'Anglade, *Un gran patrón*, 149.
50. Meyer, "Los franceses," 31.
51. Haber, *Industry and Underdevelopment*, 69.
52. D'Anglade, *Un gran patrón*, 214.
53. D'Anglade, *Un gran patrón*, 219.
54. Meyer, "Los franceses," 34–35.
55. Galán Amaro, "Estrategias," 120.
56. Meyer, "Los franceses," 35.
57. D'Anglade, *Un gran patrón*, 218.
58. D'Anglade, *Un gran patrón*, 219–20.
59. D'Anglade, *Un gran patrón*, 334.
60. Enrique Canudas Sándoval, quoted in Galán Amaro, "Estrategias," 144.
61. Meyer, "Los franceses," 35.
62. Notary Public 5 Mexico City: Bernardo Cornejo, October 28, 1909, vol. 51, deed 3542, 1–18, Archivo General de Notarías de la Ciudad de México.
63. Notary Public 5 Mexico City: Bernardo Cornejo, October 28, 1909, vol. 51, deed 3542, 1–18.
64. Archivo Histórico Banamex, Compañía Bancaria de París y México, General Assembly Reports.
65. Cosío Villegas, *Historia moderna*, 1061.
66. Haber, *Industry and Underdevelopment*, 64–65.
67. D'Anglade, *Un gran patrón*, 149.
68. Beatty, *Institutions and Investment*, presents an in-depth analysis of Díaz's protectionism of nascent industries. This work will be discussed later.
69. Though much has been written about Esteban de Antuñano and the birth of the modern Mexican textile industry, Evelyne Sánchez offers a detailed and updated character and historical analysis, including how the difficult political context presented problems for economic decision making. Her work shows how, by the mid-nineteenth century, the creation of economic activity in Mexico depended on the spaces that political authorities opened to it, as was the case in the Old Regime. See Sánchez, *Las élites empresariales*.
70. D'Anglade, *Un gran patrón*, 306–7.
71. García Díaz, "La construcción," 64.
72. D'Anglade, *Un gran patrón*, 306–7.
73. Meyer, "Los franceses," 36.
74. Notary Public 5 of Mexico City: Bernardo Cornejo, November 9, 1909, vol. 53, deed 3564, 17–25.
75. Meyer, "Los franceses," 33. The FDI/Domestic Investment ratio is unavailable.

There are only more or less informed conjectures about the FDI/Total Foreign Investment ratio, which are outlined in D'Olwer's study in Cosío Villegas, *Historia moderna*. This remains the most informative text on foreign investment in Mexico in that period. A conceptual and accounting complication for the date of 1910 comes from the case of Ferrocarriles Nacionales de México (National Railroads of Mexico); due to the "Mexicanization" of the company, those who controlled the stock packages became bondholders, thus representing an investment portfolio in a Mexican company that the government controlled. It was a large financial operation that has been studied in Valencia Islas, *El descarrilamiento*. Otherwise, one could say that FDI was clearly superior to foreign portfolio investment (which includes holdings of foreign and domestic debt and smaller holdings in Mexican financial and industrial companies) by 1910.

76. D'Anglade, *Un gran patrón*, 434.

77. Béraud-Suberville, "Centinelas," 269.

78. D'Anglade, *Un gran patrón*, 381–82.

79. Garner's story analyzes the nature of Pearson's extensive business activities during those thirty years. At the same time, Garner questions the traditional thesis about the vulnerability of developing economies and supposed exploitation by the great economic powers. Garner realizes the effectiveness of the Mexican political elite in building their nation project by taking advantage of foreign capital and technology. His study then contrasts and balances two opposing views: that of Mexican nationalist historiography, which has seen Weetman Pearson as an agent of the avaricious British Empire, and that of his English biographers, who have characterized Pearson as a prototype of the successful businessman in the golden age of British imperialism. See Garner, *British Lions*. In a recent book, Mark Wasserman reaches a similar conclusion, demonstrating that Mexicans controlled their economy from the 1880s through 1940 and that foreigners did not exploit the country. Wasserman also notes that Mexicans established, sometimes shakily, sometimes unplanned, a system of relations between foreigners, the economic elite, and the government (and later also unions and peasant organizations) that maintained checks and balances on all parties. In addition, Wasserman argues that Díaz encouraged US investors in northern Mexico into sectors like mining, where Mexican investors lacked technological knowledge and were risk averse. See Wasserman, *Pesos and Politics*.

80. Pérez Siller, "De mitos y realidades," 104.

81. Gamboa Ojeda, *Los Barcelonnettes*, 13.

82. Gamboa Ojeda, *Los Barcelonnettes*, 13–15.

83. Gamboa Ojeda, *Los Barcelonnettes*, 14.

Chapter Two

1. Zuckerman, "The Concept," 344.

2. Camp, *Mexico's Mandarins*, 11.

3. Domhoff, *Who Rules America Now?*

4. Wasserman, *Persistent Oligarchs*, 10.

5. Galindo, "Some Considerations."

6. Field, Higley, and Burton, "New Elite Framework."

7. Mexico is a country of regions, but, first, Díaz forming alliances with local strongmen—and then, Obregón, Calles, and Cárdenas using institutions (like the PNR-PRM-PRI), political practice, and in many cases coercion—succeeded in gradually imposing the will of the center over the regions.

8. This does not mean that they have not found forms of cooperation, both positive and negative, between them. Negative cooperation is generally associated with doing business together using public resources, leading to crony capitalism.

9. Camp, *Mexico's Mandarins*, 12.

10. Also, Mexico's bourgeoisie has always sought to acquire real estate because of its perceived safety and the cultural prestige associated with it. This is part of the cultural legacy of colonialism.

11. Razo, *Social Foundations*, 18.

12. Reynolds, *Mexican Economy*, 169.

13. Newell and Rubio, *Mexico's Dilemma*, 19.

14. Rajchenberg, "La industria," 274.

15. Haber, Razo, and Maurer, *Politics of Property Rights*.

16. Maurer, *Power and Money*, 15.

17. Musacchio and Read, "Bankers."

18. Collado, *Empresarios y políticos*, 329–38.

19. An interesting study offering historical context to the foundation of the Banco de México is Hall, *Oil, Banks, and Politics*.

20. Haber, *Industry and Underdevelopment*, 140.

21. The particularities of the Monterrey group and its connections to politicians, such as Saénz and Almazán, is studied in detail in Saragoza, *Monterrey Elite*, and Snodgrass, *Deference and Defiance*.

22. Haber, *Industry and Underdevelopment*, 181.

23. Building strong ties with the new revolutionary governments was not only a key aspect for those Barcelonnettes who survived the period between 1910 and 1930 in Mexico, such as members of the Jean family, but also for all of the elements of the old oligarchy that persisted over the years within the highest spheres of the Mexican economic elite.

24. Haber, *Industry and Underdevelopment*, 140.

25. Shadlen, *Democratization*, 634–41 (e-book version).

26. Medina Peña, *Hacia el nuevo estado*, 117.

27. Haber, *Industry and Underdevelopment*, 182.

28. Thorp, *Progress, Poverty and Exclusion*, 117.

29. Thorp, *Progress, Poverty and Exclusion*, 141.

30. Haber, *Industry and Underdevelopment*, 187.

31. Mosk, *Industrial Revolution*, 21.

32. Shadlen, *Democratization*, 737–44.

33. Shadlen, *Democratization*.

34. Niblo, *War, Diplomacy and Development*.

35. Medina Peña, *Hacia el nuevo estado*, 126.

36. Shadlen, *Democratization*.

37. Buve, "Un paisaje lunar," 121–51.

38. Katz, *Secret War*, 28.

39. Nickel, *El peonaje*, 14.

40. They also go deeper into the discussion of landowning elites before and after the revolution. Escobar Ohmstede and Butler, *Mexico in Transition*.

41. Tenorio Trillo and Gómez-Galvarriato Freer, *El Porfiriato*.

42. Kuntz Ficker and Speckman Guerra, "El Porfiriato," 514.

43. Chassen, "Capitalismo," 158–59.

44. Katz, *Secret War*, 11.

45. Wasserman, *Persistent Oligarchs*, 69–74.

46. Wasserman, *Persistent Oligarchs*, 69.

47. Knight, *Mexican Revolution*, 519.

48. Womack, "Mexican Revolution," 136.

49. In the vertical political integration (VPI) model, a third party (many actors can be a third party; for example, the military generals and organized labor played various third-party roles in Mexico at different times) receives an economic benefit from the second party (owners: mainly landowners, industrialists, and bankers) to ensure compliance with an informal agreement between the first party (the government) and second party (the owners). This agreement ensures governmental protection of the owners' property rights, as well as other policies favorable to their interests. In return, the owners guarantee an income for the government, generally through taxes. In practice, government officials may also receive personal economic benefits directly from the owners or participate on the boards of their companies, strengthening the alliances that guarantee owners' property rights and the viability of contracts.

50. Haber, Razo, and Maurer, *Politics of Property Rights*, 313.

51. See Galindo, "Some Aspects."

52. Paul Gillingham's work on Alejandro Mange in Veracruz shows a specific case that is an exception to the general historiography of the topic that considers that the power and influence of generals had weakened considerably as a result of the institutionalization of the Mexican military, carried out in part by Gen. Joaquín Amaro, whereby the army was professionalized and depoliticized. Gillingham shows that "General Mange's Veracruz *cacicazgo* offers an illuminating case study in military autonomy. The general powerfully influenced life in Veracruz, first as a zone and later as a regional commander, for twenty-two years [1937–59]." In addition, Gillingham shows that Veracruz gave Mange rich business opportunities as it was one of the wealthiest states. Gillingham, "Military *Caciquismo*," 228.

53. Medina Peña, *Hacia el nuevo estado*.

54. Josué Sáenz, quoted in Mosk, *Industrial Revolution*, 112.

55. Davis, *Urban Leviathan*.

56. Wasserman, *Persistent Oligarchs*, 72–73.

57. Buve, *El movimiento revolucionario*, 229.

58. Camp, *Entrepreneurs and Politics*, 80.

59. Gómez-Galvarriato Freer, "Measuring the Impact," 289–323.

60. Neo-institutionalist explanations employ a model that lacks the historical

perspective to determine how much Díaz introduced institutions, rules, and laws compared to earlier times. In addition, the narrow look at crony capitalist arrangements blinds some neo-institutionalist studies, such as Razo's, to institutions and laws and rules. Finally, most neo-institutionalist explanations ignore microlevel historical evidence. Although Beatty was formed at Stanford, the cradle of neo-institutionalist interpretations of Mexican history, he took a different perspective in his analysis of the Porfiriato.

61. Sharafutdinova, *Political Consequences*, 23.
62. Prins, *All the Presidents' Bankers*.
63. Haber, *Crony Capitalism*, 12.
64. Haber, *Crony Capitalism*.
65. Haber, *Crony Capitalism*, 16.
66. Sharafutdinova, *Political Consequences*, 23–24.
67. Sharafutdinova, *Political Consequences*, 2.
68. Haber, *Crony Capitalism*, 7–8.
69. Haber, *Crony Capitalism*, 8.
70. Haber, *Crony Capitalism*.
71. Sharafutdinova, *Political Consequences*, 27–34.
72. Sharafutdinova, *Political Consequences*.
73. North et al., "Limited Access Orders" (accessed March 6, 2019).
74. Steinmo, Thelen, and Longstreth, *Structuring Politics*.
75. Sharafutdinova, *Political Consequences*, 25.
76. Sharafutdinova, *Political Consequences*.
77. Coatsworth, "Structures."
78. Razo, *Social Foundations*, 15–16.
79. Razo, *Social Foundations*, 170.
80. Razo, *Social Foundations*, 171.
81. Gómez-Galvarriato Freer, "Review of *Social Foundations*."
82. Sergio Valero Ulloa, interview by author, Mexico City, February 6, 2015.
83. Sandra Kuntz Ficker, interview by author, Xalapa, Veracruz, October 27, 2014.
84. Humberto Morales Moreno says that, in the process of capital formation, all countries went through a similar process, from the creation of family businesses to managerial economics, passing through limited partnerships and corporations. In Mexico, managerial economics have still not been consolidated because Mexico has not gone through the process of managerial revolution. Morales Moreno also noted that, at the beginning of the process, no country meets the assumptions of neo-institutionalist theory of capital markets and competition and that this could represent a historical analysis in the case of Mexico in the early twentieth century. Humberto Morales Moreno, interview by author, Mexico City, February 6, 2015.
85. Maurer, *Power and Money*, 41.
86. Haber, *Industry and Underdevelopment*, 33.
87. Haber, *Industry and Underdevelopment*, 44.
88. After the Sherman Act, the United States gradually built a body of antitrust

regulations, including the Clayton Antitrust Act of 1914 and the Law of Bank Mergers in 1966, among others. Although not fully effective, they allowed for more control. In Mexico, it was not until 1992 that a major law to control monopolies was created. With the intention to sign a free trade agreement with the United States and Canada, the Federal Law on Economic Competition was approved—which led to the Competition Federal Commission—replacing the obsolete Organic Statute of Monopolies of 1934. Despite this, monopolies in Mexico have not been controlled the same way in practice. At the same time, the gradual strengthening of the judiciary in the United States throughout the twentieth century and the increased order imposed by its army, among many other aspects, brought results that amplified differences between the United States and Mexico in the development of formal institutions and capitalism. For example, although many monopolies persist today in the United States, it is difficult to construct a monopoly using mainly informal processes, even with ties to influential politicians. In this sense, institutions in the United States are more functional than they are in Mexico.

89. Musacchio and Read, "Bankers," 849.

90. Castañeda, "Barcelonnettes."

91. Sociologist Mark Granovetter demonstrates the great importance of social norms within a group, arguing that confidence building is a key element not only to reduce transaction and information costs but also to reduce risks and uncertainties in their business activities. Granovetter, "Weak Ties and Strong Ties."

92. Gómez-Galvarriato Freer, "Networks and Entrepreneurship," 480. There is a huge body of comparative literature on social networks in economic activity with very sophisticated analytical methods. A good account of the general bibliography available on this topic can be found in various works by Matthew O. Jackson, such as "Overview of Social Networks" and "Study of Social Networks." For the socioeconomics of property rights, see Greif, "Commitment, Coercion, and Markets."

93. Gómez-Galvarriato Freer, "Networks and Entrepreneurship," 491–502.

94. Galán Amaro, "Estrategias," 133–34. Some examples of entrepreneurs who had made great wealth and who, at the same time, were involved in politics themselves during the Porfiriato include Hugo Scherer (member of the Monetary Committee), Pablo Macedo and Joaquín Casasús (senators), Enrique Creel (Chihuahua governor and senator), Fernando Pimentel y Fogada (also member of the Monetary Committee), Porfirio Díaz Jr., Enrique Tron, and Joseph and Leon Signoret. They served as politicians as well as company directors thanks to their "high management capacity, but above all to their talent for getting loans and information." This allowed them to protect and grow their companies, directly using their privileged positions as politicians. Musacchio and Read, "Bankers," 842–80.

95. Haber, "Mercado interno," 425.

96. Archivo Histórico Banamex, Libro 6, Act. 09-10-1901.

97. Archivo Histórico Banamex, Libro 4, Act. 20-10-1891.

98. Archivo Histórico Banamex, Libro 9, Act. 05-04-1921.

99. Archivo Histórico Banamex, Libro 9, Act. 19-08-1928.

100. Archivo Histórico Banamex, Libro 9, Act. 27-12-1922.

Chapter Three

1. Bortz and Haber, *Mexican Economy*, 327.

2. Gómez-Galvarriato Freer, "Impact of Revolution," 76.

3. Notary Public 8 of Mexico City: Ignacio Alfaro, May 18, 1898, deed 38, 89–99.

4. Michel Jean, interview by author, Mexico City, September 11, 2001.

5. Notary Public 8 of Mexico City: Ignacio Alfaro, February 22, 1900, vol. 11, deed 16, 18–30.

6. Notary Public 8 of Mexico City: Ignacio Alfaro, March 4, 1903, vol. 2, deed 112, 255–78.

7. Notary Public 8 of Mexico City: Ignacio Alfaro, March 4, 1903, vol. 2, deed 112, 255–78.

8. By this point, Sebastian Donnadieu had returned to France. However, his brother Antonio became an important partner in other businesses in Mexico. For instance, he was elected a member of the board of directors of the Compañía Cervecera de Toluca y México S.A. in 1916 and he had ties to S. Robert y Compañía Sucesores, which owned the La Hormiga textile mill, the dry-goods store El Centro Mercantil, and part of one of the largest textile companies, Compañía Industrial Veracruzana S.A. (CIVSA).

9. Notary Public 8 of Mexico City: Ignacio Alfaro, March 5, 1908, vol. 25, deed 1016, 146–76.

10. Notary Public 8 of Mexico City: Ignacio Alfaro, May 13, 1914, vol. 66, deed 3270, 122–52.

11. Notary Public 8 of Mexico City: Ignacio Alfaro, April 26, 1920, vol. 77, deed 4256, 171–90. It is important to mention that many times the figures expressed in notarial deeds do not represent exact figures or hide information for legal reasons. However, they can give a clear idea of the decrease or growth of companies, as in this case.

12. Notary Public 8 of Mexico City: Ignacio Alfaro, April 26, 1920, vol. 77, deed 4256, 171–90.

13. Michel Jean interview.

14. For a better understanding of the numbers and situation of the textile industry, please refer to Galindo, "Economic Expansion."

15. José Conde Cervantes, interview by author, Mexico City, August 31, 2001.

16. Notary Public 56 of Mexico City: Eduardo Chico, January 1930, vol. 53, deed 4858, 238–43.

17. Maximino was a tough revolutionary general who became governor of Puebla in 1937 and later secretary of communications and public works in 1941, when his brother Manuel was president of Mexico (1940–46). For a detailed account of Puebla's political intrigues, shifting allegiances, and violence, mainly in rural areas, see Henderson, *Worm in the Wheat*. Also, Andrew Paxman's study on Jenkins deals in detail with the type of relationships that were established between politicians and entrepreneurs in Puebla from the 1920s. Paxman shows that relationships went from being of mutual necessity (in times of political and economic uncertainty) in the 1920s and part of the 1930s to relationships of convenience afterward: exchanges of favors

between politicians and businessmen that generated mere economic advantages for both groups. See Paxman, *Jenkins of Mexico.*

18. The Barcelonnette community in Puebla was also very important and has been studied by Leticia Gamboa Ojeda, as mentioned in chapter 1.

19. José Conde Cervantes, interview by author, Mexico City, August 31, 2001.

20. Notary Public 38 of Mexico City: Luis Beltrán, April 22, 1924, vol. 55, document 3970, 43–49.

21. Notary Public 38 of Mexico City: Luis Beltrán, July 26, 1924, vol. 51, 110–33.

22. Haber, *Industry and Underdevelopment*, 181.

23. Although the Jeans kept the Santa Teresa mill until its closure in 1965, they did not expand their activities within the wool sector.

24. Michel Jean interview.

25. Notary Public 5 of Mexico City: Bernardo Cornejo, November 9, 1909, vol. 53, deed 3564, 17–25.

26. Trujillo Bolio, "La fábrica," 267.

27. Notary Public 56 of Mexico City: Eduardo Chico, August, 1932, vol. 66, deed 6106, 197–209.

28. Notary Public 5 of Mexico City: Bernardo Cornejo, April 22, 1926, vol. 153, deed 12070, 66–92.

29. Jean Hermanos sold two pieces of land located near the Río Hondo mill to Casimiro Jean, the oldest son of Adrián Jean, to be used for the construction of housing. Notary Public 56 of Mexico City: Eduardo Chico, May 1938, vol. 97, deed 8277, 268–73.

30. Notary Public 56 of Mexico City: Eduardo Chico, April 27, 1938, vol. 97, deed 8268, 232–62.

31. Notary Public 56 of Mexico City: Eduardo Chico, May 15, 1931, vol. 63, failed deed 5468, 71.

32. Notary Public 56 of Mexico City: Eduardo Chico, August 17, 1929, vol. 51, deed 4666, 65–73; and, April 27, 1938, vol. 97, deed 8268, 232–62.

33. It is not clear from the deeds consulted where La Compañía Explotadora split and sold lands, but it is quite possible that they began in Atlixco, Puebla, where they also exploited the two power plants mentioned above, according to a deed. Notary Public 56 of Mexico City: Eduardo Chico, April 27, 1938, vol. 97, deed 8268, 232–62.

34. Notary Public 56 of Mexico City: Eduardo Chico, March, 1931, vol. 64, deed 5664, 175.

35. Notary Public 33 of Mexico City: Daniel García, September 30, 1930, vols. 77 and 79, deeds 5627 and 5629, 117–29 and 138–54. Notary Public 56 of Mexico City: Eduardo Chico, May, 1938, vol. 98, deed 8283, 260–67.

36. Patrice Olsen examines direction and meaning in terms of who was given license to design and build structures in the capital city and, equally importantly, who was excluded. In her view, it was through the reshaping of Mexico City that the revolution was extended and institutionalized. Olsen, *Artifacts of Revolution.*

37. Hernández Franyuti, *El Distrito Federal*, 194–95.
38. Hernández Franyuti, *El Distrito Federal*, 195.
39. Registro Público de la Propiedad (Mexico City), Sección Primera A, tomo 138, vol. 5, 116–17.
40. Mendoza, "Biométroplis" (accessed March 7, 2019); Villegas Cárdenas, "Los terrenos Rivera Torres" (accessed March 7, 2019); Aguirre, "Joyas del Pedregal" (accessed March 7, 2019). Comuneros benefited from the agrarian reform by having property rights over communal land in a legally established agrarian community.
41. Certified copy of Notary Public 88: Jorge Tinoco Ariza, April 7, 1964, deed number 15,893.
42. Valerio Ulloa, *Los Barcelonnettes*, 284–87.
43. Notary Public 56 of Mexico City: Eduardo Chico, April, 1932, vol. 68, deed 5928, 56–73.
44. Gómez-Galvarriato Freer, "Networks and Entrepreneurship," 491.
45. By "tough bosses," I mean that, like many of their contemporaries, they were strict with their workers in terms of rigorous monitoring of compliance with internal rules established within factories and housing, and with those established in labor contracts. For example, workers were forbidden from reading newspapers, pamphlets, or books, either in the factories or in the houses that the company provided for them. This was on the pretext of protecting them from vices. In this way, the bosses imposed restrictions on workers' private lives. Leal and Woldenberg, *Colección*, 54.
46. Michel Jean and Claude Jean, interview by author, Mexico City, Mexico, August 21, 2012.
47. Palma Mora, "Asociaciones."
48. Henri Brémond (chair of the Asociación Franco Mexicana Suiza y Belga de Beneficencia), interview by author by phone, September 24, 2015.
49. Brémond interview.
50. http://www.clubfrance.org.mx (accessed April 15, 2011).
51. Michelle Jaime (director of Club France), interview by author, August 2, 2012.
52. Red Ecuestre, www.redecuestre.com (accessed April 15, 2011; URL no longer works). Other well-known members of Mexican society were Pablo García Sainz, Gerardo Rodríguez, Nancy Horton, Joaquín González, the Guash and de las Heras families, Manuel de la Peña, the Renault family, Pablo Macedo, Ricardo García Sainz, the Genovés family, Fernando Senderos, the Williams family, the Martín del Campo family, Alejandra Mulltoff, Jorge Goñi, Jorge Nasser, Miguel Heinz, the Lecuona family, the Egerstrom family, the Jaakkola family, Andrea Morandin, and Manuel and Alia Saborit.
53. Due to space concerns, the club changed its location to Atizapán de Zaragoza, in the state of México near Mexico City, in 1966. When the club ceased operating at the end of the 2000s, the Jean family still owned around 50 percent of the shares. Michel Jean and Claude Jean, interview by author, Mexico City, Mexico, August 21, 2012.
54. "Peña Nieto," *Proceso*, November 27, 2010.

55. Minouche Suberville, interview by author, Mexico City, Mexico, July 18, 2012.

56. Suberville interview.

57. Sharma, Chrisman, and Chua, "Strategic Management," 15.

58. Haber, *Industry and Underdevelopment*, 124.

59. Oropeza and Martínez, "Participación."

60. Archivo General de la Nación, Mexico City, Mexico, Departamento de Gobernación, Box 12.

61. Archivo General de la Nación, Mexico City, Mexico, DT, Box 79, Exp. 6.

62. As a result of the Mexican Revolution's social demands, the government began an agrarian redistribution process in 1915 that heightened under Lázaro Cárdenas's presidency (1934–40). During his administration, the government redistributed approximately 20 million hectares.

63. *Diario Oficial de la Federación*, January 11, 1924, and March 28, 1924, http://www.dof.gob.mx.

64. *Diario Oficial de la Federación*, April 29, 1924, http://www.dof.gob.mx.

65. *Diario Oficial de la Federación*, August 7, 1923, http://www.dof.gob.mx.

66. Ejido is defined as an area of communal land used for agriculture, in which community members individually farm designated parcels and collectively maintain communal holdings. It is a type of property established in Mexican law, mainly associated with agrarian reform. See Galindo, "Some Aspects," 133.

67. *Diario Oficial de la Federación*, May 3, 1938, http://www.dof.gob.mx.

68. *Diario Oficial de la Federación*, August 7, 1923, http://www.dof.gob.mx.

69. Notary Public 33 of Mexico City: Daniel Garcia, September 30, 1930, vols. 77 and 79, deeds 5627 and 5629, 117–29 and 138–54.

70. Camarena, "Formas y Formación," 112.

71. Durand, cited by Camarena, "Formas y Formación," 112.

72. We do not know the exact amount of land that was sold to the Martínez Alemáns, but looking at a map attached to the deeds of the sale, it seems to have been around half of the acreage of their ranches. Notary Public 33 of Mexico City: Daniel García, September 30, 1930, vols. 77 and 79, deeds 5627 and 5629, 117–29 and 138–54.

73. Notary Public 56 of Mexico City: Eduardo Chico, December 1937, vol. 97, deed 8147, 137–41.

74. Notary Public 5 of Mexico City: Bernardo Cornejo, October 28, 1909, vol. 51, deed 3542, 1–18.

75. Génin, *México Contemporáneo*.

76. There were ten vocal positions (voting members) in addition to the president and vice president of the company. Archivo Histórico Banamex, Compañía Bancaria de París y México, *General Assembly Report* of June 5, 1915.

77. Notary Public 5 of Mexico City: Bernardo Cornejo, October 28, 1909, vol. 51, deed 3542, 1–18.

78. Anaya, "Colapso y reforma," 109–10.

79. Anaya, "Colapso y reforma," 108.

80. Maurer, *Power and Money*, 93.

81. Maurer, *Power and Money*, 94.

82. Del Ángel, "La paradoja," 644.

83. Archivo Histórico de Banamex, vol. 13, January 31, 1911, to May 21, 1912.

84. Archivo Histórico de Banamex, Libro de Actas de la Compañía Bancaria de París y México, vol. 13, January 31, 1911, to May 21, 1912.

85. Limantour, who himself was of French descent, was the head of a group called the Científicos, the technocratic branch of the Porfirian government. They managed to exert influence on other political actors through use of their substantial cultural capital and the moral leadership of Limantour. Proof of such leadership is the large amount of correspondence he exchanged with other members of the group, who asked for the opinion of "the chief" or "blessing" of "the Lord" before proceeding. See María y Campos Castelló, *José Yves Limantour*, 95. There were additional factors that allowed the Cientificos to prevail in the Porfiriato, such as the creation of a broad network that facilitated their access to strategic positions in the public and private sectors. Alvarez Garibay, "Letrados," 7–8.

86. Information obtained from the Archivo Centro de Estudios de Historia de México, CARSO. Collection José Y. Limantour, Fund CDLIV, 1880–1934, December 1911 and March 1912.

87. Archivo Centro de Estudios de Historia de México, CARSO. Collection José Y. Limantour, Fund CDLIV, letter from Scherer to Limantour, July 22, 1911, rollo 72.

88. Anaya, "Colapso y Reforma," 106.

89. Archivo Histórico de Banamex, Libro de Amortización de Acciones de la Compañía Bancaria de París y México.

90. Subscriptions refer to the process of investors signing up and committing to invest in a financial instrument, before the actual closing of the purchase; stock represents the capital paid or invested into the business. Archivo Centro de Estudios de Historia de México, CARSO. Collection José Y. Limantour, Fund CDLIV, 1880–1934, January 26, 1912.

91. Notary Public 38 of Mexico City: Luis Beltrán, May 8, 1925, vol. 53, document 4108, 196–99.

92. Anaya, "Colapso y Reforma," 109–10.

93. Archivo Histórico de Banamex, Libro de Actas del Banco Nacional de México, Libro 12, 99.

94. Archivo Histórico de Banamex, Libro de Amortización de Acciones de la Compañía Bancaria de París y México.

95. Turrent, *Historia sintética*, 7.

96. Hamilton, *México*, 264–67.

Chapter Four

1. Mutual aid societies were voluntary organizations in which workers made periodic monetary contributions to create savings funds, primarily for medical care and life insurance.

2. This labor organization was created in 1876. According to Hart, anarchist leaders managed it. Hart, *El anarquismo*, 79.

3. Hart, *El anarquismo*, 60.

4. Lear, *Workers*, 111.

5. Anderson argues that the origins of workers' anger at that time was clear: they were underpaid, overworked, mistreated, and discriminated against in favor of foreign workers. Anderson, *Outcasts*, 311.

6. Anderson, *Outcasts*, 301.

7. Anderson, *Outcasts*, 301–2.

8. Hart, *El anarquismo*, 99.

9. Lear, *Workers*; Anderson, *Outcasts*, 306.

10. Friedrich Katz, quoted in Bethell, *Mexico since Independence*, 105.

11. Bortz, "Without Any More Law," 263.

12. Lear, *Workers*, 137.

13. Lear, *Workers*, 146; *El Imparcial* (various issues) quoted by Bortz, "Without Any More Law," 264–65.

14. Archivo General de la Nación, DT, box 16, file 14, FS. 2, 3.

15. *El Imparcial*, August 2, 1912.

16. Bortz, "Genesis," 47.

17. Letter from the manager of the San Ildefonso mill to the Labor Department, quoted by Bortz, "Without Any More Law," 268.

18. Archivo General de la Nación, DT, Caja 32, Ex. 11.

19. Archivo General de la Nación, DT, Caja 211, Ex. 21.

20. Anarcho-syndicalism was a more militant ideology against capitalism. It used means such as general strikes and direct control of the factories by workers. In theory, workers organized in unions would acquire sufficient power to control the means of production by using what they called *la acción directa* (direct action).

21. Lear, *Workers*, 361.

22. Oropeza and Martínez, "Participación."

23. Lear, *Workers*, 364.

24. Bortz, "Without Any More Law," 270.

25. Bortz, "Without Any More Law," 280.

26. Gómez-Galvarriato Freer, *Political Economy*, 29.

27. Q. Rivero, quoted by Gómez-Galvarriato Freer, *Political Economy*, 30.

28. Araiza, *Historia*, 91.

29. Río Hondo was acquired in 1923.

30. Bortz, "Genesis," chart with important CGT factories, 54.

31. Hart, *El anarquismo*, 195.

32. Salazar, *Historia*, 119–25.

33. Hart, *El anarquismo*, 204.

34. Jean Meyer, cited in Bethell, *Mexico since Independence*, 229.

35. Salazar, *Historia*, 196–210.

36. Salazar, *Historia*.

37. Salazar, *Historia*.

38. Bortz, "Genesis," 48.

39. Haber, *Industry and Underdevelopment*, 33–34.

40. Haber, *Industry and Underdevelopment*, 158.

41. Departamento de Estudios Económicos, *La industria textil*, 48.

42. Bortz, "Genesis," 48.

43. The wage list in the textile industry was very extensive because wages were differentiated by activity and by state. However, on average, Federal District salaries were 18.8 percent higher than Puebla's and 5 percent lower than Veracruz's by 1923. Departamento de Estudios Económicos, *La industria textil*, 24, 52.

44. Bortz, "Genesis," 51.

45. Gómez-Galvarriato Freer, *Political Economy*, 30–31.

46. Gómez-Galvarriato Freer, *Political Economy*, 7–10.

47. Haber, *Industry and Underdevelopment*, 180.

48. The CTM was maintained as one of the pillars of the PRI for many years. It began to lose influence by the end of the 1980s with the introduction of neoliberalism in Mexico.

49. Bortz, "Genesis," 54.

50. *El Gráfico Vespertino*, quoted in Bortz, "Genesis," 55.

51. Industrialists proposed a minimum wage of 2 pesos, while the majority of labor delegates demanded 4.50 pesos.

52. Gómez-Galvarriato Freer, *Political Economy*, 38.

53. Cárdenas, *La hacienda pública*, 96.

54. Michel Jean interview.

55. Cárdenas, *La hacienda pública*, "Statistical Appendix Table A.6."

56. Gómez-Galvarriato Freer, *Political Economy*, 38–39.

57. The International Bank for Reconstruction and Dev., quoted in Gómez-Galvarriato Freer, *Political Economy*, 39.

58. Archivo General de la Nación, Presidentes: Ruiz Cortines, Caja 432/135 (June 1953).

59. Archivo General de la Nación, Presidentes: Ruiz Cortines, Caja 432/135 (June 1953).

60. Segunda Ponencia de la Compañía Industrial de Orizaba, cited in Gómez-Galvarriato Freer, *Political Economy*, 43.

61. Archivo General de la Nación, Presidentes: Ruiz Cortines, Caja 432/135 (June 1953).

62. Archivo General de la Nación, Presidentes: Ruiz Cortines, Caja 432/135. Leg. 1–6 (November 1953).

63. Archivo General de la Nación, Presidentes: Ruiz Cortines, Caja 432/135 (March 27, 1954).

64. Archivo General de la Nación, Presidentes: Ruiz Cortines, Caja 432/135 (May 31, 1954).

65. Archivo General de la Nación, Presidentes: Ruiz Cortines, Caja 432/135 (April 1955).

66. Michel Jean and Claude Jean, interview by author, Mexico City, Mexico, August 21, 2012.

67. Michel Jean interview.

68. Syrian and Lebanese migrations to Mexico had begun in the 1890s.
69. Haber, *Industry and Underdevelopment*, 186.
70. Medina Peña, *Hacia el nuevo estado*, 115.
71. United Nations, quoted in Gómez-Galvarriato Freer, *Political Economy*, 44.
72. Mosk, *Industrial Revolution*, 136.
73. Durand, "Auge y crisis," 75.
74. Durand, "Auge y crisis."
75. Heath, "Crisis."
76. Cámara Nacional de la Industria Textil, *Memoria estadística*, 16–17.
77. Registro Público de la Propiedad, Sección Comercio, Tomo 3, vol. 72, no. 508.
78. Michel Jean interview.
79. Michel Jean interview.
80. In an interview, Mario Cerutti confirms that these elements have always been fundamental for Mexican entrepreneurs to maintain privileged positions within the economic elite when they have faced adverse conditions. Cerutti in *Clío*, "La hazaña de Monterrey." As we saw in Chapter 2, Wasserman also considers this a fundamental variable for the persistence of the elite.
81. Paxman, "Televisa," 488–89.
82. Paxman, "Televisa," 488–89.
83. Archivo Histórico Banamex, Libro de Actas del Consejo de Administración, Libro 21 (March 24, 1943), 139.
84. Urbano, "CDMX."
85. D'Anglade, *Un gran patrón*, 398.
86. Gouy, *Pérégrinations*, 93.
87. D'Anglade, *Un gran patrón*, 508–11.
88. Michel Jean interview.
89. Roberto Jean, interview by author, Mexico City, Mexico, December 14, 2015.
90. Michel Jean interview.
91. Archivo de Celanese Mexicana S.A., annual reports for multiple years.
92. Archivo Histórico Banamex, Libro de Actas del Consejo de Administración, Libro 30 (March 27, 1957), 103, and Informe Anual de Banamex (1980), 43–56.
93. Camp, *Los empresarios mexicanos*, 201.
94. Archivo Histórico Banamex, Libro de Actas del Consejo de Administración, Libro 33 (October 28, 1959), 66–71.
95. Fernández and Paxman, *El Tigre*, 133–34.
96. Pamela Jean, interview with author by phone, November 2013. In fact, not all first-generation Jean family members had come to Mexico. Leon and Rosa Jean remained in Europe. They were financially supported by their brothers established in Mexico and inherited some of the wealth left by them. Notary Public 56 of Mexico City: Eduardo Chico, June 1935, volume 81, deed 7211, 147–54. Camilo Jean's will.
97. Michel Jean and Claude Jean, interview by author, Mexico City, Mexico, August 21, 2012.
98. Michel Jean and Claude Jean interview.
99. Michel Jean and Claude Jean interview.

100. Notary Public 56 of Mexico City: Eduardo Chico, December 1937, vol. 97, deed 8147, 137–41: sale of land in Oaxaca. Notary Public 56 of Mexico City: Eduardo Chico, June 1937, vol. 98, deed 7988, 8–10: purchase in 1932 and sale in 1937 of a house by Jean Hnos in Michoacán. Notary Public 56 of Mexico City: Eduardo Chico, July 1937, vol. 98, deed 8073, 90–93: purchase in 1937 of 75 hectares of the Hacienda de los Morales, in the state of México, to expand Jean Hnos's land holdings. Notary Public 56 of Mexico City: Eduardo Chico, July 1936, vol. 88, deed 7643, 273–83: purchase by Alfonso Jean, as a representative of Inmobiliaria Comercial, of 69 hectares of land, also in the state of México.

101. Notary Public 56 of Mexico City: Eduardo Chico, July 20, 1940, vol. 112, deed 9087, 130–38. For example, Eva Gonzales, a resident of Villa de Juarez, to whom Camilo Jean granted a credit line with the limit of 15,000 pesos to buy some goods from La Francia Marítima, had to leave her property "La Ladrillera" in Naucalpan, state of México, as a mortgage bond for this credit.

102. Notary Public 56 of Mexico City: Eduardo Chico, December 1937, vol. 97, deed 8147, 137–41.

103. Bourdieu, "Forms of Capital," 241–58.

104. Diggins, *El bardo*, 37–49.

105. Bell, *Las contradicciones*, 26–33.

106. Adler de Lomnitz and Pérez Lizaur, *Una familia*, 238.

107. Balmori, Voss, and Wortman, *Las alianzas de familiares,* 203.

108. Adler de Lomnitz and Pérez Lizaur, *Una familia,* 237.

109. Bourdieu, "Forms of Capital," 241–58.

110. Among other causes of the already explained decline of some members of the family, in the cotton and wool textile business the Jeans experienced the so-called Buddenbrooks Effect, which is defined as the tendency among family-run companies to decline over a period of about three generations. Colli, *History of Family Business*, 13–15. Their decline in the traditional textiles sector was in part due to the lack of an adequate succession plan—that is, they faced difficulties in delegating the business to new generations.

111. Adler de Lomnitz and Pérez Lizaur, *Una familia*, 234.

112. Lenguaje Persuasivo, http://www.lenguajepersuasivo.com/.

113. "Biografía: Reyno."

114. Mepsa, About Us, http://www.mepsa.com.mx.

115. Spika, http://spikaart.com/.

116. Galán Amaro, "Estrategias," 94.

117. Galán Amaro, "Estrategias," 93.

118. "Billionaires 2015." After the death of Max Michel Suberville, his nephew Max David Michel replaced him.

119. Henri Brémond, interview with author by phone, September 24, 2015. Henri Bremond also served as vice-chairman of Hospital ABC and COPARMEX and chairman of the Grupo Educativo Franco Mexicano.

120. The interview took place in September 2015, when Peña Nieto was still the president of Mexico.

121. Minouche Suberville, interview by author, Mexico City, Mexico, July 18, 2012.

Chapter Five

1. For a detailed overview of crony capitalism and social networks from a global perspective, see Galindo, "Algunas conclusiones." This paper explains cases of crony capitalism in the United States, South Korea, the Philippines, Russia, and the United Kingdom, among other countries, comparing the degrees of crony capitalism across the globe and establishing the main differences between nations.

2. There are certainly reasons other than crony capitalism why formal institutions remained relatively weak in Mexico. These include the political culture of the PRI, the United States' unwillingness to press for judicial reform in Mexico during the Cold War for fear of enabling a leftist party to take power, the "partidocracy" that impeded reform after 2000, and the growth of drug trafficking, to name a few. However, crony capitalism was the main reason.

3. For a more detailed explanation of this process, see Galindo, "La Conferencia de Chapultepec."

4. Susan Gauss's book *Made in Mexico* makes a detailed characterization of the policies behind the implementation of the ISI in Mexico. She studies the different actors (heterogeneous groups within the government, the business community and its associations, and labor), conflicts, and negotiations involved in its shaping and implementation. As Gauss points out, protectionist policies in Mexico became more than a means to increase revenues or strengthen industry: "They became the cornerstone of ruling-party efforts to forge political unity, achieve economic independence from the United States, and improve national standards of living." Gauss, *Made in Mexico*, 5.

5. During the 1970s, Presidents Luis Echeverría and José López Portillo expanded government spending in an attempt to regain popular support, lost in part as a result of the repressive events that took place in 1968 and 1971. However, instead of increasing taxes or using other funding sources to keep balanced public finances, they borrowed vast amounts of money, enabled by the discovery of massive new oil deposits.

6. Galindo, *La CNDH*, 104–5.

7. Corporate governance, which was established in Mexico in the second stage of Mexican industrialization (ISI), centered around the economic and political power of banks. The latter were the most influential actors due to the overlaps between their boards of directors and those of various companies or the Council of Businessmen. The strong connection between bankers and industrial and political groups is evident in the cases of Banamex and Bancomer. Banamex (Legorreta, Deutz) participated in about 300 of the largest companies in the country, controlling full or partial corporations. Bancomer (Espinosa Yglesias) was the most important bank system, with a presence throughout almost all of the Republic and involving the major industrialists and merchandisers from many regions. Reyes Hernández and Morales Moreno, *La reconfiguración*, 9.

8. Morales Moreno, "La organización actual."

9. Morales Moreno et al., *La nacionalización*.

10. Castañeda, "Evolución," 604–5.

11. Chandler, *Visible Hand*, 2.

12. "Cantidad de millonarios."

13. Fernández-Vega, "Los buenos negocios."

14. James Kenneth Galbraith, interview by author, Austin, Texas, October 26, 2015.

15. Corruption is the phenomenon by which a public official, in the exercise of their duties, illegitimately appropriates what belongs to all the inhabitants of a nation (the public), following or not the regulatory standards of a system, to favor his individual interests. Corruption erodes governmental authority, affects the credibility of instruments of power, and becomes a threat to the democratic governance of a country because it corrodes the ethical values on which the community organization is founded. Escudero Morales and Galindo, *Transparencia*, 13–14.

16. The failure of the National Anti-Corruption System is due to many complex reasons. Crony capitalism might be the most important, but the fact that rule federalism grew under the Partido Acción Nacional (PAN), even as almost half of the states failed to fulfil their legal obligations to create state-level equivalents of the national system, is important as well. This has been the story of many other autonomous systems that have been created in Mexico, such as the nonjudicial system for the protection of human rights, which includes the Comisión Nacional de los Derechos Humanos (CNDH) and all state commissions for the protection of human rights.

17. According to Transparency International, "behind these numbers is the daily reality for people living in these countries. The index cannot capture the individual frustration of this reality, but it does capture the informed views of analysts, businesspeople and experts in countries around the world." Transparency International, "Corruption Perceptions Index."

18. Vera, "Corrupción."

19. Transparency is a concept that indicates the clarity of government and public administration procedures. This implies the possibility for the community to view actors with complete clarity by thorough planning and implementation, as a means of ensuring accuracy and honesty. For a broader definition, see Escudero Morales and Galindo, *Transparencia*, 10. Accountability is an obligation for people who act on behalf or in the interest of others and who have performed acts of administration or management in relation to goods that do not belong exclusively to them. Accountability is a "to do" obligation, which consists of the obligation to present a detailed statement of the information requested to the party that is entitled to request information. This information shall be submitted within a reasonable period of time. Applied to public issues, we understand accountability as a system that, on the one hand, forces the public servant to report in detail their actions and the results thereof and, on the other, provides citizens with mechanisms to monitor the performance of public servants.

20. This does not mean that there are no new sectors being privatized; some likely include the energy sector and possibly the water supply, which will almost definitely enrich old and new entrepreneurs and politicians.

21. Presidencia de la República Mexicana, "Decreto de Presupuesto."

22. Granovetter, *Getting a Job.*

23. Pérez Islas, *Encuesta nacional de juventud*, 2005.

24. Croda, "Vida y muerte."

25. Croda, "Vida y muerte."

26. Croda, "Vida y muerte."

27. A final general conclusion also related to these social differences and social mobility is that it has been proved that positive economic cycles (improvements in economic growth) do not result in greater upward mobility. Most of the wealth generated when there is a positive economic growth rate during a particular period of time is concentrated in the power elite. What we can conclude, according to recent studies, is that less economic inequality enables greater social mobility, partly because of more widespread equal access to opportunities, including labor opportunities, which at the same time results in higher economic growth. In other words, under more equal socioeconomic conditions, economic growth reaches a greater percentage of society. For a more in-depth discussion of these topics, see Piketty, *Capital*; Esquivel, "Desigualdad"; also Vélez Grajales, "La movilidad social."

28. See Galindo, "Capitalismo de amigos," and Ramírez Tamayo, "Aún está a prueba."

29. Animal Político, "AMLO."

Conclusion

1. Unlike leaders, followers (most of the rest of society) adapt to any conditions, for good or ill, as long as there is a guarantee of certain aspects to ensure their survival. Perhaps some of them will not violate their ethical principles, but the need to subsist prevails in most cases.

Bibliography

Archival Material

Archivo Centro de Estudios de Historia de México, CARSO. Fondo José Y. Limantour. Mexico City, Mexico.

Archivo de Celanese Mexicana S.A. Mexico City, Mexico.

Archivo de la Cámara Nacional de la Industria Textil (CANAITEX). Mexico City, Mexico.

Archivo de la Secretaría de Hacienda y Crédito Público. Mexico City, Mexico.

Archivo de la Secretaría de la Economía Nacional. Mexico City, Mexico.

Archivo del Centro de Estudios de Historia de México, CARSO. Mexico City, Mexico.

Archivo Familia Couttolenc, accessed March 30, 2015, http://www.couttolenc.org.

Archivo General Agrario. Mexico City, Mexico.

Archivo General de la Nación. Mexico City, Mexico.

Archivo General de Notarías de la Ciudad de México. Gobierno de la Ciudad de México. Mexico City, Mexico.

Archivo Histórico Banamex. Mexico City, Mexico.

Archivo Museo de San Rafael, historical collection. Veracruz, Mexico.

Instituto Nacional de Estudios Históricos de las Revoluciones de México. Diario de Debates del Congreso Constituyente de 1917. Tomo 2 (1985). Mexico City, Mexico.

Liste Approximative des Intérets Francais Engagés au Mexique. MS of the "Asociación Nationale des Porteurs Francais de Valeurs Mobiliéres" (at Banco de México). Mexico City, Mexico.

Registro Público de la Propiedad. Mexico City, Mexico.

Acemoglu, Daron, and James A. Robinson. *Why Nations Fail: The Origins of Power, Prosperity, and Poverty*. New York: Crown Publishers, 2012.

Adler de Lomnitz, Larissa, and Marisol Pérez Lizaur. *Una familia de la élite Mexicana, 1820–1980: Parentesco, clase y cultura*. Mexico City: Alianza Editorial Mexicana, 1993.

Aguilar Álvarez de Alba, Javier B. *La libre competencia*. Mexico City: Oxford University Press/Harla Mexico, 2000.

Aguirre M, Alberto. "Joyas del Pedregal." *El Economista*, August 10, 2014. https://www.eleconomista.com.mx.

Alvarez Garibay, Jaime Manuel. "Letrados de fines de siglo XIX y principios del XX, los científicos." PhD diss., Universidad Iberoamericana, Mexico City, 2011. http://192.203.177.185/handle/ibero/505.

Anaya, Luis. "Colapso y reforma: La integración del sistema bancario y las finanzas públicas en el México Revolucionario, 1913–1932." PhD diss., Colegio de México, Mexico City, 2000.

Anderson, Rodney D. *Outcasts in Their Own Land: Mexican Industrial Workers, 1906–1911*. Dekalb: Northern Illinois University Press, 1976.

Animal Político. "AMLO otorga el 74% de los contratos por adjudicación directa al igual que EPN y Calderón." *Animal Político*, July 8, 2019. https://www.animalpolitico.com.

Araiza, Luis. *Historia del movimiento obrero mexicano*. Mexico City: Casa del Obrero Mundial, 1975.

Aristegui Noticias. "En México, 200 millones de actos de corrupción al año: IMCO." *Aristegui Noticias*, November 28, 2015. http://aristeguinoticias.com.

———. "Por violar normas y reglamentos, ordenan cierre de Banco Azteca en Brasil." *Aristegui Noticias*, January 9, 2016. http://m.aristeguinoticias.com.

———. "'Si le queda dignidad, renuncie,' la carta de Layda Sansores a Peña Nieto." *Aristegui Noticias*, November 12, 2015. http://aristeguinoticias.com.

Arnaud, François. *Les Barcelonnettes au Mexique. récits et témoignages*. Barcelonnette, France: Sabença de la Valéia, 1994.

Arreola, Federico. "Tigres campeón y otra vez, Televisa de @eazcarraga ignoró al 'Bronco' @JaimeRdzNL." *SDP Noticias*, December 14, 2015. http://www.sdpnoticias.com.

Austin, Lisa M. "Property and the Rule of Law." *Legal Theory* 20, no. 2 (2014): 79–105. https://doi.org/10.1017/S1352325214000056.

Ballinas, Christopher. "Reseña de 'Corrupción y cambio' de Juan Octavio López Presa (coord.)," *Perfiles Latinoamericanos*, no. 15 (1999).

Balmori, Diana, Stuart F. Voss, and Miles L. Wortman. *Las alianzas de familias y la formación del país en América Latina*. Mexico City: Fondo de Cultura Económica, 1990.

Barragán, Daniela. "El Senado alista 'Ley Casa Blanca' para esconder aún más contratos de obra: ONGs." *Sin Embargo*, September 21, 2015. http://www.sinembargo.mx.

Barragán, Daniela, and Xanath Lastiri. "OHL nunca obtuvo contratos en Pemex, pero llegó Lozoya y hoy suman casi 10 mil millones." *Sin Embargo*, November 27, 2015. http://www.sinembargo.mx.

Beatty, Edward. *Institutions and Investment: The Political Basis of Industrialization in Mexico Before 1911*. Stanford, CA: Stanford University Press, 2001.

Beezley, William H. "Kaleidoscopic Views of Liberalism Triumphant, 1862–1895." In *The Divine Charter: Constitutionalism and Liberalism in Nineteenth-Century Mexico*, edited by Jaime E. Rodríguez O., 167–80. Lanham, MD: Rowman and Littlefield Publishers, 2005.

Bell, Daniel. *Las contradicciones culturales del capitalismo*. Translated by Néstor Míguez. Mexico City: Alianza, 1996.

Bethell, Leslie, ed. *Mexico since Independence*. Cambridge, UK: Cambridge University Press, 1991.

Béraud-Suberville, Geneviéve. "Centinelas del pasado: Del cajón de ropa a las tiendas-ancla." In *Los Barcelonettes en México: Miradas regionales, siglos XIX–XX*, edited by Leticia Gamboa Ojeda, 247–73. Puebla, Mexico: BUAP, 2008.

"Billionaires 2015: #1312 Max Michel Suberville." *Forbes*, March 2, 2015. http://www.forbes.com.

Bingham, Tom. *The Rule of Law*. London: Penguin, 2011.

"Biografía: Reyno, el mundo introspectivo del rock." *Excelsior*, November 12, 2014. http://www.excelsior.com.mx.

Blake, Charles H., and Stephen D. Morris, eds. *Corruption and Democracy in Latin America*. Pittsburgh: University of Pittsburgh Press, 2009.

Blanco Moheno, Roberto. *La corrupción en México*. Mexico City: Bruguera Mexicana de Ediciones, 1979.

Borgatti, Stephen P. "Centrality and Network Flow." *Social Networks* 27, no. 1 (2005): 55–71. https://doi.org/10.1016/j.socnet.2004.11.008.

Bortz, Jeffrey L. "The Genesis of the Mexican Labor Relations System: Federal Labor Policy and the Textile Industry 1925–1940." *Americas* 52, no. 1 (1995): 43–69.

———. "'Without Any More Law than Their Own Caprice': Cotton Textile Workers and the Challenge to Factory Authority during the Mexican Revolution." *International Review of Social History* 42, no. 2 (1997): 253–88. https://doi.org/10.1017/S0020859000114907.

Bortz, Jeffrey L., and Stephen Haber, eds. *The Mexican Economy, 1870–1930: Essays on the Economic History of Institutions, Revolution, and Growth*. Stanford, CA: Stanford University Press, 2002.

Bourdieu, Pierre. "The Forms of Capital." In *Handbook of Theory and Research for the Sociology of Education*, edited by John G. Richardson, 241–58. Westport, CT: Greenwood Publishing Group, 1986.

Burnham, William. *Introduction to the Law and Legal Systems of the United States*. St. Paul, MN: West Academic Publishing, 2011.

Buve, Raymond. *El movimiento revolucionario en Tlaxcala*. Mexico City: Universidad Autónoma de Tlaxcala/Universidad Iberoamericana, 1994.

———. "Un paisaje lunar habitado por bribones y sus víctimas: Mirada retrospectiva al debate sobre las haciendas y los pueblos durante el Porfiriato (1876–1911)." In *Don Porfirio Presidente . . . nunca omnipotente: Hallazgos, reflexiones y debates.*

1876–1911, edited by Romana Falcón and Raymond Buve, 121–51. Mexico City: Universidad Iberoamericana, 1998.

Buve, Raymond, and Heather Fowler-Salamini, eds. *La Revolución Mexicana en el oriente de México (1906–1940)*. Madrid: AHILA/Iberoamericana/Vervuert/ Bonilla Artigas, 2010.

Cámara Nacional de la Industria Textil. *Memoria estadística*. Mexico City: Cámara Nacional de la Industria Textil, 1975.

Camarena, Mario. "Formas y formación: Historia social de los obreros textiles de San Ángel." PhD diss., Escuela Nacional de Antropología e Historia, Mexico City, 1999.

Camp, Roderic Ai. *Entrepreneurs and Politics in Twentieth-Century Mexico*. New York: Oxford University Press, 1989.

———. *Los empresarios mexicanos y la política en México: Una visión contemporanea*. Mexico City: Fondo de Cultura Económica, 1990.

———. *Mexico's Mandarins: Crafting a Power Elite for the Twenty-First Century*. Berkeley: University of California Press, 2002.

Campos, Mariana. *MeTrOP: Antídoto vs. la corrupción*. Mexico City: México Evalúa, 2016.

Campos Garza, Luciano. "El Bronco denuncia 100 actos de corrupción en sexenio de Rodrigo Medina." *Proceso*, December 7, 2015. http://www.proceso.com.mx.

Campoy, Ana. "Mexico Would Be an Economic Superstar without Corruption." *Quartz*, November 11, 2015. http://qz.com.

"Cantidad de millonarios creció 32% en México en cinco años: Estudio." *Proceso*, November 28, 2015. http://www.proceso.com.mx.

Carbajal, J. Antonio Fernandez. "Veinte años de política de competencia económica en México." In *La política de competencia en el umbral de la consolidación*, edited by Comisión Federal de Competencia. Mexico City: Porrúa, 2013.

Cárdenas, Enrique. *La hacienda pública y la política económica, 1929–1958*. Mexico City: Colegio de México and Fondo de Cultura Económica, 1994.

Carrillo Flores, Antonio. "La constitución en el desarrollo económico y social de México." In *Las experiencias del proceso político-constitucional en México y España*, edited by Jorge Carpizo, 307–26. Mexico City: Universidad Nacional Autónoma de México, 1979.

Casar, María Amparo. *México: Anatomía de la corrupción*. Mexico City: Centro de Investigaciones y Docencia Económicas, 2015.

Castañeda, Gonzalo. "The Barcelonnettes: An Example of Network-Entrepreneurs in Nineteenth-Century Mexico. An Explanation Based on a Theory of Bounded Rational Choice with Social Embededness." Working paper, Document de treball no. 04/2. Department d'Economia de l'Empresa, Universitat Autònoma de Barcelona, 2004.

———. "Evolución de los grupos económicos durante el período 1940–2008." In *Historia económica general de México: De la colonia a nuestros días*, edited by Sandra Kuntz Ficker, 603–33. Mexico City: Colegio de Mexico, 2010.

Cerruti, Mario. "Regional Studies and Business History in Mexico since 1975." In

Business History in Latin America: The Experience of Seven Countries, edited by Carlos Dávila and Rory Miller, 116–27. Liverpool, UK: Liverpool University Press, 1999.

Chandler, Alfred D., Jr. *The Visible Hand: The Managerial Revolution in American Business*. Cambridge, MA: Belknap Press, 1977.

Chassen, Francie R. "Capitalismo o comunalismo? Cambio y continuidad en la tenencia de la tierra en la Oaxaca porfirista." In *Don Porfirio Presidente . . . nunca omnipotente: Hallazgos, reflexiones y debates. 1876–1911*, edited by Romana Falcón and Raymond Buve, 153–200. Mexico City: Universidad Iberoamericana, 1998.

Coatsworth, John. "Structures, Endowments, and Institutions in the Economic History of Latin America." *Latin American Research Review* 40, no. 3 (2005): 126–44.

Cochran, Thomas C. *Estados Unidos en el siglo XX: El sistema socioeconómico*. Buenos Aires, Argentina: Paidós, 1968.

Collado, María del Carmen. *Empresarios y políticos, entre la restauración y la revolución 1920–1924*. Mexico City: Instituto Nacional de Estudios Históricos de la Revolución Mexicana, 1996.

Colli, Andrea. *The History of Family Business, 1850–2000*. Cambridge, UK: Cambridge University Press, 2003.

Cortez, Willy W. *Ensayos sobre victimización, percepción de inseguridad y corrupción en México*. Jalisco, Mexico: Universidad de Guadalajara, 2015.

Cosío Villegas, Daniel, ed. *Historia moderna de México. El Porfiriato: Vida económica*. Mexico City: Hermes, 1965.

Croda, Rafael. "Vida y muerte de un ejecutivo de Slim (Primera Parte)." *Proceso*, October 16, 2015. http://www.proceso.com.mx.

Cruz Rodríguez, María Soledad. *Crecimiento urbano y procesos sociales en el Distrito Federal, 1920–1928*. Mexico City: Universidad Autónoma Metropolitana, 1994.

Dam, Kenneth W. *The Law-Growth Nexus: The Rule of Law and Economic Development*. Washington, DC: Brookings Institution Press, 2006.

D'Anglade, Jean-Louis. *Un gran patrón Barcelonnette en México: Joseph Ollivier y su familia, 1850–1932*. Translated by Leticia Gamboa Ojeda. Nuevo León, Mexico: ABZAC, 2012.

Davidson, James West, Brian DeLay, Christine Leigh Heyrman, Mark H. Lytle, and Michael B. Stoff. *US: A Narrative History*. Vol. 1, *To 1877*. New York: McGraw-Hill Education, 2008.

———. *US: A Narrative History*. Vol. 2, *Since 1865*. New York: McGraw-Hill Education, 2014.

Davis, Diane. *Urban Leviathan: Mexico City in the Twentieth Century*. Philadelphia: Temple University Press, 1994.

DeHart, Monica C. *Ethnic Entrepreneurs: Identity, and Development Politics in Latin America*. Stanford, CA: Stanford University Press, 2010.

Del Ángel, Gustavo. "La paradoja del desarrollo financiero." In *Historia económica general de México, de la colonia a nuestros días*, edited by Sandra Kuntz Ficker, 635–66. Mexico City: Colegio de Mexico, 2010.

Delgado, Álvaro. "El PRI emprende el asalto al INE." *Proceso*, September 27, 2014. http://www.proceso.com.mx.

De Mora, Juan Miguel. *Ladrones en el gobierno: México, la corrupción*. Mexico City: EDAMEX, 1979.

Departamento de Estudios Económicos. *La industria textil en México*. Mexico City: Secretaría de la Economía Nacional, 1934.

Diario Oficial de la Federación. 1923, 1924. http://www.dof.gob.mx.

Diez de Urdanivia, Mario, dir. *Clío*. "La hazaña de Monterrey." Aired 2001.

Diggins, John P. *El bardo del salvajismo: Thorstein Veblen y la teoría social moderna*. Translated by Eduardo L. Suárez. Mexico City: Fondo de Cultura Económica, 1983.

Dillon, Sam. "Drug Ties Taint 2 Mexican Governors." *New York Times*, February 23, 1997. http://www.nytimes.com.

Dolia, Estevez. "Mexican TV Tycoon Azcarraga to Expand Televisa's Reach to U.S. English-Speakers." *Forbes*, January 24, 2013. https://www.forbes.com.

Domhoff, William. *Who Rules America Now? A View for the 80s*. Englewood Cliffs, NJ: Prentice-Hall, 1983.

Durand, Jorge. "Auge y crisis: Un modo de vida de la industria mexicana." In *Relaciones. El Colegio de Michoacán* 7, no. 28 (1986): 61–84.

Echánove Trujillo, Carlos A. *Manual del extranjero*. Mexico City: Porrúa, 1973.

Escobar Ohmstede, Antonio, and Matthew Butler, eds. *Mexico in Transition: New Perspectives on Mexican Agrarian History, Nineteenth and Twentieth Centuries*. Mexico City: CIESAS, 2013. https://repositories.lib.utexas.edu.

Escudero Morales, Pablo, and José Galindo. *Transparencia y rendición de cuentas en la CNDH, así como su función transversal de control en la administración pública*. Mexico City: CNDH, 2007.

Esquivel, Gerardo. "Desigualdad extrema en México: Concentración del poder económico y politico." *Reporte de Oxfam Mexico* 23 (2015): 1–43.

Fallaw, Ben, and Terry Rugeley, eds. *Forced Marches: Soldiers and Military Caciques in Modern Mexico*. Tucson: University of Arizona Press, 2012.

Faya, Alejandro. "Kia, Nuevo León e incentivos." *El Norte*, accessed March 11, 2019. http://www.negocioselnorte.com.

Fernández, Claudia, and Andrew Paxman. *El Tigre: Emilio Azcárraga y su imperio Televisa*. Mexico City: Grijalbo Mondadori, 2000.

Fernández Christlieb, Federico. "La influencia francesa en el urbanismo de la ciudad de México: 1775–1910." In *México Francia: Memoria de una sensibilidad comun siglos XIX–XX*, vol. 1, edited by Javier Pérez Siller, 227–65. Mexico City: Centro de Estudios Mexicanos y Centroamericanos/El Colegio de San Luis A.C./Benemérita Universidad Autónoma de Puebla, 1998. https://books.openedition.org.

Fernández-Vega, Carlos. "Los buenos negocios de los bancos, sólo para privilegiados." *La Jornada*, March 11, 2003. http://www.jornada.unam.mx.

Field, G. Lowell, John Higley, and Michael G. Burton. "A New Elite Framework for Political Sociology." *Revue Européenne des Sciences Sociales* 28, no. 88 (1990): 149–82.

Figueroa Esquer, Raúl, "El tiempo eje de México, 1855–1867." *Estudios* 100, no. 10 (2012): 25–45.

Flap, Henk, Adem Kumcu, and Bert Bulder. "The Social Capital of Ethnic Entrepreneurs and Their Business Success." In Rath, *Immigrant Businesses*, 142–61.

Galán Amaro, Erika Yesika. "Estrategias y redes de los empresarios textiles de la Compañía Industrial de Orizaba SA 1889–1930." PhD diss., Universidad Veracruzana, Xalapa, Mexico, 2010.

Galindo, José. "Algunas conclusiones sobre el 'crony capitalism' y las redes sociales a escala global durante el siglo XX y hasta la actualidad." *El Capitalismo de Cuates en Perspectiva Global, ISTOR-CIDE* no. 68 (2017): 7–28.

———. "Capitalismo de amigos, ¿motor de desarrollo o lastre económico?" *Forbes México*, May 10, 2018. https://www.forbes.com.mx.

———. "The Economic Expansion of an Elite Business Family of French Origin in Central Mexico in the First Half of the Twentieth Century." *Enterprise and Society* 14, no. 4 (2013): 794–828. https://doi.org/10.1093/es/kht039.

———. *La CNDH: Una consecuencia de la política económica y social de México (1970–1990)*. Mexico City: Miguel Ángel Porrúa, 2011.

———. "La Conferencia de Chapultepec (1945): El nacionalismo económico latinoamericano frente a la política librecambista de Estados Unidos." *América Latina en la Historia Económica* 24, no. 2 (2017): 35–58. http://dx.doi.org/10.18232/alhe.v24i2.800.

———, ed. *México contemporáneo: Aspectos económicos, políticos y sociales*. Xalapa, Mexico: Universidad Veracruzana, 2018.

———. "Some Aspects on the Failure of Agrarian Reforms in Mexico and Other Latin American Countries." *Forum for Development Studies* 46, no. 1 (2008): 131–46. https://doi.org/10.1080/08039410.2018.1519516.

———. "Some Considerations Regarding the Persistence of the Economic Elite in Mexico in the First Half of the Twentieth Century." *Bulletin of Latin American Research* 32, no. 2 (2013): 149–62. https://doi.org/10.1111/j.1470-9856.2012.00769.x.

Gamboa Ojeda, Leticia. *Au-delà de l'océan: Les Barcelonnettes à Puebla, 1845–1928*. Puebla, Mexico: Benemérita Universidad Autónoma de Puebla, 2004.

———, ed. *Los Barcelonnettes en México: Miradas regionales, siglos XIX–XX*. Puebla, Mexico: Benemérita Universidad de Puebla, 2008.

Gamboa Ojeda, Leticia, Guadalupe Rodríguez, and Estela Munguía, eds. *Franceses del México colonial al contemporáneo*. Puebla, Mexico: Benemérita Universidad de Puebla, 2011.

García Díaz, Bernardo. "La construcción de la fábrica y la invención del pueblo de Santa Rosa, Veracruz." In *México Francia: Memoria de una sensibilidad común siglos XIX–XX*, vol. 2, edited by Javier Pérez Siller and Chantal Cramaussel, 61–80. Puebla, Mexico: BUAP/El Colegio de Michoacán/CEMCA, 2004.

Garner, Paul. *British Lions and Mexican Eagles: Business, Politics, and Empire in the Career of Weetman Pearson in Mexico, 1889–1919*. Stanford, CA: Stanford University Press, 2011.

———. *Porfirio Díaz*. London: Pearson Education Limited, 2001.

Garner, Paul, and Marcela Martínez Rodríguez. "Fomento de la inversión británica en el Porfiriato. El caso de Pearson y de la concesión a The Santa Gertrudis Jute Mill Company, Limited." *Revista de El Colegio de San Luis* 16 (2018): 75–102. http://dx.doi.org/10.21696/rcsl9162018.

Gaulot, Pablo. *Sueño de un Imperio*. Translated by Enrique Martínez Sobral. Mexico City: A. Pola, 1905.

Gauss, Susan M., *Made in Mexico: Regions, Nation, and the State in the Rise of Mexican Industrialism, 1920s–1940s*. University Park: Pennsylvania State University Press, 2010.

Génin, Auguste. *México Contemporáneo 1921*. Mexico City: A.F. Salazar and Cía, editores, 1922.

Gillingham, Paul. "Military *Caciquismo* and the PRIísta State: General Mange's Command in Veracruz." In Fallaw and Rugeley, *Forced Marches*, 210–37.

Gómez Durán, Thelma. "Corrupción: La pandemia acaba al país." *Newsweek México*, November 1, 2015. https://newsweekespanol.com.

Gómez-Galvarriato Freer, Aurora. "The Impact of Revolution: Business and Labor in the Mexican Textile Industry, Orizaba Veracruz 1900–1930." PhD diss., Harvard University, Cambridge, MA, 1999.

———. "Industrialización, empresas y trabajadores industriales, del Porfiriato a la Revolución: La nueva historiografía." *Historia Mexicana* 52, no. 3 (2003): 773–804.

———. "Los Barcelonnettes y la modernización de la comercialización y de la producción de textiles en el Porfiriato." In *Los Barcelonnettes en México: Miradas regionales, siglos XIX–XX*, edited by Leticia Gamboa Ojeda, 189–231. Puebla, Mexico: Benemérita Universidad de Puebla, 2008.

———. "Measuring the Impact of Institutional Change in Capital-Labor Relations in the Mexican Textile Industry, 1900–1930." In *The Mexican Economy, 1870–1930: Essays on the Economic History of Institutions, Revolution, and Growth*, edited by Jeffrey Borzt and Stephen H. Haber, 289–323. Stanford, CA: Stanford University Press, 2002.

———. "Networks and Entrepreneurship: The Modernization of Textile Business in Porfirian Mexico." *Business History Review* 82, no. 3 (2008): 475–502. https://doi.org/10.1017/S0007680500082611.

———. *The Political Economy of Protectionism: The Evolution of Labor Productivity, International Competitiveness, and Tariffs in the Mexican Textile Industry, 1900–1950*. Mexico City: Centro de Investigación y Docencia Económicas, 2001.

———. "Review of *Social Foundations of Limited Dictatorship: Networks and Private Protection During Mexico's Early Industrialization*, by Armando Razo." *EH.net* (2008). http://eh.net.

Gómez-Galvarriato Freer, Aurora, and Bernardo García Díaz. "El escenario industrial." In *La huelga del Río Blanco 1907–2007*, edited by Bernardo García Díaz, 45–72. Veracruz, México: SEV, 2007.

González Navarro, Moisés. "Las ideas raciales de los científicos, 1890–1910." *Historia Mexicana* 37, no. 4 (1988): 565–83.

Gouy, Patrice. *Pérégrinations des "Barcelonnettes" au Mexique.* Grenoble: Presses universitaires de Grenoble, 1980.

———. "Peregrinaciones de Barcelonnettes a México." *Artes de México, Francia-México. Imágenes Compartidas* 39 (1997): 62–67.

Grajales Porras, Agustín, and Lilián Illades Aguilar. "Sobre franceses en Nueva España: Represalia, composición e inquisición." In *Franceses del México colonial al contemporáneo,* edited by Leticia Gamboa Ojeda, Guadalupe Rodríguez, and Estela Munguía, 11–35. Puebla, Mexico: Benemérita Universidad de Puebla, 2011.

Granovetter, Mark S. *Getting a Job: A Study of Contacts and Careers.* 2nd ed. Chicago: University of Chicago Press, 1995.

———. "Weak Ties and Strong Ties." *American Journal of Sociology* 78 (1973): 1360–80.

Greif, Avner. "Commitment, Coercion, and Markets: The Nature and Dynamics of Institutions Supporting Exchange." In *Handbook of New Institutional Economics,* edited by Claude Ménard and Mary M. Shirley, 727–86. Dordrecht, Netherlands: Springer, 2005.

Haber, Stephen H. "The Commitment Problem and Mexican Economic History." In *The Mexican Economy, 1870-1930: Essays on the Economic History of Institutions, Revolution, and Growth,* edited by Jeffrey Borzt and Stephen Haber, 324–36. Stanford, CA: Stanford University Press, 2002.

———, ed. *Crony Capitalism and Economic Growth in Latin America: Theory and Evidence.* Stanford, CA: Hoover Institution Press, 2002.

———. "Industrial Concentration and the Capital Markets: A Comparative Study of Brazil, Mexico, and the United States, 1830–1930." *Journal of Economic History* 51, no. 3 (1991): 559–80. https://doi.org/10.1017/S0022050700039565.

———. *Industry and Underdevelopment: The Industrialization of Mexico, 1890-1940.* Stanford, CA: Stanford University Press, 1989.

———. "Mercado interno, industrialización y banca, 1890–1929." In *Historia económica general de México, de la colonia a nuestros días,* edited by Sandra Kuntz Ficker, 411–36. Mexico City: Colegio de Mexico, 2010.

———. *Political Institutions and Financial Development: Evidence from the Economic Histories of Mexico and the United States.* Working Paper, Stanford University, Stanford, CA, 2005.

Haber, Stephen H., Armando Razo, and Noel Maurer. "Political Instability, Credible Commitments and Economic Growth: Evidence from Revolutionary Mexico." Working Paper, Stanford University, Stanford, CA/Instituto Tecnológico Autónomo de México, Mexico City, 1999.

———. *The Politics of Property Rights: Political Instability, Credible Commitments, and Economic Growth in Mexico, 1876-1929.* Cambridge, UK: Cambridge University Press, 2003.

Hale, Charles A. "José María Luis Mora and the Structure of Mexican Liberalism." *Hispanic American Historical Review* 45, no. 2 (1965): 196–227.

———. *The Transformation of Liberalism in Late-Nineteenth-Century Mexico.* Princeton, NJ: Princeton University Press, 1989.

Hall, Linda B. *Oil, Banks, and Politics: The United States and Postrevolutionary Mexico, 1917–1924*. Austin: University of Texas Press, 1995.

Hamilton, Nora. *México: Los límites de la autonomía del Estado*. Translated by Ana María Palos. Mexico City: Ediciones Era, 1983.

Hart, John Mason. *El anarquismo y la clase obrera mexicana: 1860–1931*. Translated by María Luisa Puga. Mexico City: Siglo XXI, 1980.

Heath, Hilaria. "La crisis de la industria textil del algodón: 1960–1970." *Revista Mexicana de Ciencias Políticas y Sociales* 21, no. 83 (1976): 187–225.

Henderson, Timothy J. *The Worm in the Wheat: Rosalie Evans and Agrarian Struggle in the Puebla-Tlaxcala Valley of Mexico, 1906–1927*. Durham, NC: Duke University Press, 1998.

Hernández Franyuti, Regina. *El Distrito Federal: Historia y vicisitudes de una invención, 1824–1995*. Mexico City: Instituto Mora, 2008.

Hernández Laos, Enrique. "Convergencias y divergencias entre las economías de México y Estados Unidos en el siglo XX." *Investigación Económica* 63, no. 250 (2004): 87–129.

Hunter, Alex, ed. *Monopolio y competencia*. Madrid: Tecnos, 1974.

INEGI. "Censo de Población y Vivienda 1910." Accessed November 5, 2014. https://www.inegi.org.mx.

Jackson, Matthew O. "An Overview of Social Networks and Economic Applications." In *Handbook of Social Economics*, edited by Jess Benhabib, Alberto Bisin, and Matthew O. Jackson, 511–86. Amsterdam, Netherlands: North Holland, 2011.

———. "The Study of Social Networks in Economics." In *The Missing Links: Formation and Decay of Economic Networks*, edited by James E. Rauch, 19–43. New York: Russell Sage Foundation, 2007.

Joireman, Sandra F. "Colonization and the Rule of Law: Comparing the Effectiveness of Common Law and Civil Law Countries." *Constitutional Political Economy* 15, no. 4 (2004): 315–38.

Jones, Peter D. A. *La sociedad consumidora*. Mexico City: Pax/México, 1968.

Josephson, Matthew. *The Robber Barons*. New York: Harcourt, Brace, 1934. https://decryptedmatrix.com.

Kahhat, Farid, and José Alberto Moreno. "La inmigración árabe hacia México (1880–1950)." In *Los árabes en América Latina. Historia de una emigración*, edited by Abdeluahed Akmir, 317–63. Madrid: Siglo XXI de España Editores, 2009.

Kaiser Aranda, Max. *El combate a la corrupción: La gran tarea pendiente en México*. Mexico City: ITAM, 2014.

Katz, Friedrich. *The Secret War in Mexico: Europe, the United States, and the Mexican Revolution*. Chicago: University of Chicago Press, 1981.

Kenny, Michael, Virginia García Acosta, Carmen Icazuriaga, Clara Elena Suarez, and Gloria Artís. *Inmigrantes y refugiados españoles en México, siglo XX*. Mexico City: Centro de Investigaciones del INAH/Ediciones de la Casa Chata, 1979.

Khan, B. Zorina. "Antitrust and Innovation before the Sherman Act." *Antitrust Law Journal* 77, no. 3 (2011): 757–86.

Kloosterman, Robert, and Jan Rath. *Immigrant Entrepreneurs: Venturing in the Age of Globalization*. Oxford: Berg, 2003.

Knight, Alan. *The Mexican Revolution*. Vol. 2, *Counter-revolution and Reconstruction*. Lincoln: University of Nebraska Press, 1990.

Kovacic, William E., and Carl Shapiro. "Antitrust Policy: A Century of Economic and Legal Thinking." *Journal of Economic Perspectives* 14, no. 1 (2000): 43–60.

Kuntz Ficker, Sandra. "De las reformas liberales a la gran depresión, 1856–1929." In *Historia económica general de México: De la colonia a nuestros días*, edited by Sandra Kuntz Ficker, 305–52. Mexico City: El Colegio de México, 2010.

Kuntz Ficker, Sandra, and Elisa Speckman Guerra. "El Porfiriato." In *Nueva Historia General de México*, edited by El Colegio de México, 487–536. Mexico City: El Colegio de México, 2010.

Lagace, Martha. "Innovation Corrupted: How Managers Can Avoid Another Enron." *Working Knowledge, Business Research for Business Leaders*, July 7, 2008. https://hbswk.hbs.edu.

Leal, Juan Felipe, and José Woldenberg. *Colección la clase obrera en la historia de México*. Vol. 2, *Del estado liberal a los inicios de la dictadura Porfirista*. Mexico City: Siglo XXI, IIS-UNAM, 1981.

Lear, John. *Workers, Neighbors, and Citizens: The Revolution in Mexico City*. Lincoln: University of Nebraska Press, 2001.

Lomnitz-Adler, Claudio, ed. *Vicios públicos, virtudes privadas: La corrupción en México*. Mexico City: Centro de Investigaciones y Estudios Superiores en Antropología Social, 2000.

López Presa, José Octavio. *Corrupción y cambio*. Mexico City: Fondo de Cultura Económica, 1998.

Luhnow, David. "Cómo Guatemala tercerizó la lucha contra la corrupción." *Wall Street Journal*, September 14, 2015. https://www.wsj.com.

Machlup, Fritz. *The Political Economy of Monopoly: Business, Labor, and Government Policies*. Baltimore: Johns Hopkins Press, 1952.

Mandujano, Isaín. "El círculo de Manuel Velasco se enriquece con obra pública." *Proceso*, November 26, 2015. http://www.proceso.com.mx.

María y Campos Castelló, Alfonso de. *José Yves Limantour: El caudillo mexicano de las finanzas (1854–1935)*. Mexico City: Grupo Condumex, 1998.

Márquez Colín, Graciela. "La institucionalización de una política." In *La política de competencia en el umbral de la consolidación*, edited by Comisión Federal de Competencia. Mexico City: Miguel Ángel Porrúa, 2013.

Maurer, Noel. *The Power and the Money: The Mexican Financial System, 1876–1932*. Stanford, CA: Stanford University Press, 2002.

Medina Peña, Luis. *Hacia el nuevo estado: México, 1920–1994*. 2nd ed. Mexico City: Fondo de Cultura Económica, 1995.

Mendoza, Elva. "Biométroplis a la congeladora por litigio." *Contralínea*, May 14, 2013. https://www.contralinea.com.mx.

Merino Huerta, Mauricio. "Prólogo: El combate a la corrupción." In *Transparencia, rendición de cuentas y combate a la corrupción. El municipio en la encrucijada*, edited by Mauricio Merino Huerta, Jaime Hernández Colorado, and Ezequiel Avilés Ochoa, 15–21. Mexico City: Centro de Investigación y Docencia Económicas, 2017. http://pirc.cide.edu.

The Mexican Yearbooks. London: McCorquodale, 1908–1914.

Meyer, Jean. "Los franceses en México durante el siglo XIX." Translated by Pastora Rodríguez. *Relaciones* 1, no. 2 (1980): 5–54.

Mills, C. Wright. *The Power Elite*. New York: Oxford University Press, 1956.

Molina Enríquez, Andrés. *Los grandes problemas nacionales*. Mexico: A. Carranza e Hijos, 1909.

Morales, Filiberto Ney. "Los monopolios en Mexico." PhD diss., Escuela Nacional de Economia, Universidad Nacional Autonoma de Mexico, Mexico City, 1949.

Morales Moreno, Humberto. "La organización actual de los grupos económicos después de la privatización de la banca mexicana: 1988–2014." Paper presented at the Third Session of Economic History, organized by the Mexican Association of Economic History and El Colegio de Mexico. Mexico City, 2015.

Morales Moreno, Humberto, Carlos Encinas Ferrer, Miguel Ángel Corona Jiménez, and Miguel Santiago Reyes Hernández. *La nacionalización de la banca como mecanismo de reconfiguración de los grupos económicos*. Mexico City: Centro de Estudios Espinosa Yglesias, 2012.

Morera Camacho, Carlos. *El capital financiero en México y la globalización: Límites y contradicciones*. Mexico City: Ediciones Era, S.A. de C.V./Instituto de Investigaciones Económicas/Universidad Nacional Autónoma de México, 1998.

Morris, Stephen D. *Corruption and Politics in Contemporary Mexico*. Tuscaloosa: University of Alabama Press, 1991.

———. "La corrupción en México a través de los años: Continuidad y cambio (primera de dos partes)." *Este País*, October 1, 2016. http://www.estepais.com.

———. *Political Corruption in Mexico: The Impact of Democratization*. Boulder, CO: Lynne Rienner Publishers, 2009.

Mosk, Sanford. *Industrial Revolution in Mexico*. Berkeley: University of California Press, 1950.

Mueller, Dennis C. "Lessons from the United States's Antitrust History." *International Journal of Industrial Organization* 14, no. 4 (1996): 415–45. https://doi.org/10.1016/0167-7187(95)00490-4.

Musacchio, Aldo, and Ian Read. "Bankers, Industrialists and Their Cliques: Elite Networks in Mexico and Brazil during Early Industrialization." *Enterprise and Society* 8, no. 4 (2007): 842–80. https://doi.org/10.1017/S1467222700006479.

Narváez Medécigo, Alfredo. *Rule of Law and Fundamental Rights: Critical Comparative Analysis of Constitutional Review in the United States, Germany, and Mexico*. Berlin: Springer International, 2016.

Newell G., Roberto, and Luis Rubio F. *Mexico's Dilemma: The Political Origins of Economic Crisis*. Boulder, CO: Westview Press, 1984.

Niblo, Stephen R. *War, Diplomacy and Development: The United States and Mexico 1938–1954*. New York: Scholarly Resources, 1995.

Nickel, Herbert J. *El peonaje en las haciendas mexicanas: Interpretaciones, fuentes, hallazgos*. Mexico City: Universidad Iberoamericana, 1991.

"Noam Chomsky: 'La corrupción fue tan grande en Sudamérica que se desacreditaron a sí mismos y desperdiciaron grandes oportunidades.'" *Perfil*, October 27, 2015. http://www.perfil.com.

North, Douglass C. "Institutions." *Journal of Economic Perspectives* 5, no. 1 (1991): 97–112. http://pubs.aeaweb.org.

———. *Institutions, Institutional Change, and Economic Performance*. Cambridge, UK: Cambridge University Press, 1990.

North, Douglass C., John Joseph Wallis, Steven B. Webb, and Barry R. Weingast. "Limited Access Orders in the Developing World: A New Approach to the Problems of Development." Policy Research Working Paper 4359, World Bank, Washington DC, 2007. https://doi.org/10.1596/1813-9450-4359.

Olsen, Patrice Elizabeth. *Artifacts of Revolution: Architecture, Society, and Politics in Mexico City, 1920–1940*. Lanham, MD: Rowman and Littlefield, 2008.

Organisation for Economic Co-operation and Development [OECD]. *Consequences of Corruption at the Sector Level and Implications for Economic Growth and Development*. Paris: OECD Publishing, 2015. https://dx.doi.org/10.1787/9789264230781-en.

Oropeza, Eduardo, and Magdalena Martínez. "Participación de Contreras en la Lucha Zapatista." *La Voz de Contreras* no. 28 (1986).

"Our Crony-Capitalism Index: Planet Plutocrat." *Economist*, March 15, 2014. http://www.economist.com.

Palma Mora, Mónica. "Asociaciones de inmigrantes extranjeros en la ciudad de México. Una mirada a fines del siglo XX." *Migraciones Internacionales* 3, no. 2 (2005): 29–57.

Pani, Erika. *Para mexicanizar el Segundo Imperio: El imaginario político de los imperialistas*. Mexico City: Colegio de México/Instituto Mora, 2001.

Pardinas, Juan E. "La corrupción en México: Transamos y no avanzamos." *Instituto Mexicano para la Competitividad A.C*, November 15, 2015. http://imco.org.mx.

Paxman, Andrew. "Entre siglos: Elementos para cotejar la industrialización en los Estados Unidos y México." In *Conference for the Instituto de Investigaciones Históricas*. Mexico City: UNAM, 2013.

———. *Jenkins of Mexico: How a Southern Farm Boy Became a Mexican Magnate*. New York: Oxford University Press, 2017.

———. "Televisa de 1997 a 2018: El socio fallido de la democratización." In *México contemporáneo: Aspectos económicos, politicos y sociales*, edited by José Galindo, 457–91. Xalapa, Mexico: Universidad Veracruzana, 2018.

Paxman, Andrew, and José Galindo, eds. "El Capitalismo de Cuates en Perspectiva Global." *ISTOR* 68 (2017).

"Peña Nieto: Su boda-show, al filo del pecado." *Proceso*, November 27, 2010. https://www.proceso.com.mx.

Pérez Islas, José Antonio. *Encuesta nacional de juventud, resultados preliminares*. Mexico City: Instituto Mexicano de la Juventud, 2005.

Pérez Siller, Javier. "De mitos y realidades: La emigración Barcelonnette a México, 1845–1891." In *Los Barcelonnettes en México: Miradas regionales, siglos XIX–XX*, edited by Leticia Gamboa Ojeda, 103–35. Puebla, Mexico: Benemérita Universidad de Puebla, 2008.

———. "Los franceses en México: Una comunidad, su estudio y sus problemas." In *Extranjeros en México: Continuidades y nuevas aproximaciones*, edited by Ernesto Rodríguez Chávez, 331–65. Mexico City: Instituto Nacional de Migración /SEGOB, 2010.

———, ed. *México Francia: Memoria de una sensibilidad común, siglos XIX–XX*. Mexico City: Centro de Estudios Mexicanos y Centroamericanos/El Colegio de San Luis A.C./Benemérita Universidad Autónoma de Puebla, 1998.

Pietschmann, Horst. "Corrupción en el virreinato novohispano: Un tercer intento de valoración." *e-Spania, revue interdisciplinaire d' études hispaniques médiévales et modernes* 16 (2013). https://journals.openedition.org.

Piketty, Thomas. *Capital in the Twenty-First Century*. Cambridge, MA: Harvard University Press, 2014.

Presidencia de la República Mexicana. "Decreto de Presupuesto de Egresos de la Federación para el Ejercicio Fiscal 2015: Título Primero de las Asignaciones al Presupuesto de Egresos de la Federación." September 5, 2014. http://www.diputados.gob.mx.

Prins, Nomi. *All the Presidents' Bankers: The Hidden Alliances That Drive American Power*. New York: Nation Books, 2014.

Quiroz, Alfonso W. *Historia de la corrupción en el Perú*. Lima: Instituto de Estudios Peruanos, 2013.

Rajchenberg, Enrique. "La industria durante la Revolución Mexicana." In *La industria mexicana y su historia, siglos XVIII, XIX y XX*, edited by Eugenia Romero Sotelo, 253–307. Mexico City: UNAM, 1997.

Ramírez Tamayo, Zacarías, "Aún está a prueba la relación entre AMLO y empresarios." *Forbes México*, July 30, 2018. https://www.forbes.com.mx.

Rath, Jan, ed. *Immigrant Businesses: The Economic, Political, and Social Environment*. Basingstoke, UK: Palgrave Macmillan, 2000.

Rath, Jan, and Robert Kloosterman. "The Economic Context, Embeddedness, and Immigrant Entrepreneurs." *International Journal of Entrepreneurial Behavior and Research* 8, no. 1/2 (2002). https://doi.org/10.1108/ijebr.2002.16008aaa.001.

Ratz, Konrad. *Tras las huellas de un desconocido: Nuevos datos y aspectos de Maximiliano de Habsburgo*. Mexico City: Siglo XXI, 2008.

Razo, Armando. *Social Foundations of Limited Dictatorship: Networks and Private Protection during Mexico's Early Industrialization*. Stanford, CA: Stanford University Press, 2008.

Reyes, Gerardo, and Peniley Ramírez. "Influyente empresario mexicano afronta demande por fraude en Estados Unidos." *Univisión*, June 6, 2015. http://www.univision.com.

Reyes Hernández, Miguel Santiago, and Humberto Morales Moreno. *La reconfiguración de los grupos económicos en México a partir de la nacionalización bancaria de 1982*. Puebla, Mexico: Universidad Iberoamericana, 2014.

Reynolds, Clark Winton. *The Mexican Economy: Twentieth-Century Structure and Growth*. New Haven, CT: Yale University Press, 1970.
Riguzzi, Paolo. "From Globalisation to Revolution? The Porfirian Political Economy: An Essay on Issues and Interpretations." *Journal of Latin American Studies* 41, no. 2 (2009): 347–68. https://doi.org/10.1017/S0022216X09005598.
Roazen-Parrillo, Diane. "Las élites de México durante el siglo XIX en una economía regional: El ascenso de la familia Olegario Molina Solís de Yucatán hasta 1902." In *Sociedad, Estructura Agraria y Estado en Yucatán*, edited by Othón Baños Ramírez, 257–79. Mérida, Mexico: Universidad Autónoma de Yucatán, 1990.
Robinson, Edward Austin Gossage. *Monopolio*. Mexico City: Fondo de Cultura Económica, 1950.
Rodríguez Nieto, Sandra. "La élite del 'México S.A.' brinca de gobiernos a negocios a gobiernos." *Sin Embargo*, September 29, 2015. http://www.sinembargo.mx.
———. "2015: La corrupción roba portadas, pero nadie va a la cárcel." *Sin Embargo*, December 17, 2015. http://www.sinembargo.mx.
Rosenmüller, Christoph. *Corruption and Justice in Colonial Mexico 1650–1755*. Cambridge, UK: Cambridge University Press, 2019.
———. "El grave delito de . . . corrupción. La visita de la audiencia de México (1715–1727) y las repercusiones internas de Utrecht." In *Resonancias Imperiales. America y el Tratado de Utrecht de 1713*, edited by Francisco Ivan Escamilla González, Matilde Souto Mantecón, and Guadalupe Pinzón Ríos, 79–118. Mexico City: Instituto de Investigaciones Dr. José María Luis Mora/CONACYT, 2015.
Rosenmüller, Christoph, and Stephan Ruderer, eds. *"Dádivas, dones y dinero": Aportes a una nueva historia de la corrupción en América Latina desde el imperio español a la modernidad*. Madrid: Editorial Iberoamericana, 2016.
Sabido Méndez, Arcadio. *Los hombres del poder; monopolios, oligarquía y riqueza en Yucatán, 1880–1990*. Mérida, Mexico: Universidad Autónoma de Yucatán, 1995.
Sáenz, Citlalli. "Destapan nuevo escándalo de OHL; Lozoya habría mediado a favor del consorcio, acusan." *MVS Noticias*, November 27, 2015.
Salazar, Rosendo. *Historia de las luchas proletarias, 1923 a 1936*. Mexico City: Avante, 1938.
Sánchez, Evelyne. *Las élites empresariales y la independencia económica de México: Estevan de Antuñano o las vicisitudes del fundador de la industria textil moderna (1792–1847)*. Puebla, Mexico: Benemérita Universidad Autónoma de Puebla, 2013.
Sanders, Elizabeth. *Roots of Reform: Farmers, Workers, and the American State, 1877–1917*. Chicago: University of Chicago Press, 1999.
Sandoval, Irma Eréndira, ed. *Corrupción y transparencia: Debatiendo las fronteras entre Estado, mercado y sociedad*. Mexico City: Siglo XXI Editores, 2009.
Saragoza, Alex M. *The Monterrey Elite and the Mexican State, 1880–1940*. Austin: University of Texas Press, 1988.
Schmelzer, Franz Leopold. "Maximiliano de México: Sueños de poder." Produced by ORF Austria and tvUNAM. Video, 52:57. https://www.youtube.com.
Secretaría de la Función Púbica. *Transparencia, buen gobierno y combate a la*

corrupción en la función pública. Mexico City: Secretaría de la Función Púbica, 2005.

Shadlen, Kenneth C. *Democratization without Representation: The Politics of Small Industry in Mexico*. University Park: Pennsylvania State University Press, 2004. Kindle.

Sharafutdinova, Gulnaz. *Political Consequences of Crony Capitalism Inside Russia*. Notre Dame, IN: University of Notre Dame Press, 2010.

Sharma, Pramodita, James J. Chrisman, and Jess H. Chua. "Strategic Management of the Family Business: Past Research and Future Challenges." *Family Business Review* 10, no. 1 (1997): 1–35. https://doi.org/10.1111/j.1741-6248.1997.00001.x.

Sierra Moncayo, María Julia. *Atlas histórico de México*. Mexico City: ITAM, 2006.

Sims, Harold D. *Descolonización en México: El conflicto entre mexicanos y españoles (1821–1831)*. Mexico City: Fondo de Cultura Económica, 1982.

Skerritt Gardner, David. *Colonos franceses y modernización en el Golfo de México*. Veracruz, Mexico: Universidad Veracruzana, 1995.

"Slim paga 40 mdd en EU por 'engañar' con internet ilimitado." *El Financiero*, January 28, 2015. http://www.elfinanciero.com.mx.

Snodgrass, Michael. *Deference and Defiance in Monterrey: Workers, Paternalism, and Revolution in Mexico, 1890–1950*. Cambridge, UK: Cambridge University Press, 2003.

Society for Latin American Studies. *Bulletin of Latin American Research, Journal Citation Reports*. 2013.

Steinmo, Sven, Kathleen Thelen, and Frank Longstreth, eds. *Structuring Politics: Historical Institutionalism in Comparative Analysis*. New York: Cambridge University Press, 1992.

Stiles, T. J. *The First Tycoon: The Epic Life of Cornelius Vanderbilt*. New York: Vintage Books, 2010.

Stucke, Maurice E. "Behavioral Antitrust and Monopolization," *Journal of Competition Law and Economics* 8, no. 3 (2012): 545–74. https://doi.org/10.1093/joclec/nhs018.

Tamames, Ramón. *La lucha contra los monopolios*. Madrid: Tecnos, 1966.

Tamanaha, Brian Z. *On the Rule of Law: History, Politics, Theory*. Cambridge, UK: Cambridge University Press, 2004.

Tannenbaum, Frank. *The Mexican Agrarian Revolution*. New York: Macmillan, 1929.

"10 casos de corrupción muy, pero muy cercanos al poder político." *Sin Embargo*, November 12, 2015. http://www.sinembargo.mx.

Tenorio Trillo, Mauricio, and Aurora Gómez-Galvarriato Freer. *El Porfiriato*. Mexico City: Centro de Investigación y Docencia Económicas/Fondo de Cultura Económica, 2006.

Thorp, Rosemary. *Progress, Poverty, and Exclusion: An Economic History of Latin America in the Twentieth Century*. New York: Inter-American Development Bank, 1998.

Topik, Steven C. "When Mexico Had the Blues: A Transatlantic Tale of Bonds, Bankers, and Nationalists, 1862–1910." *American Historical Review* 105, no. 3 (2000): 714–38. https://doi.org/10.1086/ahr/105.3.714.

Transparency International. "Corruption Perceptions Index 2014: Results." 2014. https://www.transparency.org.

Trujillo Bolio, Mario. "La fábrica la Magdalena Contreras (1836–1910): Una empresa textile precursora en el Valle de México." In *Historia de las grandes empresas en México, 1850–1930*, edited by Carlos Marichal and Mario Cerruti, 245–74. Nuevo León, Mexico: Universidad Autónoma de Nuevo León, 1997.

Turlington, Edgar. "Foreign Investments." *Annals of the American Academy of Political and Social Science* 208, no. 1 (1940): 103–11. https://doi.org/10.1177%2F000271624020800111.

Turrent, Eduardo. *Historia sintética de la banca en México*. Mexico City: Banco de México, 2007. http://www.banxico.org.mx/sistema-financiero/material-educativo/basico/%7BFFF17467-8ED6-2AB2-1B3B-ACCE5C2AF0E6%7D.pdf.

Urbano, Horacio. "CDMX . . . Una ciudad que sobrevive sin planeación urbana." *SDP Noticias*, July 31, 2018. https://www.sdpnoticias.com.

Utley, Robert M. *The Indian Frontier, 1846–1890* Rev. ed. Albuquerque: University of New Mexico Press, 2003.

Valencia Islas, Arturo. *El descarrilamiento de un sueño: Historia de Ferrocarriles Nacionales de México, 1919–1949*. Mexico City: Secretaría de Cultura, Centro Nacional para la Preservación del Patrimonio Cultural Ferrocarrilero, 2017.

Valerio Ulloa, Sergio. *Los Barcelonnettes en Guadalajara, siglos XIX y XX*. Guadalajara: Instituto Mora-CONACYT, 2015.

Vázquez, Josefina Zoraida, and Lorenzo Meyer. *The United States and Mexico*. Chicago: University of Chicago Press, 1985.

Vélez Grajales, Roberto. "La movilidad social en México durante la segunda mitad del siglo XX: Cohortes de nacimiento 1947–1986." Presented at the Nineteenth International Reunion of Historians of Mexico. Chicago, Illinois, September 18–21, 2014.

"Ventilan en la OCDE contratos marco de la CFE." *El Economista*, March 6, 2015. eleconomista.com.mx.

Vera, Rodrigo. "Corrupción corroe hasta el Vaticano, alerta el Papa Francisco en Kenia." *Proceso*, November 27, 2015. http://www.proceso.com.mx.

Villegas Cárdenas, Claudia. "Los terrenos Rivera Torres." *Crónica*, April 29, 2016. http://www.cronica.com.mx.

Waldinger, Roger, Howard Aldrich, and Robin Harwood Ward. "Opportunities, Group Characteristics, and Strategies." In *Ethnic Entrepreneurs: Immigrant Business in Industrial Societies*, edited by Roger Waldinger, Howard Aldrich, and Robin Harwood Ward, 13–48. London: Sage, 1990.

Walker, David Wayne. *Parentesco, negocios y política: La familia Martínez del Rio en México, 1823–1867*. Mexico City: Alianza Editorial, 1991.

Ward, Robin. "Economic Development and Ethnic Business." In *Paths of Enterprise: The Future of the Small Business*, edited by James Curran and Robert A. Blackburn, 51–66. London: Routledge, 1991.

Wasserman, Mark. *Persistent Oligarchs: Elites and Politics in Chihuahua, Mexico, 1910–1940*. Durham, NC: Duke University Press, 1993.

———. *Pesos and Politics: Business, Elite, Foreigners, and Government in Mexico 1854–1940*. Stanford, CA: Stanford University Press, 2015.

White, Richard. "*It's Your Misfortune and None of My Own*": *A New History of the American West*. Norman: University of Oklahoma Press, 1993.

Womack, John, Jr. "The Mexican Revolution 1910–1920." In *Mexico since Independence*, edited by Leslie Bethell, 125–200. Cambridge, UK: Cambridge University Press, 1991.

"The World's Billionaires." *Forbes*. Accessed on December 2, 2015. http://www.forbes.com.

Zarco, Francisco. *Historia del Congreso Extraordinario Constituyente, 1856–1857*. Mexico City: El Colegio de México, 1956.

Zinn, Howard. *A People's History of the United States, 1492–Present*. New York: HarperCollins, 1980.

Zuckerman, Alan. "The Concept 'Political Elite': Lessons from Mosca and Pareto." *Journal of Politics* 39, no. 2 (1997): 324–44.

Index

Page numbers in italics refer to illustrations.